We Are the Crisis of Capital

KAIROS

In ancient Greek philosophy, *kairos* signifies the right time or the "moment of transition." We believe that we live in such a transitional period. The most important task of social science in time of transformation is to transform itself into a force of liberation. Kairos, an editorial imprint of the Anthropology and Social Change department housed in the California Institute of Integral Studies, publishes groundbreaking works in critical social sciences, including anthropology, sociology, geography, theory of education, political ecology, political theory, and history.

Series editor: Andrej Grubačić

Kairos books:

Practical Utopia: Strategies for a Desirable Society by Michael Albert

In, Against, and Beyond Capitalism: The San Francisco Lectures by John Holloway

Anthropocene or Capitalocene? Nature, History, and the Crisis of Capitalism edited by Jason W. Moore

Birth Work as Care Work: Stories from Activist Birth Communities by Alana Apfel

We Are the Crisis of Capital: A John Holloway Reader by John Holloway

Archive That, Comrade! Left Legacies and the Counter Culture of Remembrance by Phil Cohen

Beyond Crisis: After the Collapse of Institutional Hope in Greece, What? edited by John Holloway, Katerina Nasioka, and Panagiotis Doulos

Re-enchanting the World: Feminism and the Politics of the Commons by Silvia Federici

Occult Features of Anarchism: With Attention to the Conspiracy of Kings and the Conspiracy of the Peoples by Erica Lagalisse

Autonomy Is in Our Hearts: Zapatista Autonomous Government through the Lens of the Tsotsil Language by Dylan Eldredge Fitzwater

The Battle for the Mountain of the Kurds: Self-Determination and Ethnic Cleansing in the Afrin Region of Rojava by Thomas Schmidinger

We Are the Crisis of Capital

A John Holloway Reader

John Holloway

KAIROS

PM

Many of the essays in this volume have appeared in slightly different form in earlier publications, as listed below. Previously unpublished pieces collected here are: "Go on Now, Go" (2010), "Rage against the Rule of Money" (Leeds Lectures, 2011), and "Opening Speech" (Elevate Festival, Graz, October 2014).

"The State and Everyday Struggle," in *The State Debate*, ed. Simon Clarke (London: Macmillan, 1991 [1979]), 225–59.
"The Red Rose of Nissan," *Capital and Class* 11, no. 2 (Summer 1987): 142–64.
"Note on Marxism," published as "Marxism: A Theoretical and Social Programme," *Common Sense* 7 (1989): 59.
"In the Beginning Was the Scream," *Common Sense* 11 (1992): 69–78.
"The Abyss Opens: The Rise and Fall of Keynesianism," in *Global Capital, National State and the Politics of Money*, eds. Werner Bonefeld and John Holloway (London: Macmillan, 1995), 7–34.
"Capital Moves," *Capital and Class* 19, no. 3 (Autumn 1995): 137–44.
"Dignity's Revolt," in *Zapatista! Reinventing Revolution in Mexico*, eds. John Holloway and Eloína Peláez (London: Pluto, 1998), 159–98.
"Zapata in Wall Street," in *The Politics of Change: Globalization, Ideology and Critique*, eds. Werner Bonefeld and Kosmas Psychopedis (London: Palgrave, 2000), 173–95.
"Where Is Class Struggle?" in *Anti-Capitalism: A Marxist Introduction*, ed. Alfred Saad-Filho (London: Pluto, 2003), 224–34.
"Zapatismo and the Social Sciences," *Capital and Class* 26, no. 3 (Autumn 2002): 153–60.
"Zapatismo Urbano," *Humboldt Journal of Social Relations* 29, no. 1 (2005): 168–79.
"Stop Making Capitalism," in *Human Dignity: Social Autonomy and the Critique of Capitalism*, Werner Bonefeld and Kosmas Psychopedis (London: Ashgate, 2005), 173–80.
"1968 and the Crisis of Abstract Labour" [original title, "1968 and Doors to New Worlds"], *Turbulence* 2 (2008): 9–14.
"Crisis and Critique," *Capital and Class* 36, no. 3 (October 2012): 515–19. First presented in a different form at the Historical Materialism Conference, London, 2010.
"Communise," in *Communism in the 21st Century*, vol. 3, ed. Shannon Brincat (Santa Barbara: Praeger, 2014), 213–21.

We Are the Crisis of Capital: A John Holloway Reader
John Holloway
© 2019 PM Press.

ISBN: 978-1-62963-225-4
Library of Congress Control Number: 2016948156

Cover by John Yates / www.stealworks.com
Interior design by briandesign

10 9 8 7 6 5 4 3 2 1

PM Press
PO Box 23912
Oakland, CA 94623
www.pmpress.org

Printed in the USA by the Employee Owners of Thomson-Shore in Dexter, Michigan.
www.thomsonshore.com

Contents

PREFACE

From Nouns to Verbs

Spread our wings and fly.[1]

We are passengers in an aeroplane that is out of control and spiralling downwards toward the ground: How can we avoid annihilation? The only way is for us all to spread our wings now and flap them so hard that we break through the fuselage and away we go. That would be nonsensical if we were not already doing it.

Flying is a verb. We fly. At the moment we are entrapped in nouns (the aeroplane). Or better: we are attacked by verbs congealed into nouns, to paraphrase Marx's *Capital*. The lines between anarchism and Marxism blur, as they should.

First, a stepping forward in the dark, a venturing beyond, as Ernst Bloch puts it—and then a path that is made by walking, *un camino que se hace al andar*.

Turning to the verb was the step in the dark, the venturing beyond. This is the first article in this collection, presented as a paper to a conference in Puebla in 1979, published in Spanish in 1980 and in English not until 1991: such was the hesitancy of my stepping.

I had already collaborated with Sol Picciotto in trying to open up new approaches to the state. We edited a book, *State and Capital*, in which we introduced the German state derivation debate into English, and wrote an article published in *Capital and Class*, entitled "Capital, Crisis and the State." The debate on the derivation of the state started with an article published in 1970 by Wolfgang Müller and Christel Neusüß that opened a new

---

1   Many thanks to Panos Doulos for his comments on an earlier version.

and much more rigorous way of thinking about the capitalist nature of the state. Drawing on the resurgence of interest in *Capital* in those years, they argued that in order to understand the state, its limits, and its impulses, it was essential to understand it as a particular *form* of capitalist social relations, like money, value, capital, rent, and so on, and for this it was necessary to derive it logically from the nature of the capital relation in the same way that Marx had derived those other forms. It was, in other words, necessary to derive the *particularisation* of the state, its existence as a particular form of capitalist social relations distinct from money or rent.

This was to return to the long-neglected approach of the Russian jurist Evgeny Pashukanis, who, in his book *Marxism and the General Theory of the Law*, published in 1924, had derived the form of law and of the state from the nature of the commodity and had posed the question: "Why does the dominance of a class not continue to be that which it is— that is to say the subordination in fact of one part of the population to another part? Why does it take on the form of official state domination?" The link to Pashukanis was important both theoretically and politically. Pashukanis had insisted on the specifically capitalist nature of the state form just at the time when Stalin was consolidating the idea of the Soviet Union as a socialist state, and for his pains he was eventually executed in 1937. A similar fate befell Itzhak Rubin, who, in his *Essays on Marx's Theory of Value*, published at much the same time as Pashukanis's book, had theorised value as a specifically capitalist form of social relations. It was clear that to pose the concept of *form* as central to Marxist theory was not only to stimulate a new reading of Marx and particularly of *Capital*, where "form" plays a central part, but also to mark a rupture with the whole theoretical tradition of the communist parties.

The state derivation debate had important theoretical and political implications, which were generally not spelled out in the articles that were part of the debate. In general terms, the debate was a rejection of the old idea that the state is simply an instrument of the ruling class: that simplification does not help us to understand the limits and contradictions of state action and is difficult to reconcile with the many examples of state actions that do not seem to coincide with the interests of capital. The influential work of Ralph Miliband, *The State in Capitalist Society*, which highlighted the personal connections between members of the ruling class and the senior positions in the state, suggested by implication that if those personal connections were abolished, the state could be quite different: in other words, it paid little attention to the structural constraints on state action arising from the nature of capitalist society. The theoretically more demanding and also very influential work of Nicos Poulantzas emphasised above all the "relative autonomy" of the state: since it is not simply the instrument of the ruling class but relatively autonomous from it, there is room for left parties to take control of the state and use this "relative autonomy" to push the state in a different direction. This is still an influential approach among the world's left parties. Poulantzas is much cited by Álvaro García Linera, the vice president of Bolivia, for example. The state derivation debate does not distance the state from its capitalist character (as the notion of "relative autonomy" does), but rather emphasises its "particularisation," or the unity-in-separation, separation-in-unity of state and capital.

The state derivation debate was criticised for adopting a capital-logic approach of assuming that historical development could be understood as simply the unfolding of the logic of capitalist development. The objection to such an approach is that it leaves no place for class struggle. At best, struggle takes place within the interstices of the unfolding of the laws of capital—a point that Sol Picciotto and I made in the Introduction to *State and Capital*.

The issue can be seen in terms of the cohesion and dynamic of the society in which we live. The state appears to be the crucial force of social cohesion: the fact that we commonly speak of Mexican society, British society, U.S. society, and so on makes that clear. The state derivation debate, by insisting that the starting point must be not the state itself but the capital relation, points us in a different direction, arguing that the cohesion and dynamic of society is constituted by the capital relation. The term "capital relation" is open to differing interpretations, but basically it refers to the fact that social relations in this society are mediated through the sale and purchase of labour power as a commodity: this implies that our products relate to one another as commodities, and therefore through money. Put simply, it is money that holds the world together, and our understanding of the world must start from there. It is this basic structure of social relations that constitutes the cohesion and therefore the dynamic of social development. The state is one moment of that overall social cohesion, but it does not constitute it.

It is the existence of money as the social gel (the fact that human richness exists as an immense pile of commodities, as Marx puts it in the first sentence of *Capital*) that allows us to speak of the "laws of capitalist development" or the "logic of capital." The question is: How do we understand the force of these laws? If we understand them in the strong sense of laws independent of human volition, then this leads easily to the view that little can be achieved as long as that basic structure exists, and that struggle should be focused above all on preparing the conditions for the future overthrow of this structure. There is a clear distinction between structure (the logic of capital) and struggle.

In the essay "The State and Everyday Struggle," I took a tentative step beyond the capital-logic approach, and sometimes I feel that everything else I have written has been an attempt to understand the implications of that step. The crucial sentence reads: "It is essential, then, that we conceive of these forms not as static entities but as 'form processes' (Sohn-Rethel 1978, 17), as processes that seek to impose ever-changing but always fragmented forms of social relations upon the resistance inevitably aroused by class oppression. The determinate forms of capital are not only the forms of existence of capital but the form-processes through which capital is reproduced. Capital is reproduced through the constant form-processing (processing into certain forms, *Formierung*, forming) of social activity" (1991, 239). Possibly it is this sentence that provides the underlying unity of the different articles in this book.

An interlude: this "I took a step" is an egocentric academic way of expressing what happened. It is true, I did not put the argument forward consciously as the outcome of a collective discussion nor was it an argument directed at influencing some party decision. Yet the individualistic formulation expresses a broader social trend. I, like many others, was trying to think a way forward: the old patterns of revolutionary-party thought were breaking down. The idea of a state-centred revolution in the future was losing ground among the many of us who thought (and still think) that capitalism is a disaster and that we must find a way of breaking capital's logic of death. The feminist movement had focused attention on the importance of the everyday and of prefiguration. The "workerist" (*operaista* or autonomist) revolts in Italy had emphasised the need to think from struggle, not from capital. In that sense the essay's title, "The State and Everyday Struggle," was a reflection of the way that anti-capitalist thought was moving. I remember still with terror that, as part of the events surrounding the congress in Puebla, I found myself in a panel with a French Trotskyist leader where we were asked, without preparation, to give our evaluation of the present crisis of capitalism. He gave a very articulate presentation of the party line, and fortunately I have no memory at all of what I said. The point is not that this is a tale of personal inadequacy, but that discussions have moved on since then, and that my apparently individual step has proved to be part of a more general movement. Of course party leaders and their self-confident certainties still exist, but there is a more general sense of taking tentative steps, of having to make the paths we walk on, of the Zapatista "asking we walk."

The shift from "form" to "form-process" or, better, from "form" to "forming," was part of the crisis of the party-centred thinking that had dominated Marxist discussion until then. If capitalism is understood as a closed system governed by the "laws of capitalist development," then class struggle will be focused on building the organisation that can break this system with its laws and logic, and this organisation is generally understood to be the Party. However, if the nouns are changed into verbs, if all the forms of capitalist social relations are understood as form-processes, so that commodity is understood as commodifying, money as monetising, capital as capitalising, state as statifying, and so on, then all this changes. (And, of course, aeroplane becomes aeroplaning, and, if we understand the aeroplane hurtling us toward our mass self-destruction as the logic of capital, then the logic is a logicising.)

The first thing that changes is the direction of struggle. Instead of thinking of struggle as being our struggle against an established system of domination, we come to understand that this "established system" is a constant and desperate struggle to impose itself as a coherent logical system and reproduce itself as such. Money is not a thing, nor is it a stable form of social relations, it is a constant struggle to form people's behaviour in a certain way, a struggle that involves the employment of millions and millions of police, supported by psychologists, teachers, parents, and so on, and that quite literally leads to the death of thousands and thousands of people each day from violence, starvation, and untreated curable diseases. Capital is an attack, an unceasing aggression against us, forcing us out of bed and off to work each morning, pushing us to work faster in the factory or the office or the university, coercing students and teachers to direct their concerns to that which will increase the profitability of capital, driving peasants off the land, destroying communities. It is an attack that constantly provokes resistance-and-rebellion and is never sure of its outcome. This does not mean that our thinking starts with capital:

no, our thinking is part of the resistance-and-rebellion, it is part of a dissonant chorus of screams against the capitalist attack that is killing us.

The logic of capital is not separate from struggle: it *is* struggle. Marx gives a succinct summary of the laws of capitalist development: "Accumulate, accumulate! That is Moses and the Prophets!" (Marx 1990 [1867], 742). But accumulation is constant struggle; there is nothing automatic about it. Society is shaped by capital's ceaseless drive to accumulate more surplus value, and this is a constant attack on working conditions, education, healthcare, the environment, everything, in order to shape them in a way that promotes the profitability of capital. This is a fragmented attack in which the different states compete to provide the most favourable conditions for capital accumulation, each trying to attract capital to its territory.

The logic of capital is attack, and the force of the attack lies in its coherence and its logic, but its success is never automatic. It is constantly confronted by resistance-and-rebellion. Resistance-and-rebellion: a hyphenated word that I picked up from talks given by Subcomandante Moisés of the Zapatistas, but I do not know if it originates with him. Resistance-and-rebellion is a fundamental concept because it refers us back to the attack: we resist-and-rebel because we are attacked. In the first place this is very often a conservative defence of what exists, what we are used to or attached to. Our teaching or learning conditions in the university are attacked by cuts or new administrative measures: our first reaction is to defend them; the structure of collective property that was the material basis of peasant and indigenous communities was attacked by a change in the Mexican constitution, and the reaction was to defend them—a strong impulse behind the Zapatista uprising in 1994; a mining company announces that it is going to start an opencast mine in a small community, and the inhabitants mobilise to defend their peasant way of life; a car company says that it is going to introduce new working practices, and the workers organise to defend their old practices and rhythms of work; a property development company plans to destroy the house in which we live, and we round up the other residents to defend the building. In all of these cases the distinction between conservatism and rebellion blur. One is reminded of the famous first sentence of John Womack's book on the Mexican Revolution: "This is a book about peasants who did not want to change and for that reason made a revolution." It is important to question the traditional distinction between a "Left" that is looking for change and a conservative "Right" that wants things to stay the same: this assumes a stable world. In reality, we are all under attack, our first reaction is generally a conservative one of resistance, and in many cases this overflows, leading on to more general questioning of the logic of the attack, the logic of profit. The first part of the word reaches out for its complement: resistance becomes resistance-and-rebellion.

This is an opening. We are under attack, and this attack has a coherence: the logic of capital. Without a concept of capital, we cannot understand the dynamic of attack that shapes our lives and structures the movement of the world. But this logic of capital is a logicising that is constantly confronted by resistance-and-rebellion, by a million refusings of this logic, a million attempts to create the world on a different basis. It is confronted by an un-logicised world. The capitalist forms of social relations are confronted by an unformed world of misbehaving, of misfitting, of disobeying. Forming against misfittings: that is the central antagonism of capitalism. If we remain at the level of *form* rather than *forming*, then this antagonism is closed.

The logic of capital does exist, and any attempt to understand social development that is not centred on a concept of capital will lose touch with the overall dynamic, but working out this logic is constantly at issue, constantly a struggle. The logic is a logicising, the totality of social relations is a totalising, the social cohesion of capital is a social cohering: they are never complete, always resisted, always in need of being reproduced. The struggle against capital is the refusal to accept the reproduction of its logic; it is the breaking of its cohering, the cracking of its totalising. These refusals, this breaking, this fragmenting, have not yet broken the constantly renewed drive of the logic of capital, but they do suggest a very different concept of revolutionary politics. The possibility of revolution is not a question of building the organisation that will one day take state power and break capital: rather it is the recognition, creation, expansion, multiplication, and confluence of all these breakings of the logic of capital, all these creatings of different ways of doing things.

The attack comes from capital, or rather, capital *is* the attack. Our thinking, though, arises from our reaction to that attack. We are the attacked, the violated, the misfitting, raging, refusing, the resisting-rebelling, the screaming-against, the pushing against-and-beyond. Understanding capital as a verb pushes us into a different world, *our* world, the world of We, the world of insubordination and nonsubordination. *Our* world does not stand outside: this is no innocent, pure world of community; it is a world being attacked and corrupted by the attack, an angry world of cripples maimed by capital. Our world is a world of rage and, in spite of everything, a world of hope. Of hope: but how?

Is this a helpful way of rethinking revolution? We do not know because capital still exists, still keeps on destroying the world, and very often it is difficult to see how we can stop it completely. We have learned from dread experience that revolution cannot be brought about through the state, but that does not tell us how to go. The argument against the traditional concept cannot take the form of "you are wrong, we are right," but at most "you are wrong, we are exploring."

The articles reproduced in the rest of the book are part of this exploring. A central theme is understanding crisis as an intensification of struggle and a manifestation of the fragility of capital. Crisis is the expression of capital's incapacity to exploit us sufficiently to secure its own profitability, of its inability to submit us totally to its logic, to shape our daily activity in a way that guarantees its constant expansion: in that sense we are the crisis of capital, and capital's struggle is the struggle to subordinate us more effectively. This is what is explored in "The Red Rose of Nissan," which centres on the struggles in the car industry in Britain and on the opening of the Nissan factory in Sunderland as a very conscious introduction of a new mode of subordination, which found a parallel in the rebirth of the Labour Party as "New Labour," a reorientation led at that time by Neil Kinnock, but which was later to find expression in the war crimes of Tony Blair. Both the managerial and the political changes analysed in the article are attempts to overcome insubordination. Insubordination is the central problem for any system of domination.

And insubordination is we. We are the object of attack, the subject of hope. If we understand capital and its forms of existence as verbs rather than nouns, then we put antagonism not domination in the centre. Capital is not just domination, it is antagonism. We take sides in this antagonism. By writing this I declare that I am on the side of insubordination, that I am against the subordination of humanity to capital. And you, dear reader, if you exist, make the same declaration by reading this. If you do exist, this already constitutes us as a we—and who knows, there may be more? We know that the attack comes from above, that we are the object of the attack, that our activities from day to day are shaped by that attack, by the totalising discipline of capital. But the very fact that we are writing/

reading this tells us that we are more than the object, that we overflow. We are subordinate to capital, but we are also insubordinate. And this is what interests us: our insubordinating, our not-fitting. That is what interests us, because that is where we are, where we live, but also because the possibility of a different form of society springs from there. Our not-fitting is the present existence of a society that does not yet exist but could be created, to draw from Ernst Bloch (a constant influence). Our not-fitting is filled with the dream, the promise, the present creation of a world that does not yet exist, but in the first place it is a horror, a refusal, a scream: in the beginning is the scream.

I go no further. I do not want to spoil the excitement of the book that follows by telling you the whole story.

Yet, yes, one more thing. In the beginning is the scream, and what is it that we scream? We scream "¡Ya basta! Enough!" just as the Zapatistas did when they rose up on the first day of January 1994. I was already living in Mexico at the time (and have continued to do so ever since), but the waves of that great ¡Ya basta! roll beyond all frontiers. It is not just the power of the Zapatista refusal but also their extraordinary creativeness and openness. They have created hope where hope seemed gone. They have digested the failure of the state-centred revolutions of the twentieth century and have worked out a new grammar of resistance-and-rebellion, with their jokes, their stories, their concepts and principles: dignity; to rule by obeying (*mandar obedeciendo*); walking not running, because we are going very far; walking at the pace of the slowest; we are ordinary people, that is to say, rebels; and the wonderful "asking we walk" (*preguntando caminamos*). If their inspiration resonates in some of the articles that follow, and not just those that deal specifically with them, then I am happy indeed.

And now the Zapatistas confront us with the storm (*la tormenta*). In their presentation of the seminar on "Critical Thought against the Hydra of Capitalism" in May 2015, they confront us with a question: "The thing is that what we Zapatistas see and hear is that a catastrophe in all its senses is coming.... So we Zapatistas think that we must ask others from other calendars, distinct geographies, what is it that you see."[2] What do we think?

---

2   "El asunto es que lo que nosotros, nosotras, zapatistas, miramos y escuchamos es que viene una catástrofe en todos los sentidos, una tormenta.... Entonces nosotros, nosotras, zapatistas, pensamos que tenemos que preguntar a otros, a otras, a otro/as, de otros calendarios, de geografías distintas, qué es lo que ven."

What do we think of the storm that we are living, that we feel all around us, that is taking us closer and closer to total destruction? And how can we think of that storm not just as a disaster but as a midwife helping with the birth of a different world? And how do we think of that storm as ours, knowing that *we* are the crisis of capital? Questions, questions, questions.

And yes, another thing—because any list must contain more than one—thank you, thank you, thank you to so many people that I have decided to give no names, but just to mention our permanent seminar here in the university in Puebla, where for years and years now we have been thinking all these things.

With that, we are back in the aeroplane, spiralling out of control down, down, down toward the final crash. Only now we know that it is not a structure but a structuring, not a logic but a logicising, confronted by a million refusings to submit, a million raging-hoping flappings of wings. And away we fly.

?

References

Holloway, John. "The State and Everyday Struggle." In *The State Debate*, edited by Simon Clarke. London: Macmillan, 1991.

Holloway, John, and Sol Picciotto. *State and Capital: A Marxist Debate*. London: Edward Arnold, 1978.

Marx, Karl. *Capital*, vol. 1. London: Penguin Books, 1990 [1867].

Miliband, Ralph. *The State in Capitalist Society*. New York: Basic Books, 1969.

Müller, Wolfgang, and Christal Neusüß, "Die Sozialstaatsillusion und der Widerspruch von Lohnarbeit und Kapital." *Sozialistische Politik*, 1970. Partly translated into English in John Holloway, and Sol Picciotto. *State and Capital: A Marxist Debate*. London: Edward Arnold, 1978.

Pashukanis, Evgeny. *Law and Marxism: A General Theory*. London: Ink Links, 1978 [1924].

Rubin, Isaak Illich. *Essays on Marx's Theory of Value*. Montreal: Black Rose Books, 1973 [1924].

Sohn-Rethel, Alfred. *Intellectual and Manual Labour*. London: Macmillan, 1978.

Womack, John. *Zapata and the Mexican Revolution*. New York: Vintage, 1969.

ONE

The State and Everyday Struggle

Introduction

The last fifteen years or so have seen the rapid development of new forms of working class struggle around the state.[1] The battlefront between the working class and the state has been extended far beyond what are sometimes thought of as the traditional areas of conflict—conflict over the regulation of wages and working conditions and tension with the overtly repressive part of the state apparatus. The growth, and especially the

---

1   This essay is the individual formulation of the outcome of many collective discussions within the framework of the Conference of Socialist Economists (CSE). In particular, it is a critical development of two earlier essays, one by the Edinburgh CSE Cuts Group on "The Crisis of the State and the Struggle against Bourgeois Forms," one by me on "The State as Class Practice." It would be dishonest not to acknowledge my considerable debt to the work done in cooperation with Sol Picciotto, with the Edinburgh CSE Cuts Group (John Macdonald, Richard Paine, Olga Stassinopoulou) and with the London-Edinburgh Weekend Return Group (Cynthia Cockburn, Neil McInnes, Jeannette Mitchell, Kathy Polanshek), as well as to those who took the trouble to write substantial comments on the earlier essays: Simon Clarke, James Donald, Ben Fine, Bob Fine, the Frankfurt state group, Bob Jessop and Mike Williams. Since most of the comments were critical, it is clear that responsibility for the essay remains mine. Some of the ideas sketched here are developed more fully in Edinburgh CSE Cuts Group, I. "State Form and State Apparatus"; II. "The Cuts and the Crisis of the State Form"; III. "State, Crisis and Transport"; IV. "The Crisis of the State and the Struggle against Bourgeois Forms," *CSE Conference Papers*, 1978; London CSE Group, "Crisis, the Labour Movement and the Alternative Economic Strategy," *Capital and Class*, 8 (1979): 68–93; the present essay is critical of the earlier versions in several respects.

1

retrenchment, of the "welfare state" has brought an enormous growth in struggles over the state's role in housing, health, transport, education, etc. Many of these struggles have been fought outside of traditional working-class structures, with parties and trade unions often seeming peripheral at best. There has been a sense of developing new forms of struggle against the state, but often with considerable confusion about how to understand the state.

The development of new forms of working-class struggle is the counterpart of the development of the state itself. The growth of the "welfare state" and "state intervention" and the rise in state employment have meant an increasing permeation of the state in daily life. Over a quarter of the working population in Britain are now employed by the state and are in daily contact with the state as their employer. For many of these workers (especially those employed in the public service rather than the nationalised industries), the fact that they are employed by the state (rather than by an individual capital) is of fundamental importance for the nature of their day-to-day activity. But clearly it is not only state employees who are affected: workers not employed by the state come into much more frequent direct contact with the state apparatus than was previously the case. This is most obviously true of the various activities affecting the reproduction of labour power: education, health, social welfare, housing— all these bring the worker into constant direct contact with various parts of the state apparatus. This is also true of the immediate sphere of production. Although the immediate antagonist for workers employed by individual capital is still the individual capitalist, the relation between capitalist and worker is increasingly influenced by the state: through pay policy, the granting of subsidies and loans conditional on "good behaviour," planning agreements, safety regulations, etc. *For more and more socialists, the state has become a problem of everyday practice.*

Undoubtedly it is these developments that account for the great surge of interest in Marxist state theory in the last few years. For socialists brought by their employment or political activity into direct and routine contact with the various agencies of the state, an understanding of the state is a matter of direct practical significance for their everyday lives. Yet it is hard to see what practical support they can have drawn out of the recent debates on state theory. This is not only because of the language in which the debates have been conducted, a factor making even the best theoretical contributions fairly inaccessible; it is also because of the questions that the theorists have addressed: In what way is the state a capitalist state? What are the structural limitations on state action? How does state expenditure relate to the reproduction of capital? In what way is the development of the state determined by the laws of motion of capital? All these questions are very important, but their relation to the political practice of socialists working in and around the state is a very indirect one. The discussion of the role of state expenditure on social services in the reproduction of capital, for example, certainly has political implications of a general nature, but it is hard to see its relevance to the nine-to-five practice of a social worker. Again it is hard to see how the knowledge that the state is a capitalist state or the injunction to "smash the state" can guide the socialist teacher in her daily confrontation with her pupils. Much of the writing on the state has tended to approach the subject from above, trying to supply answers to the questions that bourgeois theory has failed to solve; or, insofar as it has explicitly discussed, the implications of the analysis of the state for working-class action, it has tended to conceptual-ise working-class struggle solely in terms of party strategy. Consequently, although the resurgence of Marxist state theory has undoubtedly received much of its impetus and support from the development of new forms of struggle (generally non-party struggle) around the state and from the concerns of the large number of socialists in daily engagement with the state, it does not seem likely that the work of the theorists has contributed very much to the development of those forms of struggle.[2]

What we need is a theory of the state as the day in, day out class prac-tice of the bourgeoisie. If state theory is to have any significance for those in daily engagement with the state, it must be able to throw light on the developing class practices implicit in the state and on the possibilities of countering them.

---

2   The lack of contact between recent development in state theory and the devel-oping struggles around the state is brought to the fore by some of the analy-ses of the struggles around the state that have appeared in the last few years. Although these analyses often give excellent accounts of particular struggles, whenever the authors have tried to theorise their experience, they have done so by reference to the work of the state theorists and the result, not surpris-ingly, has been unsatisfactory. Cynthia Cockburn's deservedly popular book *The Local State* (London: Pluto, 1977), which provides a very stimulating account of housing struggles in London, with a quite inadequate theoretical reliance on an amalgam of Miliband and Poulantzas, is an excellent example of this.

This essay does not aim to solve these problems; but it does aim to develop, in still rudimentary form, a framework within which we can begin to talk about the everyday practice of the state and the everyday struggles of socialists against the state.

The State as a Form of Social Relations

1. In order to answer this question—i.e., in order to understand the state as a form of everyday bourgeois class practice—we must try to build more explicitly on recent experiences of class struggle against and around the state. This is not to suggest an anti-theoretical position or a complete rejection of the last few years of debate about the nature of the state. On the contrary, the deficits of the recent accounts of particular struggles around the state underline the importance of developing much more explicitly certain concepts employed or implied in the best of the recent work on the state: namely the concepts of fetishisation and state form and the distinction between state form and state apparatus. The task is not to reject state theory but to draw out and develop the political implications of some recent developments. I refer in particular to the recent "state derivation" debate that developed in West Germany and has now been taken up in other countries.[3] The German academics, true to their historical traditions, have been adept in theorising in highly abstract form the concrete struggles of others. Without always drawing out the political implications of their work, they have created a new framework for our understanding of the state, a framework that, if properly developed, can permit us to move toward an understanding of the state as class practice.

2. The starting point of the German debate was the critique of those theorists (in this case Offe and Habermas) who divorce the study of politics from the analysis of capital accumulation. However, instead of simply reiterating the connection between capital and the state, the contributors to the debate accepted the separation of the economic and the political and tried to establish, logically and historically, the foundation of that separation in

---

3   For a more comprehensive account of the debate and an assessment of its significance that does not stress quite the same points as the present essay, and for a translation into English of the most important contributions to the debate, see John Holloway and Sol Picciotto, eds., *State and Capital: A Marxist Debate* (London: Edward Arnold, 1978).

the character of capitalist production relations. They argued that, in order to understand the "relative autonomy of the state"—or, better, the separation or particularisation of the state from the economic—it is necessary to derive that "relative autonomy" (particularisation, separation) from the basic structure of capitalist production relations: in order to understand the relation between two "things," it is necessary to understand their unity.

In *Capital*, Marx developed his critique of bourgeois political economy from the most basic forms of capitalist social relations. To understand the relation between the state and capital, it is necessary to extend that procedure to the critique of the categories of bourgeois political science. They too must be derived from the basic structure of social relations under capitalism. The attempt to derive the state from capital (the focus of the German debate) is not an attempt to derive the political from the economic but the separation of the political and the economic (and therefore to derive both the political and the economic in their constitutive separate existence—since it is just their separation that constitutes them as "political" and "economic") from the structure of the social relations of capitalist production, i.e., from the particular historical form of class exploitation. The task is not to develop an "economic" or "reductionist" theory of the state but to develop Marx's method in the *materialist* critique of political economy to construct a *materialist* critique of the political. The state, in other words, is not a superstructure to be explained by reference to the economic base. Like value, money, etc., it is a historically specific form of social relations. As a category of political science, the state is a form of thought expressing with social validity the features of a discrete form assumed by the social relations of bourgeois society: "The categories of bourgeois economy consist of such like forms (value, money etc.). They are forms of thought expressing with social validity the conditions and relations of a definite, historically determined mode of production" (Marx 1965, 80). The German debate is concerned with developing Marx's method in the critique of the value-form, the money-form, etc. to elaborate a materialist critique of the state-form.[4]

A materialist critique is not only an analytical process; it is not just a question of piercing the state form and unmasking its content as capitalist

---

4   Note that the term "state-form" in this essay refers to the state understood as a form of social relations and not to what we may call the "type" of state (e.g., the fascist as opposed to the democratic state).

state. It is also what Rubin calls a dialectical process (1978 [1927], 109 ff.), a process of deriving (logically and historically) the genesis of that form from the most basic forms of social relations. Indeed, Marx distinguished his method from the method of bourgeois political economists on precisely those grounds: "Political Economy has indeed analysed, however incompletely, value and its magnitude, and has discovered what lies beneath these forms. But it has never once asked the question why labour is represented by the value of its product and labour-time by the magnitude of that value" (Marx 1965, 84–85).

Accordingly, the task that the German theorists set themselves was not only to discover "what lies beneath" the state form (the fact that it is a capitalist state) but to derive that form (the existence of the state as a particular instance, separate from the economic) from capitalist commodity relations. The debate produced various answers but the most fruitful approach would seem to be that of Hirsch (1978), who derives the particularisation of the state from the fact that under capitalism the exploitation of the working class by the ruling class is mediated through the sale and purchase of labour-power as a commodity. It follows from the nature of this form of exploitation that the social coercion essential for class domination cannot be directly associated with the immediate process of exploitation but must be located in an instance separated from individual capitals—the state. The existence of the state as a separate instance is thus dependent upon the capital relation and its reproduction dependent upon the reproduction of capital. In this perspective, the existence of the political and the economic (for it is only their separation that constitutes their existence as distinct spheres) is but an expression of the particular historical form of exploitation (the mediation of exploitation through commodity exchange). The political and the economic are thus separate moments of the capital relation.

3. Where do the German debate and its subsequent developments take us?[5] In what way does it provide a basis for theorising the state in a manner more adequate to the current phase of class struggle? One of the problems of the debate is that its political implications are never discussed openly by the authors. This, combined with the fact that the authors do not always

---

5   This is a question to which the participants in the German debate themselves have provided no clear answer.

make a clear distinction between "materialist" and "economic," has left their work open to various interpretations and developments (both by the "supporters" of this approach and by its critics, and indeed by the authors themselves in their subsequent work) that often obscure the significance of analysing the relation between the state and capital.

One such misunderstanding is to see the debate on the relation between capital and the state as being concerned solely with the "economic role of the state." Thus, for example, Poulantzas, referring to the debate, could praise "work on the state in Germany, where Marxist discussion of the economic role of the state is probably the most advanced in Europe" (1976, 81). A separate but related misunderstanding is the accusation of "economic determinism" or "economic reductionism": in this view the attempt to relate the state to capital is an attempt to "reduce" the political to the economic, which ignores the "relative autonomy of the state."

Both of these reactions to the German debate come from a perspective that bases its analysis of the political on the "relative autonomy of the state." While the latter response is a straightforward rejection of the "state derivation" approach, the former is far more insidious: instead of confronting the "state derivation" approach as an approach incompatible with its own premises, it seeks to casually integrate the approach by curtailing it to a specific area—"the economic role of the state." What both reactions have in common is a narrow conception of capital and of the relations of production. Capital is seen, if not as a thing, then at best as an economic relation, rather than as a historically specific form of the relations of class domination. But, as Marx pointed out: "Capital is not a thing, but rather a definite social production relation, belonging to a definite historical formation of society, which is manifested in a thing and lends this thing a specific social character" (*Capital*, vol. 3, 814). In analysing the state as a moment of the capital relation, therefore, we are analysing its place in the production relations of capitalism. This is very important, because it is the only way in which the development of the state can be analysed as part of the overall development of the capitalist mode of production.

However, to see the state as a moment of the relations of production is very far from "reducing" the state to the economic. Crucial here is the conceptualisation of the "relations of production."[6] For Marx, the relations

---

6   On the contrast between Marx's concept of "relations of production" and
    Poulantzas's interpretation of that concept, see Clarke (1977).

of production are not simply relations of the immediate labour process but are the relations constituted by the valorisation process, relations of a total process of social production. The relations of production are not distinct from society: rather "the relations of production in their totality constitute what are called the social relations, society, and specifically, a society at a definite stage of historical development" (Marx 1962a, 90). As Lukács has pointed out (1978, 20), Marx's starting point is the "sum total of relations of production"; it is only vulgar materialism (from the period of the Second International through to the Stalin period and its consequences) that made the relationship between the economy and other aspects of society a unilateral and direct causal one.

Many of the theories of the Marxist renaissance have sought to escape from the vulgar materialist heritage. This has not been simply a movement of ideas. All the new forms of struggle referred to in the Introduction called for an analysis that could relate them to the dynamics of capitalism as a total system, yet did not reduce them to mere epiphe- nomena incidental to the "real" struggle at the "point of production."

It is in this context that we must see the popularity of theories that emphasise the "relative autonomy" of the state, ideology, and much else from capitalist accumulation. In this view the notion of relations of pro- duction is limited to the narrow sphere of the direct production of com- modities, what Marx called the "immediate process of production." Given this narrow concept of production (a concept derived from the vulgar materialists whom they criticise), the state is seen as *external* to the rela- tions of production and the analysis is left with no way in which the devel- opment of the state can be grasped as part of the historical development of the capitalist mode of production.[7]

The analysis of the state as a form of the capital relation, therefore, is not specifically concerned with the "economic role of the state," nor is it an attempt to "reduce" the state to the economic. Rather it is an attempt to analyse the place of the state in the relations between capital and labour, conceived of as a historically specific form of class domination with its own laws of motion.

---

7   The foregoing passage is a gross plagiarism, with permission, of Sol Picciotto, "The Theory of the State, Class Struggle and the Rule of Law," mimeo, 1979.

4. The other crucial question overlooked by both the "relative autonomy" school and the vulgar materialists is the concept of form. It is characteristic of capitalist relations of production that they do not express themselves in any simple way as relations of domination. Rather they are expressed in a whole series of discrete forms that appear not as forms of class domination but as disconnected things—commodity, money, capital, rent, etc. The process of capitalist production "gives rise to ... formations, in which the vein of internal connections is increasingly lost, the production relations are rendered independent of one another, and the component values become ossified into forms independent of one another" (*Capital*, vol. 3, 828). Marx's analysis of capitalism in *Capital* can be described as a "science of forms," an analysis and critique of this "enchanted and perverted world" (*Capital*, vol. 3, 827) of disconnected forms, a critique directed not only at revealing the content but at tracing the genesis of and internal connections between those forms. This theme is made explicit at the beginning of volume 1 in the section on commodity fetishism, and the course of its elaboration throughout the three volumes is traced at the end of volume 3, in the chapter on the "trinity formula" (esp. 826–30). This critique (i.e., establishing the genesis and interconnections of the forms) is an essential part of the struggle for socialism. Capital lives by breaking the totality of our existence into apparently timeless, unhistorical fragments. An understanding of the movement for socialism presupposes establishing the unity of those fragments as a historically specific and transitory form of domination. The critique does not dispel the forms, but it is an integral part of the struggle to do so, to transform society.

The critique cannot dispel the forms, because the categories being criticised (value, money, state, etc.) are not mere forms of appearance. They are rather thought-forms that express the specific forms taken by relations between people under capitalism. Thus the money-form refers neither to a thing nor to a mere concept but to the way in which the relations between producers have developed in commodity producing societies. It and the other forms are "forms of social life" (Marx 1965, 75), the forms in which capitalist social relations are reproduced.

It follows that the forms cannot be treated as empty logical abstractions. As forms of social life they can only be understood historically. The scientific analysis of social forms cannot be a purely logical exercise but is a "matter of 'reflection post festum' on an actual process of history" (Picciotto 1979, 120). Marxist categories are not logical abstractions but aids to understanding historical processes: "These abstractions in themselves, divorced from real history, have no value whatsoever. They can only serve to facilitate the arrangement of historical material" (Marx and Engels 1976, 37).

Marx's method is essentially a historical method. Indeed, it is only by approaching historically the forms in which social relations present themselves that they can be revealed as just that: historically specific forms of social relations. It is precisely their inability to analyse value historically, and consequently their inability to conceptualise it *as a form*, that constitutes one of the principal barriers to the understanding of the classical bourgeois political economists:

> It is one of the chief failings of classical economy that it has never succeeded, by means of its analysis of commodities, and, in particular, of their value, in discovering that form under which value becomes exchange-value. Even Adam Smith and Ricardo, the best representatives of the school, treat the form of value as a thing of no importance, as having no connection with the inherent nature of commodities. The reason for this is not solely because their attention is entirely absorbed in the analysis of the magnitude of value. It lies deeper. The value-form of the product of labour is not only the most abstract, but is also the most universal form, taken by the product in bourgeois production, and stamps that production as a particular species of social production, and thereby gives it its special historical character. If then we treat this mode of production as one eternally fixed by Nature for every state of society, we necessarily overlook that which is the differentia specifica of the value-form, and consequently of the commodity-form, and of its further developments, money-form, capital-form etc. (Marx 1965, 80–81)

The analysis of forms must therefore be a historical analysis[8] and not simply a process of logical derivation. This approach has, therefore, little

---

8   See Rosa Luxemburg, *Reform or Revolution?* (New York: Pathfinder, 1988 [1899]): "The secret of Marx's theory of value, of his analysis of the problem of money, of his theory of capital, of the theory of the rate of profit and consequently of the entire economic system, is found in the transitory character of the capitalist economy. . . . It is only because Marx looked at capitalism from the socialist's viewpoint, that is, from the historical viewpoint, that he was enabled to decipher the hieroglyphics of the capitalist economy."

to do with "capital logic"—a third false interpretation that does much to obscure its implications.[9] The historical dimension is essential if we are to develop beyond purely formal argument about the nature of the state; and it is also essential if the approach is to retain its critical edge.

Being historical, the concept of form is essentially critical. The purpose of Marx's analysis was to undermine the apparent solidity of the bourgeois categories, to show that they were not given by nature but expressed historically specific and transitory forms of social relations. Thus, for example, Marx's analysis of money shows that it is neither a thing nor a natural phenomenon but a historically determinate form specific to societies based on commodity production. Similarly, the emphasis on the state as a form of social relations is essentially critical. The state is neither simply an institution nor a phenomenon pertaining to all societies but a historically determinate and transitory form of social relations. Consequently, it cannot be discussed simply as an apparatus or broken down into a conglomeration of apparatuses, ideological, mass-integrative, repressive, or whatever. Nor can the state simply be analysed in terms of its functions. What is important is not just the functions performed but the historical form in which they are performed.

Seen in the context of Marx's method of analysing the genesis of and (hence) the internal connections between forms, the emphasis on the analysis of the state as state form is critical in a double sense of the bourgeois conception of the state as an autonomous institution. Inherent in the concept of form is, first, an emphasis on the interconnection between the different forms, on the unity-in-separation of the different forms assumed by the relations between capital and labour, and hence on the capitalist nature of the state in capitalist society. And, second, the concept of form when associated with the state draws attention to the historical and transitory character of the capitalist state. Both aspects of this critical dimension are absent from the concept of "relative autonomy."

---

9 For a criticism of some of the German contributions from this perspective, see the Introduction in Holloway and Picciotto, *State and Capital*; cf. John Holloway and Sol Picciotto, "Capital, Crisis and the State," *Capital and Class*, 2 (1977); Picciotto, "The Theory of the State."

Fetishism and Fetishisation

1. The previous section underlined the importance of approaching the analysis of the state through the study of its historical development as a form of the capital relation.[10] However, if the concept of form is to be made relevant to the developing forms of struggle referred to in the introduction, it is essential to see history as relating not only to the past but to the continuing process of social development. The development of the forms of social life is not an ideal process that has ended harmoniously in self-consciousness but a continuing and ever-renewed process of class struggle. History is nothing but the movement of class struggle, defining and redefining the battlefronts between the classes. As the relation between classes—the capital relation—develops, so the forms in which the capital relation is expressed develop. As capital itself is challenged by class struggle, the forms of capital are challenged: they must constantly be reestablished and redefined. It would thus be quite erroneous to think of the capitalist forms of social relations as being firmly established at the dawn of capitalism, withering away with the transition to socialism but existing stably within capitalism itself. Such a conception would locate capitalism in history but ban history (and class struggle) from capitalism itself. The determinate forms of capital are not simply historically established but must constantly be reestablished in their specific determinations through class struggle. In the case of the state, for example, it would be quite wrong to think of the separation of politics and economics as having been formally established when the capitalist state first emerged. As Blanke, Jürgens, and Kastendiek point out: "The separation of politics and economics ... is not an historical act which happens once, but is constantly reproduced" (1978, 121).

If we think of the existence of the state as an apparently autonomous institution as one aspect of commodity fetishism, then it is important to grasp fetishism not as an established fact but as an ever-repeated process.

2. That fetishism can never be an established fact is obvious if one remembers that the forms are not just abstract categories but forms of social life, forms of capital, i.e., forms of class domination. Class domination

---

10 For a general sketch of the historical development of the state, see John Holloway and Sol Picciotto, "Capital, Crisis and the State," *Capital and Class* 1, no. 2 (1977).

inevitably means class struggle.[11] Being forms of class domination, the fetishised forms in which capital appears are inevitably unstable. Any system of class relations is inherently unstable, simply because it is founded on exploitation, antagonism, and therefore on resistance and revolt. To think that such a system could ever be stable, could ever be reduced entirely to routine habit, could ever reproduce itself "normally" without conflict or disruption, as the bourgeoisie would have us believe, is nonsense. We can see all around us that the "normal" condition of things is one of *instability*: factories, families, schools—all are riven by conflict, disruption, and impermanence—far from the havens of peace and tranquillity that bourgeois ideology suggests. The veneer of equality and harmony scarcely conceals the daily eruptions of state violence and discrimination, on the one hand, and, on the other, sabotage, truancy, absenteeism, vandalism, and the million other acts of rebellion that capital is constantly seeking to control or suppress.

The fetishised forms in which capitalist domination appears can never be a totally opaque cover concealing class exploitation from those who are subjected to it. The apparent neutrality and fragmentation of the forms, the mystifying disconnections, come into constant conflict with the workers' total experience of class oppression. Money, capital, interest, rent, profit, state—all are commonly experienced as aspects of a general system of oppression, even though their precise interconnections may not be understood. As Marx points out, the interconnections are clearer to "the popular mind" than to the bourgeois theorists:

> It should not astonish us . . . that vulgar economy feels particularly at home in the estranged outward appearance of economic relations in which these prima facie absurd and perfect contradictions appear and that these relations seem the more self-evident the more their internal relationships are concealed from it, although they are understandable to the popular mind. (*Capital*, vol. 3, 817)

11 The claim by the London CSE Group, in "Crisis, the Labour Movement and the Alternative Economic Strategy." *Capital and Class* 3, no. 2 (1979), 90, that we emphasise class domination to the exclusion of class struggle is absurd. They fail to recognise that the two are inseparable: just as class domination inevitably implies class struggle, so too class struggle is scarcely conceivable in the absence of class domination.

The fetishised forms of appearance should be seen less as an impregnable seal than as a thin crust on a seething, bubbling soup.

It is not only that "the popular mind" sees through the categories of the bourgeoisie: popular action constantly rebels against the forms of human life that those categories express. As forms of human life they are constantly disregarded, evaded, and resisted—shoplifting, vandalism, sabotage, tenancy, and squatting are all (or may be) more or less conscious acts of resistance to the forms assumed by production relations under capitalism. Shoplifting, for example, is an attack (conscious or not) on the commodity-form of the product; school truancy attacks the autonomisation of the state from society. Such acts generally lack political direction and rarely go beyond isolated and unconscious resistance directed at a particular manifestation of the form rather than at the form itself, so there is generally little difficulty for capital in absorbing such challenges. The last fifteen years or so have seen the development of new modes of more conscious challenge to the bourgeois forms—as witnessed not only in all the interest in "alternative" lifestyles, communes, cooperatives, etc. but also in the growth of struggles in which state workers have refused to accept their autonomisation from society, in which factory workers have refused to accept that use value production should be governed by the law of value, in which those involved in struggles of all kinds have sought to find ways of expressing the unity of their struggles as class struggles. Again, many of the movements have aimed at the evasion of bourgeois forms rather than being directed against the processes by which bourgeois forms are constituted and reconstituted, yet the significance of the development of new modes of resistance to the oppression inscribed in bourgeois forms of social relations should never be underestimated.

However one assesses the significance of these various forms of resistance, what they show is that the reproduction of the capitalist forms of domination is never simply an automatic process that can be taken for granted. In order to contain the ubiquitous resistance to class oppression, the forms of that oppression must be constantly developed and recreated.

3. It is in the face of this resistance and these attacks that capitalist social relations must be reproduced. Clearly, the reproduction of capital cannot be conceived of in any static sense as the automatic renewal of pre-given

forms of social relations for two reasons. First, as we have seen, there can be nothing automatic about it: there is constant resistance to the reproduction of capitalist domination and this resistance itself impels the constant reformulation of the relations of domination. Second, the relations are never pre-given: capital is an inherently dynamic form of social relations. Its unquenchable thirst for surplus value drives it constantly to intensify exploitation and to reformulate (especially through crisis) the relations between capital and labour. The maintenance of capital as a form of social relations, therefore, can only mean the maintenance and restructuring of capitalist social relations, the constant reformulation-through-crisis of the relations between capital and labour. Inevitably, this reformulation is always a struggle to impose or reimpose certain forms of social relations, to contain social activity within or channel social activity into those (developing) forms. Now, inevitably, the only way in which this struggle can take place is through the forms of the capital relation. It is essential that we conceive of these forms not as static entities but as "form processes" (Sohn-Rethel 1978, 17), as processes that seek to impose ever-changing but always fragmented forms of social relations upon the resistance inevitably aroused by class oppression. The determinate forms of capital are not only the forms of existence of capital but the form-processes through which capital is reproduced. Capital is reproduced through the constant form-processing (i.e., processing into certain forms, *Formierung*, forming) of social activity: but *it is essential to remember that the changing patterns of form-processing are to be understood not as a random, ahistorical process but as an interconnected historical movement structured by the laws of motion arising from the contradictions of capital.* As we have seen, it is in the nature of class antagonism that the form-processing is never completed but is an ever-renewed struggle to impose capitalist social relations upon society, a struggle that becomes more acute as the expansion of capital demands the ever-greater subordination of social relations to its sway.[12]

If the political relevance of form analysis is to be made clearer, it seems essential to develop this aspect—i.e., to analyse the reproduction of forms

---

12 This notion of capital as struggle, of form-determination as struggle, seems to be absent from Simon Clarke's otherwise excellent critique of fractionalism: see Clarke (1978, esp. 63 ff.)

and the form-processing of social activity.[13] The rest of this essay takes a few hesitant steps in that direction, with particular relation to the state.

The State as Form-Process

1. The capitalist state is constituted by the particularisation of the political and the economic as distinct forms of social relations.[14] This involves not the separation of the political from a preexisting economic sphere but the constitution of both the economic and the political through the fragmentation of the capital relation. This fragmentation of the capital relation into discrete economic and political spheres is perhaps the most important aspect of commodity fetishism. Through this fragmentation the unified expression of class relations typical of precapitalist societies is broken up. In the transition from feudalism, the serf (a term denoting totally indistinguishable political and economic subjection to the lord) becomes wage earner and citizen. On both sides of the divide, class (as an inherently antagonistic relation of production) has apparently dissolved into separate but interlocking and mutually confirming categories. The separation of economics and politics implies the separation of economic and political relations—the constitution of the proletarian as property owner (i.e., owner of the commodity labour power) and citizen (as burgher and *citoyen*, to speak the language of the young Marx [see Reichelt 1974, xxiii]).

This separation, however, is not an established fact but an ever-repeated process. The classless status of citizen comes into constant

---

13　In relation to the *Formierung* (forming or formation) of state functions, Bernard Blanke, Ulrich Jürgens, and Hans Kastendiek have this to say: "The question of how this formation takes place in detail, how it is transposed into structure, institution and process of the state, can no longer be answered by form analysis. It would have to be made the subject of historical analysis" (1978, 119). Their separation of form analysis and historical analysis (criticised generally in the Introduction to the same book) has most unfortunate consequences here, for it cuts them off from what is precisely the most important aspect of form analysis. Blanke, Jürgens, Kastendiek, "On the Current Marxist Discussion on the Analysis of Form and Function of the Bourgeois State," in *State and Capital*, eds. Holloway and Picciotto.

14　See Helmut Reichelt, *Zur logischen Struktur des Kapitalbegriffs bei Karl Marx* (Frankfurt: EVA, 1970), 21: "Marx agrees with Hegel that the state only really becomes the state when it appears as the state of bourgeois society, when it assumes the form of the political state standing outside and above bourgeois society and society can likewise appear as society."

conflict with the class experience of the bearer of that status. As Blanke, Jürgens, and Kastendiek point out:

> The emergence of a political subject of law corresponding to this economic category [property-owner], the "worker citizen" is accomplished through class struggles, because surface categories always constitute mere *formal* equality, while the *material inequality* posited in the production of surplus value continually calls this apparent equality into question. (1978, 142)

The processing of social activity into a political sphere separate from the economic and the processing of social relations into particularised political categories is a constant struggle to suppress the expression of class experience and class organisation. This process (i.e., the state understood as form-process and as a process of the particularisation of the political distinct form of the capital relation) is clearly of enormous importance in ensuring the reproduction of capital. An attempt to understand this process and its development is a necessary part of the struggle against capital.

2. Historically, the separation of economic and political relations coincided with the autonomisation of the state. This took place on the basis of the primitive accumulation of capital at a time when the direct relation of capitalist exploitation was not yet wage labour. Thus the first moment of the capitalist state is to establish and guarantee exchange as the mediation of production and consumption. This involved the creation and maintenance of individuals as economic and legal subjects, the bearers of reified property rights (see Picciotto 1979). At the same time, the establishment and guarantee of exchange implied the development of a coercive instance standing outside the exchange relation and relating to the members of society *as individual subjects* (see Blanke, Jürgens, and Kastendiek 1978; Pérez Sainz 1979). Historically, the European absolutist states provided the framework both for the spread of commodity production and the concomitant development of the individual citizen:

> The idea of a general citizenship began to penetrate into the political sphere, by virtue of the regime's absolutist nature and the unitary character of the state; to this idea the notion of general citizen rights was soon added. The population accustomed itself to fixed duties

laid down by the state, to taxation and military service, to daily
contact with the civil servants of a centralised state and, in consequence, acquired a sense of political cohesion, the rudiments of a
common political interest. The idea of a unified political order ...
became now an innermost concern of the population itself. ... *The
individuals became conscious of being a people: previously there had
been no more than a populace divided up by region and class*—a mere
object of government. (Hintze 1975 [1902], 175; emphasis added)

The centralisation of power that replaced the "parcellised sovereignties"
(Anderson 1974, 19) of feudalism found expression also in the atomisation of the population into "a multitude of *particuliers*, of private (though
sometimes privileged) individuals" (Poggi 1978, 78). This process of individualisation is the first basic moment of the state form, counterpart of
(and interlocking with and consolidating) the development of commodity
owners as economic subjects. With the increasing generalisation of production based on commodity exchange, the principle of individualisation
gradually undermined the ordered hierarchy of the old world, with its
system of representation based on "community" and "rank" (see Beer 1965,
17–18). In Britain the redefinition of society as a mass of individuals was
closely tied to the extension and reorganisation of the system of representation (see Beer 1965, 16 ff.).

In any full development of the argument of this essay, it would be
essential to trace the development of this basic moment of the state form
and the development of the changing modes of individualisation (particularly in relation to the emergence of the welfare state). Although
this attempt cannot be undertaken here, the importance of a historical
approach must be underlined, for it would be a grave error to mistake
forms of individualisation current in Western democracies, with their
parliamentary elections and rule of law, for the "most perfect" forms of
individualisation or the "normal" (as opposed to the "exceptional") expression of the capitalist state. The development of the mode of individualisation can be understood only in the context of the historical development
of capitalism as a whole.

Here, however, it is only possible to emphasise the importance of individualisation as the basic moment of the state form. The process of individualisation is enshrined in all the basic practices of the state—in the law,
in administration, in the structures of representation and intervention. In

each case, the state isolates people by treating them as individuals, not as concrete individuals with individual peculiarities but as abstract, general, de-individualised individuals: the abstract nature of commodity-producing labour is here reproduced as abstract citizenship. The relation to individuals is therefore a general relation, a relation in which individuals are distinguished neither on the basis of their peculiarities nor on the basis of their class position.

This process of individualisation finds one of its clearest expressions in the legal form and the concept of legal rights: "A right is always that of an individual subject: hence to extend or claim 'rights' for people in a bourgeois legal form is immediately to isolate them" (Picciotto 1977, 3). But the same process is at work in the daily contact between all the state's administrative agencies and the "public": schools, social work departments, housing departments, and social security offices, for example, all act in a measure that isolates the person coming into contact with them, treats that person as an individual or (as Cynthia Cockburn [1977] points out) as part of a family.

Representative elections are no exception to the form-processing inscribed in the state's practices, despite the sharp distinction that some (e.g., Foucault 1977 and apparently Poulantzas 1978) have drawn between representation and other aspects of the state's practice. In democratic elections, the population is treated as an undifferentiated mass of "voters," "constituents" defined according to arithmetical numbers rather than any membership of class or community. Similarly, the voting process itself, the institution of the secret ballot, is the supreme expression of the *privacy* of political opinion. Through the institution of the ballot box, resistance to class oppression is channelled into an act of individual private choice between two or more oppressors.

This is not to deny that the rule of law and representative democracy are generally more favourable to the working class than a regime in which neither of these prevails. The point is rather to recognise the limits, or rather the oppressive implications, of these forms and not to hypostasise them as achievements of civilisation that must at all costs be preserved. It is a mistake, for example, to make an absolute distinction between the exclusion of the working class from the state before the introduction of universal suffrage and its representation within the state after that event.

This is a mistake: first, the working class was able to ensure its representation within the state even before the extension of the franchise, as

Foster's study (1974) of early nineteenth-century working-class politics in Oldham shows; second, representation of the working class within the state through the processes of electoral democracy is simultaneously a process of fragmentation, of exclusion *as working class*. What is involved in the extension of the franchise is thus not an absolute change from exclusion to representation but a (normally very significant) change in the mode of representation and exclusion of the working class. It is not representative democracy that limits the power of the state (as Poulantzas 1978, 73, would have it) but the strength of the working class, whatever its institutional expression.

Law, administration, and representation are all practices that individualise, that treat the classes of society as a homogeneous mass of people. This individualisation is not an established fact but a process that consistently obscures the basic structures of society. Pannekoek put the point neatly when he wrote: "Democracy, they say, is government by the people, but the people as such does not exist; in reality, society is divided into classes" (1969 [1919], 136).

To see the state as a process of individualisation is not to suggest that this individualisation takes place solely in the political sphere, that classes are formed at the economic level and then fragmented at the political level. Nor, indeed, is it to suggest that the state simply consolidates an individualisation that is basically established at the economic level, as Poulantzas (1978, 65) suggests.[15] Rather it is the fragmentation of class relations into distinct but interlocking economic and political forms that brings with it the atomisation of the working class. The struggle to build up class organisation must therefore be a struggle against these forms. This is not to say that it may not be important to use legal action or parliamentary elections

---

15 Poulantzas apparently sees individualisation as taking place basically in production (which he conceptualises narrowly as the immediate process of production) and being "consecrated and institutionalised" by the state. The problem with this is that he still starts from a presupposed separation of the economic and political. His whole discussion of "individualisation" is consistently ahistorical and static, apparently leaving no space for a rupture of this "individualisation," see *State, Power, Socialism* (London: New Left Books, 1978), esp. 73–74. This may explain why there seem to be no clear conclusions for class struggle drawn from the analysis, or rather only inconsistent conclusions concerning the value of representative democracy. For a useful discussion of Nicos Poulantzas, *State, Power, Socialism* (London: New Left Books, 1978), see Barker (1979).

as part of a campaign, but, if so, it is important that it should be within the perspective of a broader movement aiming at the total transformation of social relations and with an awareness of the individualising, fragmenting implications of these forms.

3. So far we have suggested that individualisation should be seen as the first moment of the state form, corresponding to the state's basic function of establishing and guaranteeing commodity exchange. With the establishment of the capitalist mode of production on the basis of "free" wage labour, the state develops new functions and a new mode of political formation (see generally Holloway and Picciotto 1977). On the one hand, the generalisation of commodity production brings with it the clearest expression of individualist ideology in nineteenth-century liberalism and radicalism. On the other hand, with the generalisation of commodity production and the establishment of capital, "the laws of appropriation or of private property, laws that are based on the production and circulation of commodities, become by their own inner and inexorable dialectic changed into their very opposite" (Marx 1965, 583). The appearance of equality of exchange in the sphere of circulation is increasingly undermined by the inequality of production. The guarantee of the relations of exchange by the state, therefore, increasingly involves the state in the overt regulation of the conditions governing the sale and purchase of labour power. The abstentionism of the liberal ideal is at once undermined by the growth of state intervention, from the very beginning of the heyday of liberalism (see Roberts 1960). The expansion of state activity means that the state enters into more direct relations with an ever-greater number of people (see Poggi 1978, 123). Inevitably, this expansion involves not just an expansion in the quantity or density of relations between the state and individuals but the establishment of new forms of relations between the state and the "public." The development of new forms of representation/intervention/administration—for these are but three very closely interrelated aspects of the same process—becomes a problem both for the administrators and for those being administered. Individualism, as soon as it is established, is apparently undermined by the development of collective political forms.

The primary impulse to the growth in state intervention was the need to ensure the reproduction of labour power as a commodity. Consequently the patterns of intervention/administration/representation that developed were structured primarily around the sale and purchase of labour-power. The growth of state intervention led to the development of more direct relations between the state, on one hand, and workers and capitalists, on the other—defined neither as classes nor simply as individuals but as sellers and buyers of the commodity labour-power, as owners of different revenue sources (trade unions and employers' organisations). As the individual citizen is the counterpart of the individual commodity owner, so the new political collectives that began to emerge in the nineteenth century (very different from the old communities that had been undermined by the individualising effect of the spread of commodity exchange) were mostly so structured that they interlocked with the economic categorisation on the basis of revenue sources.[16]

Collectivism is, therefore, not the absolute opposite of individualism, as it is so often presented to be. Rather it complements individualism and arises on the basis of individualisation and the abstraction from the relations of production inherent in the process of individualisation. It is true that "class" emerges as a category of nineteenth-century politics (see Beer 1965; Poggi 1978), but this is class understood not as an antagonistic relation of production but as a mass of *individuals* owning the same source of revenue or enjoying a similar income. Collectivisation obscures the structure of social relations at least as effectively as individualisation. Classes are not only atomised, but the atoms are regrouped in such a way as to make the concept of class seem quite irrelevant to collective struggle.

Although it cannot be undertaken here, it would be absolutely essential in any further development of this essay to trace the changing modes of collectivisation, the changing ways in which capitalism groups us politically. In the modern capitalist state, citizens are lumped together into all sorts of groupings: they are classified first and foremost as families (an extremely important point made by Cockburn [1977]) but also as voters, taxpayers, tenants, parents, patients, wage earners, smokers, and non-smokers. Class members are categorised on the basis of consanguinity, of geographical residence, of income, of housing tenure, of parenthood, of health, of revenue form, of personal habits: never on the basis of class. Understanding the process by which classes are defined into the

---

16 The analysis of Sybille von Flatow and Freerk Huisken, in "Zum Problem der Ableitung des bürgerlichen Staates." *Prokla*, 7 (1973), has something to offer in this respect, but only if the state's relation to the owners of the revenue-sources is reinterpreted as a process of fetishisation.

different categories of bourgeois politics is a fundamental problem for state theory,[17] as this categorisation not only responds to but defines and redefines the forms of political organisation in bourgeois society. The process of categorisation can be seen as the formation of so many constituencies—the grouping together of individuals into (at least potential) "interest" groups based on their common parenthood, ill-health, predilection for tobacco, housing tenure, etc. The constituency—both in the usual sense of a geographically defined grouping together of voters and in the sense of the functional grouping of people in their relations with particular aspects of the state apparatus (the sense often given to the term by political scientists) can be seen as the basic unit within which political relations are constituted. If constituency is seen in these terms, then McConnell, the radical American political scientist, is clearly right to point to the question of constituency as the fundamental question of politics (McConnell 1966)—except that he addresses the question of the size of the constituency rather than the more fundamental question of the processes through which a constituency is defined. It is the manner in which constituencies are defined that is the crucial problem, the manner in which the massive totality of class struggle is fragmented through state administration into distinct problems for functionally defined branches of state activity—problems for the Department of Health and Social Security, for the Department of Education and Science, for the Department of the Environment, etc. and their smaller divisions right down to the division of responsibilities among individual officials—and then the manner in which this fragmentation is imposed upon those who have any dealings with the state apparatus, the manner in which "the rules and red tape that swathe the agency within... also reach out to mould the client" (Wilensky and Lebeaux 1965, 240)—and not only the "client" but the classes of capitalist society. This "moulding" is a struggle to channel class action into the fetishised forms of bourgeois politics, a struggle to constitute the state form. This struggle can only be understood in the historical context of the development of the class struggle that is the reproduction and accu-

---

17　It is an unfortunate effect of Simon Clarke's overdeterminist view of the state that the problem of representation is reduced to the secondary aspect of the way in which the state is subordinated to capital. One implication of this is to suggest that the political system should be seen simply as a transmission belt between capital and the state, rather than as an extremely important and problematic moment in the reproduction of capital.

mulation of capital. The change in the forms of collectivisation is not a random process: the developing forms of the capital relation constitute a differentiated whole.

A distinction can, perhaps, usefully be drawn between the "external" and "internal" processes of constitution, i.e., between the constitution of bourgeois political relations through the interaction of the state with those outside of the state apparatus, on the one hand, and the constitution of bourgeois relations within the state apparatus, on the other. The "internal" process of forming social relations is not necessarily less problematical for capital than the "external" process: both involve the maintenance/re-creation of bourgeois social relations in the face of a contradictory experience. The two processes are, moreover, inextricably interlocked: the transmutation of class relations outside of the state apparatus depends upon the maintenance of bourgeois relations within the state apparatus. This implies, first, bureaucratic control of the actions of the employees of the state apparatus—a problem of increasing complexity and importance as state employment expands and the state comes to play a more crucial role in the reproduction of social relations. It implies also a fragmentation of relations within the state apparatus that complements the fragmentation existing in and imposed upon class relations at large. If the fragmentation of class relations at large can be seen as being accomplished (or rather transmuted and consolidated) through the "reaching out" of "the rules and red tape that swathe the agency within ... to mould the client [or class]" (Wilensky and Lebeaux 1965, 240), then the same is true in reverse. The fetishised categories of commodity production "reach out" in transmuted form and mould the internal organisation of the state apparatus: this internal fragmentation of the state apparatus then "reaches out" in its turn to mould and reinforce the fetishised relations of bourgeois society. The question of the internal organisation of the state is thus far from being a technical question of public administration.[18] When Aristotle posed his famous question in relation to the distribution of functions in the Greek city state: "We have also to consider whether to allocate duties on the basis

---

18   It is worth noting that the rise in interest in the internal structures of the state coincided in time with the growth of the collective organisation of interests and their increasing articulation with the bureaucratic structures of the state apparatus. Generally, the analysis of the fetishised forms of public administration (so vital for an understanding of the forms of political organisation) is a task still largely untouched by Marxist theory.

of the subject to be handled, or on that of the class of persons concerned"
(*Politics*, Book IV, chap. XV), he was raising not just a problem of administration but one of the most important questions of political organisation.

4. Whether as individualisation or as collectivisation, the constitution of
the state (the process by which the structure of relations clustered around
the exercise of coercion is constituted as separate from the economic)
is a process of fetishisation, of the fragmentation of class relations into
nonclass forms.

Fetishisation refers here not just to the creation of certain forms of
thought but to the constitution of the bourgeois "forms of social life." It
involves the organisation of our lives in such a way that the important
questions (class struggle and the transition to socialism) can never be
posed in an active manner. What is important here is the material organisation of our lives rather than simply the dissemination or inculcation of
ideas. As Heide Gerstenberger puts it:

> Instead of assuming that people who do not fight have been success-
> fully trapped by the ideology of the bourgeois state, we should try to
> analyse the everyday constituents of consciousness in a bourgeois
> society. And by doing this ... we will pretty soon be confronted with
> the overwhelming presence of bureaucratic structures. Not only
> are most aspects of life administered, but the integrity of people's
> lives and the connections between their problems are split up in
> fractional aspects of administration. (Gerstenberger 1977, 7–8)

In this respect, the emphasis by Foucault (1977) on the "microphysics of
power" and the "politics of the body" is a helpful antidote to much of the
recent writing on the state. In order to contribute to a more adequate theorisation of the state, however, such an analysis would need to be extended
to the less spectacular forms of popular contact with the state and to be
established on a historical materialist basis, i.e., in relation to the development of the forms of capital seen as a totality. Nevertheless, his insistence
on the significance of the material practices of the state is an important
one, for it makes clear that the struggle against the state can be neither
simply a matter of theoretical enlightenment of the working class nor
simply of capturing control of or smashing the state apparatus but must
involve the development of material forms of counterpractice and counterorganisation. As Pannekoek puts it: "Organisation is the fundamental

principle of the struggle of the working class for its emancipation. It follows that from the point of view of the practical movement, *the most important problem is that of the forms of this organisation"* (1969 [1919], 257; my emphasis).

To this point we must return in the conclusion. The state as a process of fetishisation, then, is a process of reaching out and ordering social relations in certain ways. It is easy to overestimate the penetration of this process into society and also to overemphasise its importance vis-à-vis other forces at work (e.g., the "dull compulsion of economic relations"). Certainly, as a general trend, the expansion of capital implies the increasing permeation by capital of every aspect of our lives and this is achieved in part through the state (the growth of state intervention implying the need for a more thorough categorisation and representation of our interests); but it is clear from present experience in Britain that there is no unequivocal and irreversible trend toward the expansion of the state's role in this respect.

Some Conclusions

It is clear that this essay is very much a working paper. The purpose has been to take up a certain theoretical current (the state form debate) and suggest some ways in which it might be developed to make it more relevant to the development of new forms of struggle against the state. Its argument is that the state must be seen not just as a form of existence of the capital relation but as a moment in the reproduction of capital as a relation of class exploitation mediated through individual exchanges of the commodity labour power, as a process of forming social activity in such a way as to reproduce classes as atomised individuals and exclude the possibility of class organisation against capital. The conclusion, at its most basic level, is that the struggle to build class organisation must be directed against the state as a form of social relations and must involve the development of material forms of counterorganisation that reassert the unity of that which the state pulls asunder. But before developing this in slightly more detail, it is necessary to make two other points relating to crisis and to the distinction between state form and state apparatus.

1. *Crisis:* In many countries, the present crisis has taken the form of a fiscal crisis of the state. The state has come under attack from the bourgeoisie itself and significant cuts have been made, especially in the "welfare"

aspects of the state. It is clear that the Left must defend working-class gains that have become enshrined in the welfare activities of the state, yet any straightforward defence of the welfare state that overlooks its capitalist form is highly problematic. First, such a strategy is unlikely to mobilise wide support: the great strength of the bourgeoisie's attack in this area lies precisely in the fact that the state is widely experienced as being oppressive (as witness, the popular appeal of Mrs. Thatcher's attacks on the overmighty state in the recent election campaign). And, second, such a strategy misses an opportunity of exploiting the destabilising potential inherent in the retraction of the state.

The problem must be seen within the general context of crisis and its impact upon the stability of capitalist relations. The contradictions of the capital relation express themselves in a constant tendency toward, and periodic outbreak of, crisis. Crisis, if it is to be overcome within the framework of capitalism, involves a restructuring of the capitalist relations of production (see Hirsch 1978). The relation between capital and labour must be restructured if it is to be maintained: by increasing the rate of exploitation, altering the ratio between constant and variable capital, accelerating turnover, etc. The problem, however, from the standpoint of capital is that, although restructuring is essential for the maintenance of the capital relation, restructuring may, at the same time, imperil the continued existence of that relation. In a period of restructuring, the maintenance/reimposition of bourgeois relations becomes particularly difficult. The "dull compulsion of economic relations" either becomes so sharp (for those still employed) that it may provoke reaction, or it becomes so blunt (for the long-term unemployed) that it may lose all effectiveness (see Frith 1978). Consider the slightly different but very instructive case of poor Mr. Peel who decided that it would be more profitable to "restructure" his capital by moving it to West Australia:

> Mr. Peel . . . took with him from England to Swan River, West Australia, means of subsistence and of production to the amount of £50,000. Mr. Peel had the foresight to bring with him, besides, 3,000 persons of the working-class, men, women and children. Once arrived at his destination, "Mr. Peel was left without a servant to make his bed or fetch him water from the river." Unhappy Mr. Peel who provided for everything except the export of English modes of production to Swan River! (Marx 1965, 766)

But we need not go as far as West Australia to find the very existence of the capital relation threatened by its restructuring. It is clear that the restructuring nearly always subjects the continued imposition of the relation to a severe strain: this can be seen, for example, in all the strikes connected with "rationalisation" and wage restraint in Britain in the late 1960s and early 1970s. Crisis is not only a technical question of restructuring inputs into the process of production, it is a crisis of the social relations of capital production.

The crisis, as a crisis of productive relations, extends not only to the immediate process of production but also to the state in its various moments. Here too the bourgeois form must be restructured if it is to be maintained; here too the restructuring of the bourgeois form subjects its continued existence to particular strains. The crisis of the state form is just as inevitable as the crisis of the capital relation, is in fact one moment of that crisis. The mobilisation of the countertendencies to the tendency of the rate of profit to fall that takes the place through crisis means a massive restructuring of social relations involving, as Hirsch points out, the whole "re-organisation of a historical complex of general social conditions of production and relations of exploitation" (Hirsch 1978, 74). The fact that increasingly the mobilisation of these countertendencies is effected through the state means that inevitably the whole complex of political relations is directly permeated by the general restructuring of the relations of production. The crisis and restructuring of the capital relation as a whole is inevitably also a period of crisis and restructuring of the forms constituting bourgeois political relations. Thus, to take an obvious example, the present attempt by British capital to raise the rate of surplus value does not simply mean the introduction of new technology or the implementation of wage cuts by individual capitals; what is involved is rather a very long and extremely complex struggle conducted at all levels, embracing such elements as the repeated attempts to restructure the relations between trade unions and the state and relations within the trade unions themselves (Donovan Commission, In Place of Strife, Industrial Relations Act, Social Contract), massive ideological campaigns (on productivity, inflation, etc.), changes in state expenditure and taxation, complex interplay of political parties, plans to introduce worker directors, etc.

The point that the crisis of capital is inevitably also a crisis of the state form is perhaps worth emphasising, if only because it differs from the view taken by a number of other authors. The problem is often approached through a discussion of the relation between "economic crisis" and "political crisis." Many authors argue against the widespread but simplistic assumption that economic crisis leads more or less automatically to a crisis of the political system (see especially Gramsci's critique of Rosa Luxemburg: 1971, 233). Countering this view, however, these authors either evade the problem by emphasising the relative autonomy of the political or, in the better cases (see Autorenkollektiv 1976), suggest that whether the crisis in the economic base gives rise to a "political crisis" and "ideological crisis" will depend on the organisation and militancy of the class struggle, an organisation and militancy that cannot be derived from the capital form. Superficially, of course, that is correct. Such an approach, however, does have several weaknesses. Most fundamentally, it treats the capitalist crisis as an economic crisis rather than as a crisis of the capital relation, which inevitably involves a restructuring of that relation in both its economic and its political forms. It then presents "political crisis" as a possible catastrophic crisis of the political system rather than as an inevitable process of restructuring the forms of political constitution. Such an approach is dangerous because it tends to focus attention on the fetishised forms of bourgeois party politics and to present a "top-down" view of the political system, rather than the "bottom-up" perspective of the working class in struggle. It tends to distract attention away from the less dramatic but very significant restructuring of the political constitution, a process that is inherent in the crisis and restructuring of capital. This restructuring is of great practical importance because it poses new problems for socialist strategy and opens up new opportunities for action. The attempts to recategorise the population in terms of communities, regions, nations, consumers, parents, participants in an enterprise, social partners of one sort or another: these make up the crisis and restructuring of the political form, these are the changes that create, willy-nilly, new forms of political organisation and pose new problems and new opportunities that cannot be waved out of existence by a dismissal of the "reductionist" identification of "economic" and "political" crisis. It is important to understand the changes taking place as a process of restructuring and potential destabilisation. The problem with the simple stress on defending the old forms of state now being overcome is that it not only misses this opportunity but effectively squashes it by asserting the neutrality or potential neutrality of the state.

2. *State form and state apparatus*: The struggle to reformulate the social relations of capitalism takes place not only outside of the state apparatus, and not only through the action of the state apparatus upon society but also within the state apparatus itself. The antagonism and conflict that pervade the whole of capitalist society are present equally in the state apparatus. Resistance to the oppression inscribed in the state form is not only external to the state apparatus, it takes place also within the state apparatus, both in the actions of state employees and elected representatives and in the behaviour of state "clients" fighting back against the oppression that seems implicit in their relations with the state. Often these antagonisms are expressed simply in individual acts of rebellion with little political consequence, but sometimes they take more significant forms: organisation by claimants, community workers joining tenants in protests against state housing provision, Community Health Council workers organising workers to disrupt the activities of the Area Health Authority, etc. Each of these may be seen as attempts to confront the oppressive definitions implicit in the state and to challenge the limits of the state form while remaining within the framework of the state apparatus.

To conceptualise these struggles, it seems inevitable that we should make some distinction between state form and state apparatus. We have already seen that the concept of the state form is an essentially critical one: its purpose is to emphasise that the state cannot be understood as an autonomous institution but only in the context of its historical interconnections with the developing forms of capital. Nevertheless, this does not mean that the institution does not exist; the form must have some institutional embodiment. It is thus possible to speak of a "double dimension" of the state as relation of capitalist domination and as apparatus (see Pérez Sainz 1979). Now clearly the form cannot have a disembodied existence. It is materialised through the institutional development of the state and the activity of the state agents. Similarly, the institutional development of the apparatus can only be the expression of the historical development of social relations.

Nevertheless, the distinction between form and apparatus does acquire significance if we view the matter from the point of view of the socialist employee (or "client") of the state. For socialists in this position, there is little doubt that they work within the state apparatus. However, their problem as socialists is to shape their daily activity in such a way that they do not simply act as agents for the reproduction of capitalist social relations. Their problem, in other words, is to maintain their daily contact with the state apparatus (for this is normally a practical necessity), while combatting the processing of social activity usually implicit in the actions of the state: to work within the state apparatus, yet against the state form. The extent to which this is possible will depend on the general constellation of class forces, but for the socialist working within (or entering into routine contact with) the state apparatus who does not want her (or his) socialism to relate only to evening and weekend activity (thus consigning herself to the fate of Sisyphus, rolling the rock of socialism up the hill at night, only to see her alter ego rolling it down again during the day), this is an absolutely unavoidable problem.

In thinking about the problem of those engaged in daily contact with the state it is necessary to distinguish between the state apparatus (as an institutional network of financial and administrative controls) and the state as a form of capitalist social relations: the "double dimension" of the state must be retained and explored. This is certainly not to suggest that the state apparatus is a neutral venue for class struggle. Although the state apparatus must be distinguished from the state form, its general shape and detailed minutiae have been moulded by the past imposition of bourgeois forms upon class struggle. The state apparatus can be seen as the institutional fossil of past struggles to reproduce bourgeois forms. Thus, the conformity of behaviour within the state apparatus with bourgeois forms is normally more or less ensured not only by the informal codes of conduct but by the host of administrative and financial regulations backed by force that is the institutional outcome of those past struggles. The significance of organisational structures is constantly changing in the course of class struggle, so that it becomes, in particular circumstances, more or less meaningful to struggle within or through the state apparatus against the state form, against the constitution of social relations on a fetishised basis. The success or failure of such a struggle will always depend on the general constellation of class forces and the degree to which such a struggle is integrated into the general process of class struggle. It is impossible, therefore, to define a priori the limits of such a struggle. The point to be retained, however, is that the relation between form and its institutionalised expression is not the same in the case of the state as it is in the case of an enterprise. The imposition of the state form upon the state apparatus does not take place directly through the operation of the law of value on the market, so the problem of the limits to which the bourgeois form can be transcended is different in the case of the state apparatus than in the case of an individual enterprise.

The problem for capital is to maintain the bourgeois forms of social relations, increasingly through (and therefore also in) the activity of the state—even if it means breaking up the state apparatus in order to maintain the capitalist (and with it the state) form of social relations, as in the case of regional devolution or political independence. The problem for socialists is to break through the state form as an integral part of smashing the social relations of capitalism. For most socialists, especially those who are either employed by or come into daily direct contact with the state, this must at least occasionally involve struggle within or through the state apparatus against the state form. There is no way in which this problem can be avoided, there is no way in which one can remain class-neutral in one's contact with the state: either one is playing a part in the fetishisation of social relations or one is struggling against it. In recent years the oppressive nature of the everyday practice of the state has been more often emphasised by libertarian radicals than by socialists, who have perhaps been too aware of the limitations of radical practice. The weakness of the radical experiments of the early 1970s, however, lay not so much in the fact that they tried to develop alternative practices *before* the revolution as in the fact that, first, they did not conceive of these practices as part of a long process of *class* revolution and, second, their practices, being directed to the liberation of the individual rather than the class, were reintegrated into the normal forms of bourgeois intercourse with relative ease.

The extent to which socialists can act through particular state institutions in a manner directed against the state form (i.e., in a manner that will lead to the strengthening of *class* organisation) is always a question of tactics. The changing forms of class struggle and of the process of constituting bourgeois political relations are constantly creating new possibilities of action and closing others, as the significance of particular institutions for class struggle changes. While it is clear that any decisive rupture of the state as a form of social relations presupposes the smashing of the state as an apparatus, it does not follow that we must await the smashing of the apparatus before directing our activity against the fetishising processes implicit in the state form.

3. *Against the state form:* This essay has argued that much of the recent state theory has failed to respond to the developing forms of working-class struggle. Analyses of the state that focus on factional conflicts within the state apparatus, on the determinants and limitations of state action, or on the functions performed by the state may (or may not) be important, but they are of little direct assistance to the socialist (party member or not) who comes into daily contact with the state apparatus. It may be important for a social worker or social security claimant to understand the role of state social expenditure in the reproduction of capital, but it is never clear how any such analysis can guide the social worker or claimant in her or his daily activity. To dismiss the daily activity of the social worker or social security claimant as being irrelevant for the overthrow of capitalism or irretrievably capitalist in nature before the great day of the revolutionary event is not only unhelpful for the vast majority of socialists who are not and cannot be full-time professional revolutionaries but ultimately reactionary in effect, for there is no way in which contact with the state apparatus (or any other aspect of social activity) can stand outside the class struggle.

We have suggested that in order to begin to lay the basis for an understanding of the daily practice of the state it is necessary to focus not on the functions but on the form of the state and to develop some of the insights to be found in recent German work in a much more explicitly political manner. The state does not simply perform certain functions but performs them in a certain way that categorises (or confirms the categorisation of) classes into individuals, families, and superficial groupings of one sort or another, all of which abstract from class relations. Yet it is only by the constitution of explicitly class relations that the transition to socialism can be put firmly on the agenda.

The task, therefore, is not to work through bourgeois forms to gain positions of "power" and "influence" (the hopeless, destructive illusion of Eurocommunism) but to work *against* those forms, to develop through practice material forms of counterorganisation that express and consolidate the underlying unity of the resistance to class oppression, that stand in opposition to the fetishised and fetishising forms of bourgeois "politics" and "economics." What is revolution but the process of weakening and ultimately breaking with the bourgeois forms of intercourse, a process of the daily puncturing of bourgeois forms as a necessary prelude to that final decay that will lay a radically new basis for struggle?[19] To imagine that you can weaken the old forms of intercourse by working through them is nonsense.

It is not possible at the end of this essay to do that; the essay itself doesn't provide a basis to set forth a concrete programme for transcending the state form in daily practice. That would require a full historical analysis of the changing bourgeois forms. A theory of anti-bourgeois forms can no more be drawn out of an ahistorical hat than can a developed theory of bourgeois forms. The most basic point, however, which is valid for all bourgeois societies, is that the only way to defeat class exploitation is through class organisation. Thus, for Pannekoek, the key point about councils as a proletarian form of organisation was that, in contrast to the bourgeois forms of representative democracy, they were specifically class-based, "*founded not on persons but on Labour*" (Pannekoek 1969 [1919], 137).[20] How this is to be achieved, how we can best develop forms of organisation "founded not on persons but on Labour," how in any given situation the categories of person, community, region, parent, tenant, taxpayer, etc. are to be undermined by class organisation cannot be answered in a general essay like this. There is no timeless answer. We must beware of the hardened concepts of our revolutionary tradition.

Socialism is not a fixed, unchanging doctrine. As the world develops, people's insight increases, and as new relations come into being there arise new methods for achieving our goal (Pannekoek 1974 [1919], 52).

19 See Anton Pannekoek, "World Revolution and Communist Tactics," in *Pannekoek and Gö̈urter's Marxism*, ed. D.A. Smart (London: Pluto, 1978 [1920]), 118: "Certain conditions must be fulfilled in any society for the social process of production and collective existence to be possible, and these relations acquire the firm hold of spontaneous habits and moral norms—sense of duty, industriousness, discipline; in the first instance, the process of revolution consists in a loosening of these old relations." See also John Holloway, "The State and Everyday Struggle," in *The State Debate*, ed. Simon Clarke (London: Macmillan, 1991), 231.

20 This passage appears in Pannekoek's discussion of the Bolsheviks' dissolution of the Constituent Assembly. It is interesting to compare Pannekoek's approach with Poulantzas's treatment of the same topic (*State, Power, Socialism*, 253) and, more generally, with the latter's absurd and unfounded argument that the development of statism in Russia is to be attributed to the Bolsheviks' exclusive reliance on council democracy (the main theme of the final part of Poulantzas, *State, Power, Socialism*).

References

Anderson, Perry. *Lineages of the Absolutist State*. London: New Left Books, 1974.

Autorenkollektiv. "Klassenbewegung und Staat in der Bundesrepublik." *Gesellschaft*, Frankfurt, nos. 8–9 (1978).

Barker, Colin. "A 'New' Reformism?," *International Socialism* 2, no. 4 (1979): 88–108.

Beer, Samuel. *Modern British Politics*. London: Faber and Faber, 1965.

Blanke, Bernhard, Ulrich Jürgens, and Hans Kastendiek. "On the Current Marxist Discussion on the Analysis of Form and Function of the Bourgeois State." In *State and Capital: A Marxist Debate*, edited by John Holloway and Sol Picciotto. London: Edward Arnold, 1978.

Clarke, Simon. "Capital, Fractions of Capital and the State: 'Neo-Marxist' Analysis of the South African State," *Capital and Class* 2, no. 2 (Summer 1978): 32–77.

Clarke, Simon. "Marxism, Sociology and Poulantzas' Theory of the State," *Capital and Class* 1, no. 2 (Summer 1977): 1–31.

Cockburn, Cynthia. *The Local State*. London: Pluto, London, 1977.

CSE State Apparatus and State Expenditure Group. *Struggle over the State: Cuts and Restructuring in Contemporary Britain*. London: CSE Books, 1979.

Davis, Mike. "'Fordism' in Crisis: A Review of Michel Aglietta's *Régulation et crises: L'expérience des Etats-Unis*." *The Review* 2, no. 2 (1978): 207–69.

Edinburgh CSE Cuts Group I. "State Form and State Apparatus"; II. "The Cuts and the Crisis of the State Form"; III. "State, Crisis and Transport"; IV. "The Crisis of the State and the Struggle against Bourgeois Forms." *CSE Conference Papers*, 1978.

Edinburgh CSE Group. "State, Restructuring, Local State." *CSE Conference Papers*, 1977.

Flatow, Sybille von, and Freerk Huisken. "Zum Problem der Ableitung des bürgerlichen Staates." *Prokla* 7 (1973).

Foster, John. *Class Struggle in the Industrial Revolution*. London: Weidenfeld and Nicolson, 1974.

Foucault, Michel. *Discipline and Punish*. London: Allen Lane, 1977.

Gerstenberger, Heide. "Fetish and Control." *CSE Conference Papers*, 1977.

Gramsci, Antonio. *Selections from the Prison Notebooks*. London: Lawrence and Wishart, 1971.

Habermas, Jürgen. *Legitimationsprobleme im Spätkapitalismus*. Frankfurt: Suhrkamp, 1973. (Translated as *Legitimation Crisis*. London: Heinemann, 1976.)

Hintze, Otto. *The Historical Essays of Otto Hintze*. New York: Oxford University Press, 1975 (1902).

Hirsch, Joachim. "The State Apparatus and Social Reproduction: Elements of a Theory of the Bourgeois State." In *State and Capital: A Marxist Debate*, edited by John Holloway and Sol Picciotto. London: Edward Arnold, 1978.

Holloway, John. "The State and Everyday Struggle." In *The State Debate*, edited by Simon Clarke. London: Macmillan, 1991.

Holloway, John, and Sol Picciotto. "Capital, Crisis and the State." *Capital and Class* 1, no. 2 (Summer 1977): 76–101.

Holloway, John, and Sol Picciotto, eds. *State and Capital: A Marxist Debate*. London: Edward Arnold, 1978.

London CSE Group. "Crisis, the Labour Movement and the Alternative Economic Strategy." *Capital and Class* 3, no. 2 (Summer 1979): 68–93.

Lukács, Georg. *The Ontology of Social Being*. London: Merlin, 1978.

Luxemburg, Rosa. *Reform or Revolution?*. New York: Pathfinder, 1988 (1899).

Marx, Karl. *Capital*, vol. 1, Moscow: Progress Publishers, 1965.

Marx, Karl. "Wage Labour and Capital." In Karl Marx and Frederick Engels, *Selected Works*, vol. 1. Moscow: Foreign Languages Publishing House, 1962.

Marx, Karl, and Frederick Engels. "The German Ideology." In *Collected Works*, vol. 5. London: Lawrence and Wishart, 1976.

McConnell, Grant. *Private Power and American Democracy*. New York: Vintage Books, 1966.

Offe, Claus. *Contradictions of the Welfare State*. Edited by John Keane. London: Hutchinson, 1984.

Offe, Claus. *Strukturprobleme des kapitalistischen Staates*. Frankfurt: Campus Bibliothek, 1972. [Sections have been translated in *Kapitalistate*, 1, 109–16 and 2, 73–75, 1973; K. Von Beyme, ed., *German Political Studies*, vol. 1. London: Sage, 1974, 31–57; *Telos* 25 (Fall 1975).]

Pannekoek, Anton. "Bolchevisme et democratie." In *Pannekoek et les Conseils Ouvriers*, edited by Serge Bricianer. Paris: EDI, 1969 (1919).

Pannekoek, Anton. "Sozialdemokratie und Kommunismus." In Cajo Brendel, ed., *Neubestimmung des Marxismus*. Berlin: Karin Kramer Verlag, 1974 (1919).

Pannekoek, Anton. "World Revolution and Communist Tactics." In *Pannekoek and Göurter's Marxism*, edited by D.A. Smart. London: Pluto, 1978 (1920).

Pérez Sainz, Juan Pablo. "Commodity, State and Capital Reproduction: Basic Elements." *CSE Conference Papers*, 1979.

Picciotto, Sol. "Myths of Bourgeois Legality." *CSE Conference Papers*, 1977.

Picciotto, Sol. "The Theory of the State, Class Struggle and the Rule of Law." Mimeo, 1979.

Poggi, Gianfranco. *The Development of the Modern State*. London: Hutchinson, 1978.

Poulantzas, Nicos. "The Capitalist State: A Reply to Miliband and Laclau." *New Left Review* 95 (1976): 63–83.

Poulantzas, Nicos. *State, Power, Socialism*. London: New Left Books, 1978.

Reichelt, Helmut. *Zur logischen Struktur des Kapitalbegriffs bei Karl Marx*. Frankfurt: EVA, 1970.

Reichelt, Helmut. "Zur Staatstheorie im Frühwerk von Marx und Engels." In *Karl Marx, Friedrich Engels: Staatstheorie*, edited by Eike Hennig, Joachim Hirsch, Helmut Reichelt, and Gert Schäfer. Frankfurt: Ullstein, 1974.

Roberts, David. *Victorian Origins of the Welfare State*. New Haven: Yale University Press, 1960.

Rubin, Isaak Illich. "Abstract Labour and Value in Marx's System." *Capital and Class* 2, no. 2 (1978 [1927]): 107–39.

Sohn-Rethel, Alfred. *Intellectual and Manual Labour*. London: Macmillan, 1978.

Wilensky, Harold L., and Charles N. Lebeaux. *Industrial Society and Social Welfare*. New York: Collier-Macmillan, 1965.

TWO

The Red Rose of Nissan

The new Nissan factory in Sunderland was opened on September 11, 1986, with a great fanfare of publicity: television advertisements, documentaries, newspaper supplements, and news coverage of the formal opening by the prime minister.[1]

The theme of all this publicity was that the Nissan plant opened a new age. Here is a factory where managers and workers alike wear white coats and share the same canteen, where managers and workers alike are young (average age in the late twenties), a company where there have never been strikes, where trade unions are not forbidden but are redundant because workers enjoy good working conditions and identify with the aims of the company. The factory of the new age, of the new technology, of the new consensus. Light years away from the militancy of the car workers in the 1970s, and light years away from the macho management of Michael Edwardes, Ian MacGregor, or Rupert Murdoch.

Some weeks later, another event was surrounded by just as much glossy publicity, just as much sophisticated marketing: the launching of the new-look Labour Party at the annual conference, the party of the new Moral Majority, the party of the new consensus. Here too is a new age, a break with the past. The lid is closed on the dustbin of history, with its evil-smelling politics of conflict and trade union militancy. These evil odours are dispelled by the sweet smell of the red rose, the macho militants are replaced by the gentle man with the flower.

---

1 This essay is the product of many discussions in Edinburgh—thanks to all who took part.

The dawn of a new harmony in industry, the heralding of a new politics of consensus. Is this just coincidence, or does it tell us something about the direction being taken by capitalism in Britain?

The contrast suggested by the Nissan publicity is a contrast with the British car industry of the 1970s, and particularly with British Leyland. If British Leyland can be seen as a symbol of crisis, then Nissan symbolises its successful resolution. British Leyland symbolises not just the crisis of the car industry, not just the crisis of British capitalism, but the crisis of a particular pattern of production, often referred to as Fordism. In contrast, Nissan represents not just the success of Japanese capital but a new model of production relations, a current trend often referred to as neo-Fordism or post-Fordism.

The crisis at British Leyland in the mid-1970s is significant not only because it was a very large company and the last bastion of the British car industry, but because it stands as a stereotype of the industry associated with the long postwar boom. Production took place in large factories organised around the assembly line, very much in accordance with the principles adopted by Ford in the production of the Model T. The vast majority of the work was repetitive and required little skill. All the workers were organised in trade unions and throughout the long period of boom when any car produced could immediately be sold, they managed to achieve relatively high and constantly rising real wages.

Dull, repetitive, unskilled work in the factory compensated for by relatively high wages: the typical Fordist peace bargain was maintained. Ford's production of the Model T was trendsetting not only because of his use of the assembly line for the production of cars but also because of the way in which consumption was promoted as both reward for and stimulus to production. Ford paid his workers the high wages of five dollars a day in return for the intensive, monotonous work on the assembly line. With this wage they could become rich enough to buy a cheap car, thus stimulating demand for more Model Ts, more monotonous work, and so on.

At British Leyland the figures were different but the essence was the same, the core principle of postwar capitalist domination: accept the deadly, deadening alienation of boring work in return for high wages, which will allow you to live the life of mass consumption, which will in turn generate demand for the products of ever more alienating boring work.

Since, generally, it was men in this case who did the work in the factory, while women were seen as being more closely associated with consumption, this pattern of relations at work implied the development of a certain pattern of gender relations and a certain type of sexuality. The pattern of domination in the factory was complemented by a pattern of domination in the home, and it was on the basis of these relations that cars were produced: alienation in the factory produces alienation in the home, which in turn provides a stimulus to go out to alienated work.

The keystone holding this structure together was the trade unions and the practice of collective bargaining. Through the annual rounds of collective bargaining the trade-off between the death of alienated labour and the "life" of consumption was regularly negotiated and renegotiated.

Within this equilibrium there were, of course, conflicts and shifts in power. The long period of relative prosperity allowed the workers to build up a considerable position of strength. In British Leyland the bargaining strength of the workers (and the consequent limitations on management) were expressed most clearly in the system of mutuality. Under this system, management accepted that no new technology or reorganisation of working practices could be introduced without the prior agreement of the shop stewards. Mutuality was a striking embodiment of the strength of the workers within the Fordist equilibrium: the mutuality principle did not assert a revolutionary claim by the workers to control production but merely made clear that management's rights were limited and that any intensification of labour must be paid for. "Payment for change" was the key principle of the mutuality system.

Of course this was never the whole story. The Fordist wage contract in the factory could no more run smoothly than the marriage contract in the home. The trade-off between boredom at work and "life" outside could never be entirely successful. Inevitably, there were struggles in the factory that did not fall neatly into the Fordist pattern: struggles not just for higher wages or for the control of production but revolts against work as such: sabotage, absenteeism, wildcat strikes, etc. Revolts against work in the only form in which it existed: as death, as the negation of life and creativity.

For a long time, however, these expressions of frustration posed little threat to the structure as a whole. The Fordist peace deal was never the whole picture, but it was sufficiently real to provide a framework for the rapid and sustained growth of the British car industry (and other car industries) throughout the 1950s and much of the 1960s. However, it rested on a very fragile basis (like all social harmony in a class society): on the one hand, the balance between frustration and consumption was always a delicate (and potentially explosive) one, and, on the other hand, the whole system presupposed the expansion of the market and the relatively easy sale of the cars produced.

In the late 1960s and early 1970s the whole pattern of domination and production began to crack. Accumulated boredom made it increasingly difficult to contain frustrations within the factory. The bursting frustration found expression in high labour turnover, increasing absenteeism, and sabotage, and the frequent outbreak of strikes. In the British car industry as a whole, the level of strike activity rose markedly after 1963, and then very dramatically in the late 1960s and early 1970s: from 1969 to 1978 an annual average of more than 1,800,000 working days were lost through strikes in the car industry, as compared with an average of 377,600 working days lost per year in 1950–63 (Marsden et al. 1985, 121).

Significantly, the majority of these strikes were not for higher wages but arose out of disputes concerning conditions at work. In his Annual Report for 1976, the chairman of British Leyland (BL) recognised this: "In BL, though relatively few industrial disputes have been directly concerned with pay, so many strikes have occurred with no benefit either to the company or to the employees that one is forced to the conclusion that the underlying reason is the desire to make a protest" (quoted in Television History Workshop 1985, 81). The rising militancy of the late 1960s did not just aim at the renegotiation of the Fordist deal—more wages for nasty work. It struck at the core of Fordism itself: high wages were no longer sufficient to contain the accumulated frustration. As one BL manager commented: "This protest was, in my view, a protest against the capitalism and the democracy of this country" (Television History Workshop 1985, 81).

This was not a revolutionary situation. There was no question, at British Leyland or elsewhere in Britain, of a revolutionary assault on capital. But it would also be totally wrong to conclude from that that capital was not threatened. The structure of control that was the basis of capitalist development in the postwar period was being undermined. The capitalist class was not in imminent danger of being toppled but certainly no British Leyland manager could speak with the confidence of the centurion in the Gospels: "I say unto one, Go, and he goeth; and to another, Come, and he cometh; and to my servant, Do this, and he doeth it" (Luke 7: vii). The authority upon which the whole capitalist system of production is premised was no longer functioning.

The loss of authority within the factories blended with the collapse of the other fragile pillar of Fordism: production. Difficulties due to a combination of rising militancy and the fact that investments in new machinery were no longer leading to significant increases in productivity hit profits and brought to an end the constant expansion of the capitalist market on which the smooth functioning of the Fordist system had been premised. It was no longer true by the late 1960s that any car produced could be sold without difficulty, and by 1974, when world crisis was manifest and the rise in oil prices took its effect on motorists, car companies had to change their production methods to address intense competition. Management too was forced to attack the established patterns of work relations. From both sides of the capital-labour relation, the relative stability of Fordism was under assault. The period of compromise in which the trade unions had held the two sides together in apparent harmony gave way to a period of open conflict and open struggle for power. As the BL manager already quoted put it:

> The only thing that really stands out is the fact that both management and the shop stewards appreciated the situation—they both knew what their objectives were, and they both admitted to each other what they were doing. There was no question of it being a battle that was raging with people who were denying it—both sides openly admitted this was a struggle. Management were saying, "We are going to win." Shop stewards said, "We are going to win." (Television History Workshop 1985, 81)

The crisis at British Leyland was the breaking out of open battle. The Fordist equilibrium that had succeeded in containing frustrations and maintaining an adequate structure of control for so long that it had shaped a whole generation's image of capitalism was broken.

Capitalist crisis is never anything other than that: the breakdown of a relatively stable pattern of class domination. It appears as an economic crisis, expressed in a fall in the rate of profit, but its core is the failure of an established pattern of domination. From the point of view of capital, the crisis can be resolved only through the establishment of new patterns of domination. This does not mean that capital has new patterns ready-made to impose on the working class. For capital, the crisis can be resolved only through struggle, through the restoration of authority, and through a far from smooth search for new patterns of domination.

In the case of British Leyland, the reestablishment of control became identified with the question of raising productivity. Raising productivity was seen as the key to the survival of the company in the face of international competition. It was not just a question of introducing new machinery but of getting workers to work harder. As a Central Policy Review Staff report of 1975 said, "With the same power at his elbow and doing the same job as his continental counterparts, a British car assembly worker produces only half as much output per shift" (CPRS 1975). In these circumstances, there was little point in introducing new technology until new attitudes and a new discipline had been established. New technology would require a new type of control over the workforce, but at the same time it could also contribute to the creation of that control. As one manager in Ford put it when discussing the installation of thirty-nine new industrial robots: "We haven't got control of the labour force. We can't force each man to put each weld in the right place. So we've tried to build in quality through the machines" (Scarborough 1986, 99).

In British Leyland, the reestablishment of managerial control and the introduction of new technology were very tightly intertwined with the planning of a new car model, the Metro, to be produced at the end of the 1970s. The decision to use the most advanced technology (automated multiwelders and robots) in the production of the Metro was made in the mid-1970s, partly out of a concern for quality (machines being considered more reliable than workers) and partly because "there were felt to be unquantifiable advantages in using a technology which resulted in management having to deal with far fewer direct operatives" (Willman and Winch 1985, 50). Once the decision was taken to invest in high technology and to construct a new plant (the New West Works at Longbridge), it became more urgent than ever to establish managerial control before the new plant was opened.

The attempt by management to establish control can be seen in two phases. The first phase, running from the financial collapse of the company and the consequent takeover by the Labour government in 1974 to the appointment of Michael Edwardes as chief executive in October 1977, aimed at the incorporation of the shop stewards. When the finances of the company collapsed in December 1974, the government commissioned a report by Sir Don Ryder, chairman of the National Enterprise Board. The Ryder Plan, published in April 1975, underlined the urgency of change at British Leyland, but, recognising the strength of the shop stewards within

the company, it sought to achieve change through winning their cooperation. In particular, the Plan accepted the continuing existence of the
mutuality system and established a structure of joint management–shop
steward committees to discuss a wide range of issues relating to company
performance. After heated discussion, the shop stewards agreed to coop-
erate in the participation scheme, some even enthusiastically. As Derek
Robinson, the convenor of the shop stewards at Longbridge, put it, "If we
make Leyland successful, it will be a political victory. It will prove that
ordinary working people have got the intelligence and determination to
run industry" (*Guardian*, April 9, 1979, quoted in Scarborough 1986, 102).

Robinson's enthusiasm was not borne out by the experience.
Discussions in the joint committees took place within a framework already
tightly defined by managerial decisions, and they were separated from
the structure of collective bargaining in which the actual decisions on
working practices were made. Consequently, the shop stewards found that,
on the one hand, they had exercised little influence and that, on the other,
they were often compromised in the eyes of the workers they represented
by their participation in managerial decisions (Willman and Winch 1985;
Scarborough 1986).

From the management point of view, the participation exercise was both a success and a failure. On the one hand, it did promote
some degree of acceptance of the need for change; as one manager put
it, "Participation was a success and helped us in selling the changes we
wanted" (Scarborough 1986, 103). On the other hand, it was a slow and
cumbersome way of bringing about change, and it did not establish the
clear authority that management required: the power of the shop stewards was recognised, yet strike activity continued at a high level. In the
view of Michael Edwardes:

> The three-tier employee participation structure—a cornerstone of
> the Ryder remedy to solve the entrenched industrial relations prob-
> lems—only produced a bureaucratic paperchase dissipating man-
> agement resource and effort. Some management decisions were
> delayed by months while the joint consultative machinery tried
> unsuccessfully to grind out a consensus. Procedure and consulta-
> tion to avert industrial relations problems appeared to overwhelm
> decision-making and action-taking, yet during this time the number
> of disputes rose sharply. (Edwardes 1984, 39)

By 1977, it was clear that the Ryder strategy could not bring about the recovery of the company: productivity continued to fall and with it British Leyland's share of the market. Since effective managerial control could not be achieved through the incorporation of the shop stewards, it was necessary for management to become more openly aggressive. In October 1977, Michael Edwardes was appointed by the National Enterprise Board (with the approval of the Labour government) as chairman and chief executive of British Leyland.

For Edwardes, the key to success was the reassertion of capital's control over labour: the "sine qua non of survival was to establish the right to manage" (Edwardes 1984, 54), and this would involve "counteracting shop steward power" (Edwardes 1984, 79). Crucially, for him establishing the right to manage meant breaking the mutuality system and asserting management's right to introduce new working practices without the prior agreement of the shop stewards. Although Edwardes's managerial style was abrasive from the beginning, he first attacked the established pattern of management by taking on not the shop stewards but the managers themselves, getting rid of many and moving others to new positions. It was two years before he engaged the shop stewards in direct confrontation over the issue of mutuality. During those two years the position of the stewards had been considerably weakened by a number of plant closures, by the inflexibility of management in wage negotiations and by the sharp rise in unemployment at a national level. It was also weakened by management's new populist strategy designed to mobilise the workers against the shop stewards. Claiming that the shop stewards did not represent the wishes of their members, management developed a policy (after February 1979) of going over the heads of the shop stewards and appealing directly to the workers themselves:

> This often meant sending letters to employees' homes (where they could calmly and deliberately consider the situation with their families), the issuing of factory briefing sheets, and posters. When we felt a particular issue had wider significance we used newspaper advertisements and they seemed to be effective, for the militants invariably called "foul." (Edwardes 1984, 93)

In this way, "democracy" became a managerial strategy: direct ballots of the membership were used to counter the established patterns of trade union representation.

The confrontation over mutuality and managerial control came at the end of 1979. It began when, in response to continuing economic difficulties, Edwardes unveiled a Recovery Plan that provided for the loss of twenty-five thousand jobs and the closure or severe cutback of thirteen factories. The plan was initially opposed by the trade unions, but, in the face of management's assertion that the only alternative was closure of the company, the engineering unions decided to recommend acceptance in a ballot of the company's employees, and the ballot produced a large majority in favour. When a number of shop stewards then published a pamphlet criticising the plan (in November 1979), management responded by sacking Derek Robinson, one of the signatories of the pamphlet and chairman of the shop stewards' combine.

A strike in support of Robinson soon collapsed, although the shop stewards continued to support him and even reelected him convenor of the Longbridge stewards in January 1980. The stewards no longer wielded the same power as before. On the one hand, the national unions (particularly the engineers' union, the AUEW, of which Robinson was a member) failed to give him support: Robinson and the shop steward power he represented had long been a thorn in the flesh of the responsible national officials of the AUEW (Edwardes 1984, 117–23). On the other hand, it became clear that the shop stewards could no longer count on the active support of the union members: an important element was undoubtedly the acceptance of the Ryder strategy of involving shop stewards in a participation scheme that was not widely supported by the workers (Willman and Winch 1985, 83; Scarborough 1986). And although Edwardes's aggressive strategy appeared to be the very opposite of the Ryder approach, it actually built upon it in important respects.

Once the Recovery Plan was accepted, management spelled out some of its implications in a 92-page document on changes in working practices. In Edwardes's own words: "At the heart of the 92-page document outlining the changes we needed was the challenge to 'mutuality'" (Edwardes 1984, 133). A document circulated at the time to management throughout the company emphasised:

> It is managers who have the responsibility for managing, leading and motivating employees and for communicating on company matters ... shop stewards have the right to represent and to communicate trade union information to their members at the workplace

but only within the rules and procedures jointly established. . . . Every manager must play his part in defeating the small minority who would like to see BL fail. (quoted in Willman and Winch 1985, 130)

At issue was the extent of managerial control within the factory. Management was aiming "to change the habits of two business lifetimes" (Edwardes 1984, 133) and to recover for capital the authority of the proud centurion: I say unto one, Go, and he goeth.

Negotiations over the document broke down: the stewards could not agree to the abandonment of mutuality. Management responded by circulating the document as the "Blue Newspaper" to all employees and gave notice that it would be implemented on April 8–9, 1980: any worker arriving for work on that day would be deemed to have accepted the new working practices. The union response was uncoordinated and resistance quickly collapsed. Management had been successful, and capital had asserted its right to rule: "On those two days, Tuesday 8th April and Wednesday 9th April 1980, thirty years of management concessions (which had made it impossible to manufacture cars competitively) were thrown out of the window, and our car factories found themselves with a fighting chance of becoming competitive" (Edwardes 1984, 135). The power of the shop stewards had been effectively broken: management had won.

The way was then clear for the launching of the Metro in October 1980. Workers were carefully selected for the new plant to make sure that they had the right attitude and that anyone with a record of militancy was excluded. The success of the Metro depended on a blend of new technology and new workers: multiwelders and robots were of no use unless the workers had the right attitudes to go with them.

The key word in the reform of working practices is "flexibility." Flexibility means essentially the removal of barriers to management's right to tell the workers what to do, where to do it, and at what speed. The workers should no longer insist on job demarcations: they must be "flexible" enough to move from one job to another. As one worker from the Cowley plant commented:

There's now a constant attack, and all the protective agreements that were established in the sixties are now all gone. Workers are herded around now like cattle in those plants. The protective agreements,

the seniority agreements, which were the most important protective agreements, are now completely gone. We're seeing conditions
where workers that have worked in off-track jobs for thirty or forty
years are given five minutes' notice to get onto a track. Often with
medical conditions. Often working in a pit, with overhead conditions that make it absolutely impossible for them to do the job. And
they're just directed totally ruthlessly after forty years of working
with the company. "Get in that pit and do that job or find yourself
another job outside." And I'm not exaggerating at all—that is what is
happening every day. Every day in those plants. And the difference
between that and what existed when the trade unions had power a
few years ago is absolute difference of chalk to cheese. (Television
History Workshop 1985, 108)

Shop stewards are no longer able to exert control over the speed of
work or the mobility of the workers in the same way as before. The shop
stewards' organisation still exists, but they have far fewer facilities and a
greatly reduced role: they no longer have any part in negotiating wages,
bonuses, or effort levels, their position being reduced mainly to the representation of workers in grievance procedures. The aim of management
was never to destroy trade unionism within the company, merely to limit
its scope so that it assisted rather than challenged managerial authority.

Productivity on the Metro line surpassed even management expectations. It rose sharply in other plants as well, suggesting that the rise was
due at least as much to the new pattern of industrial relations as to the
new technology. The level of strike activity also fell. The change in the
position was so dramatic that by early 1984 Longbridge was reported to
have the highest productivity of any car plant in Europe (Willman and
Winch 1985, 155). Raising productivity to European levels, however, is
no longer sufficient to withstand international competition. BL (now the
Rover Group) continues to face acute difficulties. The current challenge is
to raise productivity and quality to Japanese standards. But that requires
further changes, not so much in technology as in workers' attitudes.

What Edwardes (whose term of office ended in 1982) achieved was the
destruction of the power of the shop stewards, the destruction of barriers
to managerial control. This sort of aggressive managerial approach could
(and did) force the workers to obey the commands of management, but it
could hardly be expected to produce a devoted and enthusiastic workforce.

It is, however, just this sort of devotion and enthusiasm that is now considered necessary to ensure the quality of the products.

The Edwardes "macho management" can now be seen as a transitional phase, necessary to destroy the obstacles to managerial control but unable to establish the basis for a new stable pattern of industrial relations. What was achieved was the destruction of the old pattern of relations and a resounding defeat for labour. What management needs to do now is build on this defeat and mould the submissive worker into an enthusiastic worker, proud of his company.

Changes in this direction are already taking place at the Rover Group. When the appointment of the new chairman and chief executive Graham Day was announced early in 1986, it was questioned whether one of Edwardes's leading collaborators, Harold Musgrove, could stay on as chairman of Austin Rover, one reason being that it was doubtful "whether Mr. Musgrove's approach—'whipping people's backsides to get the cars out of the plant' as one put it—is the right one today" (*Financial Times*, March 22, 1986). And indeed, Mr. Musgrove's resignation was one of the first consequences of Day's appointment.

A more positive indication of the same trend can be seen in Austin Rover's current "working with pride" initiative. As Andy Barr, the managing director in charge of this initiative, put it: "We need to change attitudes and not just behaviour patterns. We need total involvement to ensure that quality and reliability of our products" (*Financial Times*, September 18, 1986).

Applicants for a job on the Rover assembly line at Cowley now undergo a two-day assessment to discuss the aims and objectives of the company. Even parents or wives and children are encouraged to take part, "to come along and judge whether Austin Rover is the company for their family" (*Financial Times*, September 18, 1986). As Barr put it: "We are not looking just for manual skills and dexterity. We want to know whether their aspirations are the same as the company's. It is a two-way process. What is good for people is good for the company" (*Financial Times*, June 20, 1986).

The "macho management" style is being replaced by a new image: an image of a caring management supported by a proud and dedicated workforce.

The image to which the Rover management aspires is already being presented by the new Nissan factory opened on September 11 in

Sunderland. The company's television advertisements project a picture of a new harmony, far removed from the strike and acrimony of traditional British car manufacturing:

> Imagine a car factory where no one goes on strike, and where no one is made redundant either. Imagine if the managing director dressed just the same as the men on the line. Imagine if the management and the workers got together every day to see how they could make things better. Imagine if work wasn't just about getting a better pay packet, but about working together to make something you could be proud of. Maybe then it would be possible to make a car so good, they'd have a 100,000-mile or three-year warranty. Or is this just a day-dream? (Quoted in Bassett 1986, 148)

All the advertisements have the same theme: with Nissan, motor manufacturing enters a new world. The relationship between management and labour is transformed. The Nissan worker is a new worker, so new that he is no longer a worker. He is a staffer: "they don't have 'workers' at Sunderland" (Nissan advertisement feature, *Observer*, September 14, 1986).

The "staffers" were carefully chosen to make sure that they were really new men, that they bore no taint of the old trade union militancy. First the site for the factory was selected—"one of the most exhaustive location searches in commercial history, looking at more than fifty sites in all, with local authorities vigorously bidding against each other for the development" (Bassett 1986, 149). Once the site was chosen (a former airport near Sunderland), the company set about choosing the "staffers." Management has plenty of scope for rejecting anyone with unconstructive attitudes:

> More than 11,000 applications were received for the first 247 posts at the new plant and everyone was put through one of the most intense and vigorous selection courses imaginable. The vacancies for 22 supervisors, a kind of hybrid foreman, attracted 3,000 applications. (Advertisement feature, *Observer*, September 14, 1986)

The option of creating a non-union plant was considered but rejected by the company because it was felt that such a decision could be a constant source of friction. Instead, they decided that they would recognise only a single union and interviewed the various possible unions (T&GWU,

AUEW, GMBATU) before making a choice: "We were forced to parade before prospective employers like beauty queens," as one of the regional secretaries put it (Bassett 1986, 149). The company chose the engineering union, the AUEW, and concluded an agreement with it that virtually eliminated the possibility of a strike: all disputes are to be settled by negotiation, conciliation, or arbitration.

The question of union organisation is, in any case, peripheral if one follows the image projected by the company. Antagonism between management and labour is a thing of the past. Management and production workers wear the same clothes and eat in the same canteen; workers are not required to clock on in the mornings; wage packets are replaced by salaries paid directly into the employee's bank. All are part of a team aiming to produce cars of high quality. Job demarcation has no place here, of course: the emphasis is on flexibility of crafts, skills, and jobs. "The concept has been to create a team or small group of workers (sorry, 'production staffers') using and swapping different skills" (Advertisement feature, *Observer*, September 14, 1986).

The whole world of motor manufacturing is transformed. Class struggle has no place here: there is apparently no antagonism. Struggle as such has no place here: the New Man does not fight. This new harmonious world has been achieved not by struggle but by the rejection of struggle. Indeed, the new world represents liberation from struggle, from the old world of strife. Here at Nissan, managers and workers alike are able to do what they have always wanted to do: to make products of high quality, unhindered by union interference. In this view, the militancy of the 1970s defeated itself: it was both irrational and sterile. The New Man is not militant, he knows that all problems can be solved by communication: "'He who communicates is very much king,' advocates Peter Wickens, Nissan's personnel director. If the team leader is not happy he can chat to the supervisor and they all sit down and try to iron things out" (Advertisement feature, *Observer*, September 14, 1986).

The New Man is still a man, of course. The importance of ensuring reliability and keeping absenteeism to an absolute minimum "leads to very careful screening of recruits in order to ensure that they will have minimum distractions from the domestic sphere, which, in a patriarchal context means a stronger preference for male workers" (Sayer 1986, 67). The New Man is still a man but not an aggressive, unreliable man: he is a responsible, caring family man with a good, stable home environment.

The world of Nissan is the world of new harmony, the new consensus. Militancy has been thrown into the dustbin of history, as has macho management: the names of Derek Robinson, Arthur Scargill, as well as Michael Edwardes and Ian MacGregor, are best forgotten as aberrations in the forward march of rational common sense.

From the crisis at Leyland and the establishment of Nissan it is possible to draw some conclusions about capitalist development in Britain over the last fifteen years or so.

The most obvious point is that the changes that have taken place cannot be understood without a concept of crisis. The crisis at British Leyland was a crisis in the established methods of producing cars. It was not just that the established technology was outdated but that the patterns of relations between labour and management associated with semi-automatic assembly-line production were no longer viable. The crisis was above all a crisis in the relation of domination: the established patterns of control over labour had broken down. As such, it was necessarily also a crisis of management. New ways of managing labour had to be found (and in the process many of the old managers had to be sacked). And it was also a crisis of the trade unions, because the established trade union structure was based upon the maintenance of a certain type of equilibrium between capital and labour.

The crisis was an outbreak of open struggle between capital and labour. To reiterate, the established pattern of domination had broken down: this was not a revolutionary situation but a situation in which everything seemed possible. Capital could not allow that to continue: it needed to reassert its right to rule, its arrogantly proclaimed "right to manage," its right to determine what is possible and what is not.

There is no doubt that in this struggle capital was victorious and labour was defeated. In the case of British Leyland, managerial strategy went through various phases, the most effective of which was undoubtedly the aggressive "macho" management of Edwardes. But each apparent reversal of managerial strategy built upon the achievements of the previous phase. Edwardes was able to build upon the isolation of the shop stewards that resulted from Ryder's corporatist approach, just as the present "working with pride" approach builds upon the crushing of the workers under Edwardes.

Over the period as a whole, relations of production have changed in a way that would have been inconceivable in the mid-1970s. The reassertion of managerial authority has gone hand in hand with the exclusion of vast numbers of workers. The number of manual workers employed by BL fell from 120,000 to 26,000 in a space of eight years, a fall of almost 100,000, as compared with the 400-odd employed by Nissan. The restructuring of the labour process and of relations between management and labour is simultaneously the creation of large-scale unemployment. The two cannot be separated.

Why was labour defeated? One factor was certainly the insecurity of existence on which capitalism is based: if you do not own capital, you have to sell your labour power in order to survive at an acceptable standard. During the period of conflict at British Leyland, unemployment rose sharply and the threat of being made redundant was acute. In those circumstances it was easy for management to use the threat of closure to impose its will.

A second factor was the way in which the shop stewards (and the national trade unions) were internally weakened just at the moment when their power appeared greatest. The involvement of shop stewards and officials in the participation scheme under the Ryder Plan (and in the whole national corporatist structure of the Social Contract) led to an alienation of the workers from their "representatives." Edwardes's strategy of direct communication with the workers was able to build very successfully upon this alienation.

Participation had this effect because, inevitably perhaps, it meant participation in making the company competitive again. The stewards accepted this goal, just as they did not question the need to introduce new technology in order to achieve it: there was no obvious alternative. In the absence of an alternative, the logic of capitalist development imposed itself: cars must be made as efficiently as possible and management must manage. The law of value asserts itself as necessity in a capitalist society.

It would be wrong to think that the crisis is over. The Rover Group is still in grave difficulty and there are obviously problems in implementing the new methods that have become fashionable among managers. Edwardes's legacy is not the best basis for building up a sense of dedication and pride among the workers.

The case of Nissan is instructive because the company was able to start afresh, taking for granted the destruction of the old traditions. In Nissan it is possible to see not yet a new established pattern of relations between management and labour but trends that indicate the shape of an emergent pattern. The extensive use of new technology means that many of the problems of control (such as control of the quality of welding or painting, for example) are transferred from direct supervision of the production workers to the design and especially the programming of the multiwelder or robot.

Control of the workforce does not, in any case, present the same problems as before: establishing a new factory in a greenfield site and in an area of high unemployment means that many of the problems of managerial control can be transferred to the point of selection. By ensuring that only workers with the right attitude are employed, management is able to largely resolve not only the problem of militancy but also the questions of quality, flexibility, and discipline. It now becomes possible to expect the workers to identify with the company to the extent of being concerned about the quality of the product, to demand flexibility in the performance of jobs, and to assume the sort of discipline that makes just-in-time production (with its minimal stocking of components) possible.

In this context, trade unionism comes to have a new meaning. The new factory does not exclude trade unions, but the unions, like the workers, undergo a process of selection and have to satisfy the company that they have the right attitude. The new trade union is cooperative and identifies with the interests of the company. For the leaders of the electricians' union, the EEPTU, and the engineers' union, the AUEW—the two unions most strongly identified with this trend—militancy is irrational and outdated: it has no place in this new world. The miners' strike and the printers' struggle at Wapping are untimely relics of a buried past. The new trade union, like the new worker, is liberated from the past, free to enjoy the new harmony of suffocating conformism on the graves of the defeated and to the exclusion of millions.

Of course that is not the whole story. It cannot be.

There are striking parallels between the phases of managerial strategy in the car industry and the development of the British state. In the state too there is a certain equilibrium that holds until the mid-1970s. As in British Leyland, that equilibrium is based on a recognition of the strength of the trade unions and therefore of their importance for the whole structure of government. In British Leyland this is known as mutuality; in the state it is called Keynesianism.

Often the term "Keynesianism" is used to refer to a set of economic policies designed to ensure full employment and the even development of the economy through demand management or to the economic theory that supports those policies. The adoption of such policies and the development of Keynesian theory, however, were not just historical chance: policies and theory alike grew out of a recognition of the growing power (and therefore threat) of the working class and of the need to develop a new form of controlling and harnessing that power. In Britain it was the outbreak of the Second World War that made this need particularly urgent and led to the co-opting of trade union leaders into the government and the commitment by the state to maintain full employment and to implement welfare state policies after the war. In the postwar period, in which the expansion of mass production and the tight labour market consolidated the power of labour, Keynesianism became the established pattern of domination.

Essentially mutuality and Keynesianism are the same thing. Both principles recognize the strength of the working class and so its ability to impose limits on the power of the state (or management) to do as it wishes. At the level of the factory, it is recognised that management cannot introduce changes in technology or working practices without the prior agreement of the shop stewards. At the national level, it is accepted that the control of wages or other aspects of industrial relations cannot be imposed against the wishes of the trade unions and that this is an area in which the law should not intervene.

In both cases there is an attempt to build the power of the unions into the structure of control and to use it to capital's advantage. The key principle is the conversion of the frustrations of the workers into monetary demands and the harnessing of those demands in such a way that they become a positive force for capital accumulation. In British Leyland and other companies, this is achieved through collective bargaining and the convention of payment for change. At the level of the state, the attempts to regulate demand in the interests of capital accumulation have the same end. Demand is the frustration of the working class converted into money. Demand management is precisely what it says it is: management of the monetised frustrations of the working class in such a way as to convert them into a stimulus for capital accumulation.

In both cases it was clear by the late 1960s that the established structure of domination and compromise was obstructing the development of capitalism in Britain. However, it was still a very long way from the recognition that it was essential to break the established balance to actually being able to do so. In British Leyland, it was recognised in the late 1960s that there was serious "overmanning," but the chief executive at the time, Stokes, held back from sacking thirty thousand workers for fear of the consequences (Turner 1973), and it was not until nearly ten years later that Edwardes was able to make a serious assault on the problem. At the level of the state, the attempts of both the Wilson government (the "In Place of Strife" White Paper of 1969) and of the Heath government (the Industrial Relations Act of 1971) to radically restrict the power of the unions failed when confronted with the reality of that power. Again, it was to take ten years or more to break the pattern.

In both cases the crisis of control reached its peak in 1974-75. At the level of the state, as in British Leyland, there was no question of a revolutionary situation; but there was a serious crisis of authority and control. Events such as the failure of Heath's Industrial Relations Act after the freeing of the Pentonville Five in 1971 and the miners' strikes of 1972 and 1974 made very explicit the limits of the authority of the state. Rising inflation, soaring public expenditure, falling profits, high levels of strike activity: all made clear that the postwar equilibrium was breaking down.

The Labour government's response to this dilemma was essentially to adopt the Ryder strategy: to get the trade unions to participate openly and explicitly in the management of the country through the Social Contract. The experience of the Social Contract was remarkably like the experience of participation at British Leyland. Discussion took place within the framework of a predefined objective: restoring competitiveness and technological renewal at British Leyland and in Britain as a whole. Since this objective clearly involved reducing the power of the trade unions, participation by the unions could only mean participation in their own destruction.

And so it happened. As the crisis deepened, and especially after 1975-76, it became clearer and clearer that the Social Contract meant nothing other than the participation of the trade unions in a policy that cut working-class living standards, allowing unemployment to rise and eroding the basis of the unions' own power.

The Social Contract, from capital's point of view, was both a success and a failure, in exactly the same manner as the Ryder strategy at British Leyland. It was a very striking success. By appearing to give unions power it effectively destroyed them. When they were directly attacked in the early 1980s, it became clear that the power of the unions was hollow: like the shop stewards at British Leyland, they had been discredited by their participation in management. The Social Contract both hollowed out trade union power and puffed the unions up so that they became an easy object for attack.

The Social Contract was also a failure in exactly the same sense as the Ryder strategy at Leyland. It was expensive (because concessions had to be given to buy the unions' acquiescence) and cumbersome, and above all it could not achieve the clear reassertion of authority that was necessary if a new basis for capital accumulation was to be established.

Edwardes finds a clear counterpart in Thatcher at the national level. She came to office over a year after Edwardes was appointed chief executive at British Leyland, with very much the same image and the same message: the government would be firm, there would be no compromise; it was the government's task to govern, just as it was management's task to manage. Keynesianism and the corporatism of the Social Contract were rejected.

Thatcher, like Edwardes, was not simply attacking the trade unions. Like Edwardes, she was attacking a style of government (or management) that was based on recognition of trade union power. Just as Edwardes had first attacked management and got rid of managers too committed to established practices, one of Thatcher's first targets was the civil service and the established network of relations between civil servants, trade unionists, and employers. Capitalist crisis involves not just an intensified attack on the working class, but the destruction of a whole structure of domination. That destruction is achieved largely through the operation of money, but an important role is also played by people from outside the established power structures. That explains the particular prominence in recent years of managers brought in from outside a particular industry (like Edwardes or MacGregor) or of someone like Thatcher who came from outside the Conservative establishment. It explains also why people like Edwardes or Thatcher, although acting in the interests of capital, may be very unpopular with many individual groups of capitalists. Finally, it explains the particular importance of money under the Thatcher government: this is not because the government has been unduly influenced by finance capital rather than industrial capital, as is sometimes argued, but because money plays a central role in a period of crisis in the breaking and restructuring of patterns of domination.

The postwar equilibrium lay in ruins, at least rhetorically. In 1979, however, it was not entirely clear that the Keynesian-corporatist welfare state was as dead as Thatcher proclaimed. There were still those who claimed that the social democratisation of the British state could not be reversed and who predicted that Thatcher would have to go through the same sort of U-turn as the Heath government ten years earlier. That view was overoptimistic: the Keynesian-corporatist state rested on a recognition of the trade union power, and by the end of the 1970s that power had been substantially weakened. However, just as Edwardes had held back for two years before putting his rhetoric to the test in a direct confrontation with shop steward power, so the Thatcher government postponed its legal restriction of trade union power, preferring to introduce it little by little in the years after 1981. It postponed too, quite deliberately, its major confrontation with the miners, until 1984.

In retrospect, it seems that Mrs. Thatcher, far from being an "iron lady," was in fact very cautious in her approach to the trade unions. She waited to make sure that the enemy was really vanquished before cutting off its head. It was after the defeat of the unions that the harsh anti-union legislation became possible. It was neither primarily the Thatcher government that brought the Keynesian era to an end nor the previous Labour government: Callaghan's famous speech at the 1977 Labour Party Conference recognised (or heralded) the death of Keynesianism but did not bring it about. Though the Keynesian system of government rested on recognition of the power of unions, it was not the state that was chiefly responsible for breaking that power. The power of the unions was destroyed first and foremost in the industrial conflicts of the late 1970s and early 1980s, and the role of the state in these was important but secondary. If one had to put a date on the final death of Keynesianism, then it would neither be Callaghan's speech nor Thatcher's electoral victory but April 8, 1980, the day on which mutuality ended at British Leyland. This, along with a host of similar developments throughout industry, eliminated the possibility of a U-turn and a return to the patterns of postwar social democracy.

To say that there can be no return to the old patterns of social democracy does not, however, mean that Thatcherism will necessarily provide a long-term model for government in Britain. On the contrary, the analogy with Edwardes at British Leyland would suggest that it is better to see Thatcherism as a transitional type of government, well suited to destroying the vestiges of Fordism/Keynesianism but not suitable for establishing the political patterns of the brave new world typified by Nissan. It is premature to see in Thatcherism a model of the "post-Fordist state."

The parallels between changes in the managerial strategy and changes in state policy are striking. Striking too is the fact that the currents of influence do not run in the direction that the dominant state-centred view of society might lead one to expect. Naturally there is constant interaction, but on the whole it is changes in managerial strategy that point the way for changes in state policy. Rather than seeing Edwardes as the John the Baptist of Thatcherism, it is probably more accurate to see Thatcher as the St Paul of Edwardesism. Management leads, the state follows.

"Edwardesism" here stands for a whole sea change in managerial strategy. The changes at British Leyland are particularly clear and well-documented, but they are not untypical. Edwardes himself was very influential in setting a managerial style throughout industry: but even where management did not become so overtly aggressive, management-labour relations almost everywhere were characterised by a sharp shift in the balance toward management, a weakening of the power of shop stewards, and a tightening of managerial authority. Everywhere, the changes were helped by an environment of high unemployment and by the introduction of new technology, which both facilitates and requires changes in working practices and the undermining of the power relations associated with the old patterns of work. The changes have not all been as sharp as at British Leyland, or as conflictual: often they have been achieved without battle waged. Nor have they all been simultaneous: some groups of workers (miners and printers in particular) have managed to hold on to their old patterns of work—Keynesian rocks withstanding the incoming tide of change. For that the price was isolation: when battle came, the old world was no longer there to give them full support.

The new patterns being built on the ruins of the old do not all correspond to a strict model either; yet Nissan can fairly be seen as representative of an important trend. It represents not just the expansion of Japanese capital but, much more important, a significant trend in the structure of capitalist domination over work. The emphasis on quality and the insistence on the workers' pride in "their" products; the widespread subcontracting of component supplies to small dependent firms; the reduction of stocking so that components arrive just in time for assembly; the establishment of a factory in a greenfield site with an environment of high unemployment and no tradition of trade union militancy; the stress on careful selection of a loyal workforce and exclusion of the disloyal and unreliable; the conclusion of a strike-free deal with a cooperative trade union; the international control of geographically separated groups of workers—all of these are important trends in the current development of capitalism (see Sayer 1986).

These trends are often referred to as the "Japanisation" of production, but it is misleading to place too much emphasis on the place of origin of the managerial strategies: Nissan's management techniques in Sunderland may be of Japanese inspiration, but their real basis is the defeat of the workers at Cowley, Longbridge, and elsewhere. It is these defeats that allow management to talk of introducing Japanese management techniques and of moving from just-in-case to just-in-time production. Just-in-time production (which gets its name from the fact that components are delivered just in time for incorporation into the finished product rather than being stocked in large quantities to allow for possible disruptions) presupposes a certain, predictable environment (Graham 1986), both in the factory itself and in the factory's suppliers. It is a style of management built on the assumption that workers are disciplined and loyal, that there will be no unexpected stoppages, and that the quality of the products at every stage of the production process will be reliable. It assumes that when the manager says go, the worker goeth.

The patterns exemplified by Nissan are trends not universal reality. These trends are experiments in a new form of domination; it is still too early to say whether they will harden into a clear long-term pattern. Many firms have experienced difficulties in introducing quality control circles and just-in-time production. Not every firm has had the advantages of Nissan, yet everywhere there are movements in the same direction.

If changes in the car industry are representative of changes in the pattern of management-labour relations more generally, then it is not surprising that there are parallels between changes in managerial style and changes in the state. The parallel development of management and the state has been presented here in the form of an analogy, but the similarities are not a matter of chance. Management and the state are two aspects of the same thing, they are two forms of the capital relation, the relation of domination between capital and labour. Both work in distinct but interrelated ways to ensure the profitable accumulation of capital and the continued exploitation of labour. It cannot be otherwise. Just as management depends on the state to provide (through the maintenance of public order) a disciplined environment for the exploitation of the workforce and the accumulation of capital, the state depends equally on the success of capitalist exploitation for its own continued existence; capital accumulation is both the source of the state's income (through taxation) and the basis for the maintenance of public order. Both management and the state depend on the successful exploitation of labour. The actions of both are ultimately directed to the same end, and both are shaped by the same constant struggle for capitalist authority. It is therefore the conditions of that exploitation and the struggles around the process of work that are the key to understanding not only changes in management but also the development of the state. Moreover, since management is closer and more responsive to the labour process, it is not surprising that trends in political development should be foreshadowed by trends in management.

Aggressive management styles were effective in breaking the power of the old worker and in hacking a new sharper division between the core employed workers and the marginalised peripheral workers. The state, under both Labour and Tory governments, gave support to this approach in the late 1970s and early 1980s: through the appointment and support of people like Edwardes and MacGregor, the acceptance and promotion of high unemployment, public expenditure cuts, legislation to curb strikes, the mobilisation of the police, etc.

If people like Edwardes and MacGregor hacked their way through the workforce and excluded millions from work, then Nissan suggests that the emphasis is now on integrating those who remain. While excluding the irresponsible masses, the focus has shifted to integrating the responsible worker, to holding him up as a model of virtue. Now that the bouncers have thrown out the unruly guests, they can retreat to their normal position at the door and the party-giver can concentrate on entertaining the well-behaved guests who remain. Roughing up those excluded continues: the police, the Manpower Services Commission, and the Department of Health and Social Security see to that; but that is in the background, behind the scenes, excluded from the press and from political debate. Attention is now focused on the "moral majority"—whether they are actually a majority does not matter, since they are the only people who count. Like a mafioso in a gangster film, the party-giver's face changes suddenly. The thug turns around and smiles with charm at the remaining guests: the iron lady turns into . . . a fresh-faced boy.

Or does she? It does not really matter. It does not matter what her face, sex, or name is. The point is that at the political level too the tide is changing. Whether Mrs. Thatcher goes on or not, the aggressive façade associated with Thatcherism is giving way increasingly to a more human face. The emphasis is on the construction of a new consensus, not a consensus that will cover everybody but a consensus among the responsible moral majority. Political competition is increasingly focused on the claim to speak for that majority. Who wins that competition—whether it is Thatcher with a revamped face, a new more moderate leader of the Conservative Party, Owen, or Kinnock—matters a great deal to the participants in the competition, but it will probably not make very much difference to anybody else. Democratic elections are not much more relevant to the running of the country than to the management of a car company.

And so: the Red Rose of Nissan. The caring, conformist worker of Nissan who firmly rejects all trace of militancy finds his counterpart in the caring, conformist man with the Red Rose, who firmly rejects any irresponsible behaviour, any mindless militancy, the man who speaks for the Moral Majority, the New Man.

The New Man has strange acolytes. Not only the established bureaucrats of the labour movement but many on the intellectual "Left" clamour to participate in the construction of the new pattern of domination. To justify their position they claim to have a basis in Marxism, a new Marxism, of course, a Marxism of today. To read these analyses of the changes in capitalism, of the "new reality" (e.g., Carter 1986), one would suppose that no struggles had taken place over the last ten years. The new reality has not been created through struggle; it has just "emerged." The struggles that have taken place—the miners' strike, for example—are seen as struggles against reality. Heroic but anachronistic, they are out of tune with the new reality, "with the inescapable lines of tendency and direction, established by the real world" (Hall 1985, 15). The miners, like the rest of us, are not the creators but the victims of the new reality.

Apparently, the new reality is not constituted by the permanent conflict between capital and labour. It is a reality that emerges and confronts not classes but "people." Class has no place in this world: change takes place not through incessant class struggles but through democracy and winning the support of public opinion. In this new reality, we are all staffers.

The people of this new reality are all reasonable, gentle people. In a remarkable somersault from the feminist radicalism of the early 1970s, feminism is now used to justify passivity, and militancy is identified with machismo (Campbell 1985; Hall 1985; Carter 1986). The analysis that sees women as the victims of male violence—a strong current within the feminist movement—easily turns into the condemnation of all violence as an expression of male domination. The violence of the miners, for example, is seen not as arising from righteous anger but as an expression of a macho culture that we can (and must) condemn with a good conscience. And so the "Left" orchestrates Marxism and feminism in a remarkable concert of support for the new reality, new morality, and new sexuality: a world of suffocating oppression.

Against such views, it is important to emphasise some of the conclusions that stand out from the story of British Leyland and Nissan. Capitalism has indeed changed: capitalist society today is very different from the capitalist society of ten years ago. But many of the discussions of the "new reality," whether in *Marxism Today* or in the much richer debates on the neo-Fordist state (for an account, see Bonefeld 1987), overlook the most important features that are so striking if one focuses on the story of British Leyland and Nissan.

First, neither the car workers nor the miners nor the women are the victims of an emergent new reality. Whether we like it or not, reality is constituted by struggle, and we are part of that struggle. The "new reality" of the car industry was not something that simply emerged to confront the car workers as victims, it was constituted through the struggle of capital against labour and of labour against capital. All workers in the industry were part of that struggle, whether they wanted it or not. It was a struggle stacked against labour, because we live in a society dominated by capital. Struggle in a capitalist society is not an equal struggle, but it is always both inevitable and unpredictable. The car workers, like the miners, were undoubtedly defeated in that struggle, but there is a world of difference between being temporarily defeated in a continuing struggle and being the victims of "the inescapable lines of tendency and direction established by the real world."

Struggle implies unpredictability and instability. Patterns of domination are inherently unstable in capitalism. Periodically, it becomes clear that the established pattern of domination is no longer functioning and there is an outbreak of more intense and open struggle to restructure or to break those relations of domination. During such periods, capitalist authority is particularly fragile. That is why the concept of crisis is central to Marxist analysis: in crisis the inherent instability of capitalism, the unreality of "reality," becomes clear. It is not possible, for example, to understand the changes in the car industry since the mid-1970s without a concept of crisis, yet the proponents of the "new reality" rarely mention crisis, for they have forgotten how fragile that reality is.

For capital, recovery from crisis means above all the reassertion of its authority, its right to manage and to rule. It is in this context—in the context of crisis and not because of elections or some autonomous battle of ideas—that there is a turn in capitalist strategies toward more authoritarian ideas, more authoritarian management, and a more authoritarian state. The increased authoritarianism does not result from the success of the New Right: on the contrary, the success of the New Right is the result of pressures for more authoritarianism. For capital, the reassertion of its authority is the precondition for everything else.

The mere reassertion of authority does not yet constitute a new stable pattern of domination, however. Certainly, there are clear trends that indicate what a possible long-term pattern of domination may look like: that is the significance of Nissan and the Red Rose. But it would be wrong to see Nissanism as already established reality. For the moment it is merely an increasingly influential strategy for establishing a new pattern of domination.

The Nissan strategy is proving very effective, but there are still major obstacles to its success. It is hard to imagine that the happy party guests will go on smiling forever when the party is based on their exploitation. And it is not at all clear that the bouncers at the door will be able to suppress indefinitely the frustrations of those who have been thrown out of the party and are constantly being told how nice it is inside.

The Nissan strategy, and the just-in-time approach with which it is associated, aims at the management of an environment that is certain: it aims at replacing management against uncertainty with the management of certainty (Graham 1986). But the only thing that is certain in this world is death. The only "inescapable lines of tendency and direction" are the lines that lead to the grave. As long as there is life, it will be impossible to achieve anything other than management against uncertainty. That is why just-in-time is proving so hard to implement on a wide scale. That is also why there is a contradiction at the very heart of automation, of the attempt to subject more and more processes within society to mathematical control—a contradiction expressed in the problems of software production (Pelaez 1987). And that is why the gleam of Nissan has already been tarnished by widespread reports of discontent among both managers and workers.

To talk of "new reality" is to talk of certainty, of death. To talk of struggle is to talk of life and of the openness of the future. The working class has certainly been defeated, and the conformist world of Nissan daily declares through the mouths of Kinnock and Co. that more and more types of opposition are illegitimate, irresponsible, immoral. But for capital, the struggle to subjugate and exploit labour is endless. And oppression by capital daily meets resistance from labour. The world of Nissan is suffocating, but occasionally a scream of protest breaks the silence. The miners' scream was long and loud and heartening: it was silenced, but it echoes still—as do the riots, as do Wapping and a thousand other daily screams that fill the air with echoes of hope.

The cracks that appeared in capitalist domination in the late 1960s and early 1970s have been plastered over and it is not yet clear how they will reappear: in the inevitable resistance of the Nissan worker pushed too far or in the unpredictable explosions of those who have been excluded from the party. One thing is clear: struggle is inseparable from domination. At the centre of capitalist society is a silent but explosive scream:

> Inside our ears are the many wailing cries of misery,
> Inside our bodies, the internal bleeding of stifled volcanoes,
> Inside our heads, the erupting thoughts of rebellion.
> How can there be calm when the storm is yet to come?
> (Linton Kwesi Johnson, "Two Sides of Silence")

References

Bassett, Philip. *Strike Free: New Industrial Relations in Britain*. London: Macmillan, 1986.

Bonefeld, Werner. "Fordism and the Reformulation of State Theory." Unpublished paper. University of Edinburgh, 1987.

Campbell, Beatrix. "Politics Old and New." *New Statesman*, March 8, 1985, 22–25.

Carter, Pete. *Trade Unions—The New Reality*. London: Communist Party Publications, 1986.

Central Policy Review Staff. *The Future of the British Car Industry*. London: Her Majesty's Stationary Office, 1975.

Edwardes, Michael. *Back from the Brink*. London: Pan Books, 1984.

Graham, Ian. "JIT with Uncertain Demand." Unpublished paper. Edinburgh: Heriot Watt University, 1986.

Hall, Stuart. "Realignment for What?" *Marxism Today*, December 12–17, 1985.

Johnson, Linton Kwesi. *Dread Beat an' Blood*. London: Bogle L'Ouverture Publications, 1975.

Marsden, David, Timothy Morris, Paul Willman, and Stephen Wood. *The Car Industry: Labour Relations and Industrial Adjustment*. London: Tavistock, 1985.

Peláez, Eloína. "The GOTO Controversy and the Software Crisis." PhD diss., University of Edinburgh, 1987.

Sayer, Andrew. "New Developments in Manufacturing: The Just-in-Time System." *Capital and Class* 10, no. 3 (Winter 1986): 43–72.

Scarborough. Harry. "The Politics of Technical Change at British Leyland." In *Technological Change, Rationalisation and Industrial Relations*, edited by Otto Jacobi, Bob Jessop, Hans Kastendiek, and Marino Regini. London: Croom Helm, 1986.

Television History Workshop. *Making Cars: A History of Car Making in Cowley by the People Who Make the Cars*. London: Routledge and Kegan Paul, 1985.

Willman, Paul, and Graham Winch. (1985) *Innovation and Control: Labour Relations at BL Cars*. Cambridge: Cambridge University Press, 1985.

THREE

Note on Marxism

Marxism is a theory not of oppression but of the contradictions of oppression. Those contradictions are the expression of our strength.

FOUR

In the Beginning Was the Scream

In the beginning was the scream.

When we talk or write, it is all too easy to forget that the beginning was not the word but the scream. Faced with the destruction of human lives by capitalism, a scream of sadness, a scream of horror, above all a scream of anger, of refusal: NO. The starting point of theoretical reflection is opposition, negativity, struggle.

The role of theory is to elaborate that scream, to express its strength, and to contribute to its power, to show how the scream resonates through society and to contribute to that resonance.

That is the origin of Marxism, not just of Marx's Marxism but presumably also of our own interest in Marxism. The appeal of Marxism lies in its claim to be a theory of struggle, of opposition, of negation. But that is not what Marxism has become.

Today Marxism is probably more discredited than ever, not just in the bourgeois press or in the universities but also as a theory of struggle. The experience of the Soviet Union and Eastern Europe has been crucial in this respect; the identification of Marxism as the official ideology of the state has meant that the struggles against the state have taken the form not of struggles inspired by a "truer Marxism," as was hoped by many in the West for so long but of struggles against Marxism as such. But it is not only in the East that the statification of Marxism has led to its rejection. In the West too, the surge of Marxism into the universities in the late 1960s and early 1970s has led in some degree to its desiccation. Borne into the universities on a wave of working-class struggle, Marxist theory has tended to be sucked into the general separation of theory from practice that characterises the university as an institution. As the wave of struggle that provided the basis of Marxism has ebbed, many Marxist academics have completely abandoned Marxism; even worse, perhaps, many have not but have carried their Marxism with them as they adapt to the institutional structures and professional pressures of the university. Often this is not the result of conscious choice, but rather the result of the dynamics of non-choice; work in the university has its own dynamic that constantly tends to separate theoretical work from any political base. The result is often a Marxism that is far more sophisticated but no less determinist than the old "orthodoxy" of the communist parties.

In both cases, the state ideology of the East and the sophisticated academicism of the West, Marxism has lost its scream. Class struggle remains a category, but the simple statement at the start of the *Communist Manifesto* that "the history of all hitherto existing societies is the history of class struggle" is in fact abandoned. Class struggle in these theories is still seen as being influential but only within a broader framework, variously interpreted as the conflict between the forces and relations of production or simply as the "laws of capitalist development." Class struggle is important—of course (so "of course" that it can simply be taken for granted)—but it must submit to the "inescapable lines of tendency and direction established by the real world" (Hall 1985, 15). Struggle is subject to structure, and since structure is the structure of capitalist society (the real world), Marxism in this version becomes quite simply a theory of capitalist reproduction. The "inescapable lines of tendency and direction established by the real world" are quite simply the functional requirements of capitalist reproduction, so that these theories are not only structuralist but functionalist. And then, with all thought of rupture or revolution long forgotten, these theorists move from analysing what is necessary for capitalist reproduction to prescribing what is necessary, to making policy suggestions and advising the state, still, of course, using the language of Marxist theory and making obeisance to the importance of class struggle. It is little wonder that many who are actively involved in anti-capitalist struggle feel little attraction to such Marxism.

Yet a theory of the scream is more urgent than ever, because capitalism is both increasingly fragile and increasingly terroristic. The scream will continue as long as capitalism does, but there is a real danger that Marxism as the language of the scream, as the theory of protest, could get lost. Marxism as a theory of determinism and as an ideology of the state is discredited, but it is more urgent than ever to develop Marxism clearly as a theory of struggle. There is of course a long tradition of emphasising struggle as the central element of Marxism, a long tradition of what one might call "left Marxism," but it is a diverse and often subterranean tradition, without very clear continuities. Many of those who politically have insisted on the self-organisation of the working class have retained theoretical concepts that go against the articulation of the power of labour (as in Pannekoek's discussion of crisis, for example); and many of those who have made important contributions to theorising working-class power have adopted ambivalent political positions in practice (Adorno and Bloch, for example). The crisis of the regimes of Eastern Europe is, or can be, a liberation of Marxism from much of the baggage acquired over the last century, but it is very important to try to be clear about the foundations of this liberated Marxism.

The most obvious point to be made about a theory of struggle is that its basis is uncertainty. If the world is to be understood in terms of struggle, then there is no room for determinism of any kind. Struggle, by definition, is uncertain and open, and the categories that conceptualise it must also be understood as open. The determinism of Marx's more triumphalist moments (such as the end of section 1 of the *Communist Manifesto*, *Capital* vol. 1, chap. 32, or the 1859 "Preface to *A Contribution to Political Economy*"), which are so important for the "orthodox" Marxist tradition, must go, so must any idea of historical necessity or any suggestion of a final inevitable victory of socialism. As Adorno put it, after the experience of fascism, it is no longer possible (if it ever was) to think of a smooth dialectical progression ending with communism as the resolution of conflict, the inevitable negation of the negation. We can only think of the dialectic as being a negative dialectic, a dialectic of negation with no certain synthesis. In a world of untruth, the only concept of truth that we can have is negative. There is no certainty in Marxism: its only claim to truth is the force of its attack on untruth. This leads perhaps to a dizzy, dizzying vision of the world (see Adorno 1990, 31), but the dizziness lies not in the vision but in the reality of a world hurtling who knows where.

The dialectic of negation is the struggle of the working class. In a world of struggle, there is no neutrality. The perspective is the perspective of our struggle. As Tronti put it in an article that provided one of the starting points for the theory of *autonomia* in Italy: "We too had a conception of capitalism that put capital in first place and the workers in second.

That was a mistake. And now we must reverse the polarity and start again from the beginning. And the beginning is the class struggle of the working class." The beginning is the struggle, our struggle, our scream, the scream of negation. As Rosa Luxemburg put it, "The secret of Marx's theory of value ... was that he looked at capitalism from the point of view of its transcendence, from a socialist point of view." It is only from the standpoint of negation that Marx's categories make any sense at all: without that, they are quite literally meaningless. That is why there cannot be any continuity between bourgeois theory and Marxist theory: the basic presuppositions that underlie their categories are totally incompatible. Underlying bourgeois theory is an assumption about the stability of capitalism and the power of capital to retain control of society indefinitely. The basis of Marxist theory is just the opposite: the instability of capitalism and the power of labour to overthrow capitalism.

It is essential to retain the idea that the starting point must be the struggle of the working class. Linton Kwesi Johnson has a wonderful expression when he describes the violent reaction of a group of blacks to police harassment: "the bile of oppression was vomited" ("Five Nights of Bleeding"). If we are to avoid the structural-functionalism that characterises so much of Marxist theory, it is important to think of our work in those terms: as a vomiting of the bile of oppression.

However, there is a difficulty here, and it is a difficulty presented by a lot of left theory. The focus on the struggle of the working class leads very easily to a conception of the working class as purely external to capital. From correctly emphasising the subjectivity of labour and the antagonism between labour and capital as the starting point, such approaches easily move to simply counterposing the subjectivity of labour to the objectivity of capital. The one-sided emphasis on subjectivity (voluntarism), although it appears to be the opposite of objectivism (determinism) is actually its logical complement. Both operate with the assumption that there is a distinction between class struggle and the laws of economic development: the difference lies only in the primacy attached to one or the other. Alternately, all notion of the "logic of capital" is abandoned and capital is seen as a purely external subject, manipulating and controlling labour. Class struggle is then seen as the clash of two opposing armies, as a battle that goes back and forth, to and fro. At this level there is no history, or rather history is a formless thing, without shape, without tendency.

Marx's conception is different: in the clash of the two opposing armies of capital and labour, there is something that gives direction and shape to the struggle. The fact that the two sides are not external to each other: capital is nothing other than alienated labour and the objectivity of the "real world" is nothing than our own alienated subjectivity. The basis of both sides of the class struggle is the same: the power of labour. Capital is nothing other than alienated labour. This is the basis of the labour theory of value, seen even before Marx by both the radical Ricardians and their critics as an assertion of the power of labour. At its most basic, the power of labour is the power to create, and therefore also the power to destroy. When Marx distinguished between the worst architect and the best bee by saying that the former plans the construction before executing it, he might also have added that the architect is also more likely to fail in the construction. The power of labour is the power of uncertain creation, the power of that which is not, the power of nonidentity (Adorno), of the Not Yet (Bloch), of the working class No (Tronti).

When labour and capital confront each other, this is not an external confrontation. The power of labour meets the power of labour but in the form of its antithesis. Contradiction is "non-identity under the aspect of identity" (Adorno), negativity under the aspect of positivity, labour under the aspect of capital. The substance of capital is the power of labour; the power of labour exists under the aspect of capital: it assumes the fetish-ised form of capital. Once the relation between capital and labour is seen as an internal relation, then the question of form becomes crucial. Unlike the Ricardians, who were content to show that the substance of value was labour, Marx was concerned with the form of value, with the question why the product of labour took the form of value—and indeed he saw the question of form as being the crucial dividing line between his theory and bourgeois theory, for which the question of form is meaningless (*Capital* vol. 1, 80). The whole of Marx's *Capital* is a study of the increasingly fetish-ised forms of the power of labour. The "pivot" for an understanding of the different forms of social relations is the dual existence of concrete labour and abstract labour, the fact that concrete, useful labour takes the form of abstract labour, the fact that useful, creative labour confronts itself in meaningless, in alienated form.

If capital cannot be understood as external to labour, it cannot be understood as something economic. The movement of capital can only be understood as the movement of the contradiction (internal to capital itself) between capital and labour, the movement of struggle. The notion of "Marxist economics," one of the most unfortunate creations of the "orthodox" Marxist tradition, insofar as it suggests a separation of capital from struggle, must be abandoned. But if the movement of capital can only be understood as the movement of struggle, the movement of struggle can only be understood as a movement in-and-against capital. The notion that you can understand the movement of struggle or of society in abstraction from the particular form that it takes, the notion that underlies the concept of "Marxist sociology" must also be abandoned. (The absurd notion of a Marxist political science, an idea raised by Poulantzas, need not even be mentioned.)

Discussion of form (or form analysis) often appears to be very far removed from any political concern, so it is important to emphasise why the concept of form is important for developing Marxism as a theory of struggle. The central issue is the articulation and recognition of the power of labour. A concept that emphasises struggle but sees struggle as being external to capital, recognises only one aspect of the power of labour. It hears the scream but is deaf to the resonance of the scream within capital itself. It sees the power of labour in strikes, in demonstrations, in armed struggle but does not see it in the contradiction between productive and money capital, in the inadequacies of technology, or in the internal disorder of the state. It sees the power of labour in the response of the state to overt struggles but does not see it in the very existence of value as an uncontrollable chaos at the heart of capital. It is the presence of the power of labour within capital that makes it ineradicably crisis-ridden, and that allows us to speak not of laws of capitalist development but of certain rhythms and tendencies in the development of struggle.

It is important, to see that the concept of form here implies contradiction, instability. The power of labour appears in the form of its antithesis, the power of capital. Class struggle takes the form of relations or "things" (value, money, profit, etc.) that appear to be neither class relations nor antagonistic. Class "exists in the mode of being denied" (Gunn). As forms of class struggle that deny their own substance, the social forms of value, money, state, etc. are inevitably characterised by a constant tension between form and content. The content is not contained within the form but constantly breaks its banks and overflows. To quote Adorno again: "The name of dialectics says no more, to begin with, than that objects do not go into their concepts without leaving a remainder, that they come to contradict the traditional norm of adequacy" (1990, 5). The power of labour is not contained within the forms of capital; it constantly overflows and forces these forms to reconstitute themselves, to reform, in order to contain the uncontainable. Fetishism, in other words, is not an established fact but a constant process of fetishisation.

This distinction between fetishism and fetishisation is crucial for the way that we understand society and the way that we understand Marxism. If fetishism is total, if class antagonism is completely contained within its forms, then revolution as the self-organisation of the working class becomes theoretically impossible. If fetishism is total and the working class cannot see through the forms in which class struggle presents itself (as neutral things), then there are only two possibilities: either one sees the working class within the structures of capitalism and gives up hope of revolution—the understandable but destructive pessimism of the Frankfurt School—or else one sees the only possibility of revolution as lying in the intervention of a deus ex machina, a vanguard party who will come from the outside. But there is no outside, just as there is no inside: there is only an inside-outside, an overflowing, an in-and-against-and-beyond. The only possible way of resolving this dilemma, the dilemma common to Leninism and the Frankfurt School theory, is to see that fetishism is not total. It is not an established fact but a constant process of fetishisation. Labour does not simply exist in the form of capital: it exists in-and-against-and-beyond those forms of capital. Class struggle does not simply exist in the form of value, money, state, etc. It exists in-and-against-and-beyond those forms. The forms of value. money, state, etc., are better thought of as form-processes, as processes of valorisation, monetisation, statification.

The state, for example, is neither an institution in the sense of a thing that is outside us nor simply a form of social relations in the sense of a link in the chain of capitalist reproduction: it is rather a form-process, an active process of forming social relations and therefore social struggles in a certain way. It is not just an aspect of fetishism (the neutral state) but as part of the general struggle of capital against labour an active process of fetishisation that systematically channels class struggles into nonclass forms, into struggles on behalf of citizens, struggles for democracy, for human rights, etc.—forms that systematically deny the existence of class and therefore promote the disarticulation of the power of labour.

Or money, to take another example, is not a fetishised form of social relations. It is a process of monetising life, of subjecting human existence to the command of money, which implies a constant and violent struggle. The intensity of that struggle is reflected in all the conflicts surrounding the unprecedented expansion of debt throughout the world and in the equally unprecedented rise in theft and "crimes" against property.

Or, to make the point more generally, if the dual existence of labour as concrete and abstract labour "is the pivot on which the comprehension of political economy turns," then it is important to see the abstraction of labour (the "imposition of work" as it is sometimes called) as a process, as a struggle that permeates not only the workplace but the whole of society— a point emphasised without differentiation in the concept of the social factory.

Capital's reproduction depends on the fetishisation, on the containment of a struggle that always goes beyond it. The relation between labour and capital is neither external nor internal: it is both, but with no clear dividing line. Labour does not simply exist within capital; it exists in-against-and-beyond capital (again with no clear dividing line between in, against and beyond, and therefore no clear distinction between class-in-itself and class-for-itself). Labour overflows from capital. Capital is not simply the form of labour; it is the process of forming labour; it is the constant process of self-reconstitution to contain labour. Class struggle is the movement of the overflowing-and-containment, or, in other words, class struggle is the movement of fetishisation/defetishisation. This is not to say that class struggle is theoretical, although theoretical reflection is clearly part of it. The process of fetishisation/defetishisation is a practical one. Fetishisation is the process by which social interconnections are broken down and become impenetrable. It is the decomposition of the working class. Defetishisation is the opposite movement: the movement by which, through struggle and the theoretical reflection that is part of it, interconnections are established and the working class is recomposed. Fetishisation is the containment of the power of labour. defetishisation is the overflowing of the power of labour, the scream of negativity. Fetishisation is the smothering of the scream, the assurance that "things are so." Defetishisation is the unleashing of the scream, the awareness that the only truth is that things are not so, that truth is not yet, or simply not.

Marxism is defetishisation, the theory of the power of labour in-against-and-beyond capital, the theory of the scream that shows that the scream does not exist only in overt militancy (in what is usually called "class struggle"), but that it is much, much more powerful than that because it reverberates in the very concepts of capital, because it reverberates in the deepest silence of everyday life. As Linton Kwesi Johnson puts it:

> Inside our ears are the many wailing cries of misery,
> Inside our bodies, the internal bleeding of stifled volcanoes,
> Inside our heads, the erupting thoughts of rebellion.
> How can there be calm when the storm is yet to come?
> ("Two Sides of Silence")

The "internal bleeding of stifled volcanoes" inside our bodies, the "erupting thoughts of rebellion" inside our heads, the existence of nonidentity under the aspect of identity, the presence of the not-yet in the now, the power of labour in-against-and-beyond capital are the instability of capital, its constant tendency to crisis. Crisis is the manifestation of that power and for that reason the central concept of Marxism. Crisis is the eruption of the power of labour.

References

Adorno, Theodor W. *Negative Dialectics*. London: Routledge, 1990.

Gunn, Richard. *Marxism* and *Mediation*. Common Sense, no. 2 (1987).

Hall, Stuart. "Realignment for What?," *Marxism Today*, December 1985.

Johnson, Linton Kwesi. *Dread Beat an' Blood*. London: Bogle L'Ouverture Publications, 1975.

Marx, Karl. *Capital*, vol. l. Moscow: Progress Publishers, 1965.

FIVE

The Abyss Opens: The Rise and Fall of Keynesianism

I

Keynes lounging in an armchair, comfortable, thoughtful, and benign, a pile of books and papers beside him, against the background of a chart showing the dramatic decline in unemployment from the 1930s to the 1960s: the cover of a popular book conveys perfectly the popular image of Keynesianism. For much of the postwar period, Keynesianism was presented simply as a beneficial, rational, scientific advance in the management of the economy, as a theoretical development that provided the basis for overcoming the problem of capitalist crisis and creating a just capitalist society. Even in recent years, when Keynesianism has been so much criticised, the image remains of Keynesianism as a possibly misguided but certainly well-meaning theoretical development. In the midst of such images, it is sometimes hard to remember that the adoption of Keynesian policies was the culmination of a prolonged conflict, of violence, horror, and bloodiness quite unprecedented in the history of the world.

Keynes was, of course, an economist. "Keynesianism" refers strictly to the economic theories that he propounded and to the economic policies associated with his name, which gained influence throughout the world during and after the Second World War. These theories and policies should not, however, be seen in isolation: their adoption formed an important part of the establishment of a new pattern of relations between capital and labour, and for that reason the term "Keynesian" is often used to refer more broadly to the pattern of political and economic relations associated with those theories and policies. It is primarily in this broad sense that the term will be used here.

The central feature of Keynesianism was the acknowledgement of the organisational strength of the working class. Keynesianism made explicit in institutional form the dependence of capital upon labour and the strength of labour in-and-against capital.

The aim of this chapter is to examine the establishment and the collapse of Keynesianism as a mode of domination and a mode of containing the power of labour.

The power of labour to which Keynesianism responded was most dramatically illustrated in the "Red October" of 1917. The Russian Revolution was not an isolated event but the crest of a wave: the surface of capitalism was broken not only in St Petersburg and Moscow but, more briefly, in other places too—Berlin, Budapest, Munich, Turin, etc. These revolutionary struggles at the end of the First World War were part of a much broader change: as Woodrow Wilson put it shortly before his death, the Russian Revolution was "the symbol of the discontent of the age" (Schlesinger 1957, 94). The revolutionary movement fed from and fed into a longer-term, less spectacular surge in the power of the working class, expressed in the rise of trade unionism and social democratic parties in all the advanced capitalist countries from the end of the nineteenth century. For all the failings of the organised movement (most notably the collapse of "socialist internationalism" on the eve of the war), the visible power of the working class had grown enormously in the early years of the century.

Beneath the visible, organised power of labour lay a less visible, more insidious power: the power of the exploited to resist exploitation. The growing organisations derived much of their power from the workers' realisation that, however bad their conditions might be, there were limits to the extent to which they could be exploited. Capital might control their lives, but capital depended on their work for its survival. Power derived precisely from the condition that defined the working class: labour. This realisation was expressed not only in the withdrawal of labour in strikes but in the constant, everyday struggle for control of the process of work: the control of how things were done and at what speed. Even the most domineering capitalists were confronted with the fact that they did not fully control the work process that was the source of their own profit. As F.W. Taylor recounted of his own experience, "As was usual then ... the shop was really run by the workmen and not by the bosses. The workmen together had carefully planned just how fast each job should be done" (Braverman 1974, 102). Taylor's life work articulated the frustration of capital and was dedicated to overcoming its source, the power of labour to control the labour process.

The extent of the power of the workers to control their own labour varied according to the area, the industry, and, most importantly, the type of work involved. It was particularly the more skilled workers who played an indispensable role in the labour process and who were able to exercise most control over their own process of work. The position of the skilled workers gave a particular complexion to the working-class movement at the time, reflected in trade union organisation (based mainly on craft lines) and in the ideology of even the more revolutionary sections of the socialist movement, with their vision of socialism in terms of workers' control of the work process. For capital, the skill of the workers turned from being a necessary condition for industrial development into being an obstacle to capital accumulation (Coriat 1982, 12).

From the beginning of the century, capital was increasingly confronted with its own dependence upon labour. This expressed itself both in apprehension of the organised labour movement and in growing difficulty in raising surplus value production sufficiently to offset the rising costs of investment. The imperialist flight of capital to a new workforce, new raw materials, and new markets offset the difficulties but also raised intercapitalist competition to a new level of interimperialist rivalry and war.

The impact of the war was double-edged. On the one hand, it split the international labour movement and led to a weakening of the position of the skilled worker within the factory, as established practices were "diluted" by bringing in women to help with the war effort; on the other, it stirred up a wave of discontent throughout the world that threatened capital as it had never been threatened before.

Capital's response to this threat was complex. From the end of the war, in all the leading capitalist countries, there were voices calling for reform: bourgeois politicians and theorists who argued that the old capitalism had been discredited and that a radically new social order was necessary. These calls took many different forms and surfaced on many different occasions through the 1920s.

There were three principal issues in the strategic debates of the 1920s: international relations, the role of the state, and the control of money.

The first clash between "progressives" and "reactionaries" came immediately after the war in the negotiation of the Versailles peace treaty.

Many of the young reformers who were part of their national delegations resigned in disgust when they realised that their leaders were more interested in the "evil old conspiracy of naked force" (Schlesinger 1957, 14) than in creating a new era in world history. Among those who resigned was Keynes, who was present as part of the British delegation. One of the key issues was the attitude of the Western powers to the new revolutionary government in Russia. For the progressives, the response to the Soviet threat should be conciliatory. In the pamphlet that he wrote to justify his resignation, "The Economic Consequences of the Peace," Keynes inveighed against the old-style diplomats who "behave as if foreign policy was of the same genre as a cheap melodrama" (Keynes 1971, 185) and argued that rather than excluding Russia and taking revenge on Germany, the policy of the victorious powers should aim at reconstructing Germany and reintegrating Russia into world trade: "whether or not the form of communism represented by the Soviet government proves permanently suited to the Russian temperament, the revival of trade, of the comforts of life and of ordinary economic motives are not likely to promote the extreme forms of those doctrines of violence and tyranny which are the children of war and of despair" (Keynes 1971, 187; cf. Negri 1988, 16).

The issue of the new international order was quickly settled against the views of the progressives by the Treaty of Versailles. The second issue, the question of the role of the state, remained alive throughout the 1920s. The war had seen an unprecedented expansion in the role of the state, involving extensive control of production (see Clarke 1988, 193ff). In the years after the war, the "progressives" argued that the development of capitalism made it imperative that the state should maintain an active interventionist role in the economy. The argument took different forms and rested on different justifications, from acknowledged fear of revolution to charitable concern for the poor to the simple pursuit of economic efficiency, but there were a number of threads that ran through the debate in all countries.

The most immediate issue was the role of the state in production. Everywhere, the state had taken over, directly or indirectly, important sections of production and transport during the war. The "progressives" argued that these should not be returned to private ownership, that the modern state should control certain basic industries in the interests of the national welfare (see Schlesinger 1957, 37–45; Clarke, 1988, 200). They lost this argument: the industries taken over during the war were on the whole returned to private hands in the years immediately following. But the argument concerning the role of the state continued. It was argued that the state should be more active in providing social welfare provision for the poor, especially in the case of unemployment. It was argued too that the state should play a more active role in encouraging economic efficiency, especially through the promotion of economic "rationalisation." All the functions that are usually associated with the post-1945 "Keynesian" state were already being argued for in the 1920s.

This is also true of the general conception of the state as responsible for the management of the economy, particularly through the manipulation of demand. Such ideas were to be found not only in Keynes's early writings but also, for example, in the work of Foster and Catchings in the United States. In their book *The Road to Plenty*, published in 1928, they attacked Say's law, the foundation of orthodox economic theory, which held that total demand for goods must equal total supply, so that the financing of production automatically created enough purchasing power to purchase all the goods produced. Foster and Catchings pointed out that there was no such automatic balance, since the flow of money was constantly interrupted by saving (as indeed Marx had pointed out in Chapter 2 of *Capital* sixty years before). Hence, the only way to maintain prosperity was for the government to maintain an adequate flow of money income to consumers: its policies should be founded on the principles of "putting more money into consumers' hands when business is falling off, and less money when inflation is under way" (Schlesinger 1957, 135).

Money was central to any discussion of an expanded role for the state. Plans such as that proposed by Foster and Catchings would involve the government running budget deficits in times of recession, and such an idea was abhorrent to the more orthodox politicians and theorists of the day. The issue of financial orthodoxy during this period crystallised around discussions of the reconstruction of the gold standard, under which national currencies are tied to the price of gold, and which was seen by many as the key to the reconstruction of the international political system after the First World War and was one of the first tasks undertaken by the new League of Nations (Clarke 1988, 204). The significance (both symbolic and real) of the restoration of the gold standard was that it subordinated national currency, and hence the nation state, to the international movement of money, thereby anchoring the minimal role of the state that the conservatives wished to safeguard and imposing on governments a financial discipline that popular pressures might otherwise lead them to evade. The restoration and maintenance of the gold standard thus became a symbol for the viability of the old liberal world order, which the "progressives" claimed was doomed to extinction.

The debates of the 1920s on the international order and the role of the state and money were conducted among policymakers, advisers, and critics: the politicians, civil servants, and intellectuals of the bourgeoisie. Behind them, however, stood the unspoken (or at least rarely mentioned) subject of all bourgeois theory: the power of the working class. This is not to say that the idealists who resigned from their national delegations at Versailles were cynically concerned only with a more effective means of suppressing labour, but that the course of the argument was shaped by "reality" and that the most important feature of that "reality" was the growing difficulty experienced in dominating and exploiting labour. At issue in the debates of the 1920s was a clash between two strategic responses to the new power symbolised by the October Revolution of 1917.

The subject of the debates occasionally broke through in explicit terms. Far away from the streets of St Petersburg, Berlin, or Munich, the U.S. Attorney General A. Mitchell Palmer gave colourful expression to the fears of capital everywhere when he said, in 1920:

> Like a prairie-fire, the blaze of revolution was sweeping over every American institution of law and order a year ago. It was eating its way into the homes of the American workman, its sharp tongues of revolutionary heat were licking the altars of the churches, leaping into the belfry of the school bell, crawling into the sacred corners of American homes, seeking to replace marriage vows with libertine laws, burning up the foundations of society. (Schlesinger 1957, 42)

For politicians of the stamp of Palmer, the response was simple: suppression by force of anything remotely resembling a revolutionary threat, withdrawal of the state from the expanded role assumed during the war, exclusion of trade unionists from the policymaking process into which they had been co-opted during the fighting, and restoration of the power of money over the state. In international affairs, this position was matched by a non-conciliatory approach to the Soviet revolution, first military intervention and then diplomatic isolation. In retrospect, this approach has often been portrayed as simpleminded: it was, however, by and large the strategy that was implemented by all the major governments throughout the 1920s. The 1920s were built on the violent suppression of workers' movements, real and imagined, throughout the world.

The other response was more complex. To speak of it as a single "strategic response" is, of course, a gross simplification. It was made up of a plethora of policies, policy proposals, managerial innovations, and theoretical developments in different parts of the world, with different motivations and different implications. But the common theme everywhere was the assumption of a new role by the state, and the common background everywhere was the wave of discontent symbolised by the Russian Revolution. The starting point was an awareness that things had changed. The old balance was broken:

> The idea of the old-world party, that you can, for example, alter the value of money and then leave the consequential adjustments to be brought about by the forces of supply and demand, belongs to the days of fifty or a hundred years ago when trade unions were powerless, and when the economic juggernaut was allowed to crash along the highway of progress without obstruction and even with applause. Half the copybook assumptions of our statesmen is based on assumptions which were at one time true, or partly true, but are now less and less true day by day. (Keynes 1972, 305)

The old equilibrium had been broken by the collective power of labour. The assumption that labour power could simply be treated as any other commodity on the market was no longer valid: "the trade unions are strong enough to interfere with the free play of the forces of supply and demand" (Keynes 1972, 305). As a result, Say's law had lost its validity: it could no longer be assumed that market forces alone would ensure the most efficient use of resources: "In the economic field this means, first of all, that we must find new policies and new instruments to adapt and control the working of economic forces, so that they do not intolerably interfere with contemporary ideas as to what is fit and proper in the interests of social stability and social justice" (Keynes 1972, 306).

Whereas the "old-world party" did not recognise—or refused to recognise—the changed balance of forces within society, the progressives argued for a new accommodation with labour. This did not mean taking the side of labour. "I can be influenced by what seems to me to be justice and good sense; but the class war will find me on the side of the educated bourgeoisie," as Keynes declared in the same article (1972, 297), but developing a strategy based on the recognition of the new situation that would integrate the working class as a force for development within capitalism (see Negri 1988), that would not openly defeat but contain and redefine the power of the working class.

It was not only in discussions of state policy but also in the development of management practices that awareness was growing of a new situation. Taylor had been preaching his gospel of "scientific management" since the turn of the century: an explicit attack on the power of the skilled worker through the detailed study and the fragmentation of skilled tasks into simple and closely controlled operations. The fragmentation of tasks had been developed further by Henry Ford, who had connected it to the electrically driven conveyor belt to create the assembly line, the detailed steps in the production of the Ford cars being performed at different positions along the line. However, Ford's technological development of scientific management was soon confronted by the fact that cars are produced neither by science nor by technology but by working people. The workers, not surprisingly, found the new organisation of work unbearably boring and rarely stayed long. In 1913, for example, to maintain a workforce of fifteen thousand, it was necessary to hire fifty-three thousand workers (Coriat 1982, 56). It was in order to control this chaotic flow of labour that Ford introduced his famous "five dollars a day" wage contract in 1914.

Five dollars was more than double the previous wage at Ford's factory, but it was not given to everybody. In order to receive such a high wage, it was necessary to be a man over twenty-one and to have been working at the factory for at least six months. It was also necessary to show oneself morally worthy of such a high wage. As the director of Ford's newly created department of sociology put it:

> It was easy to foresee that in the hands of certain men, five dollars a day could constitute a serious obstacle on the path of rectitude and of a well-ordered life and could make them a menace to society as a whole; that is why it was established from the beginning that no man could receive this increase who did not know how to use it in a discrete and prudent manner. (Lee 1916, 303, quoted by Coriat 1982, 57)

The five-dollar day was extremely successful in reducing the turnover of labour: after 1914 it dropped to less than 0.5 per cent per year (Coriat 1982, 59). This created the basis for a new, more disciplined organisation of production within the factory and an intensification of work that, despite the rise in wage costs, reduced the costs of production of the Model T Ford by about 17 per cent (Beynon 1973, 24; Coriat 1982, 59). In addition, it also created a new group of relatively prosperous workers, who then provided a new market for the mass-produced Model T.

The striking feature of the Ford contract is the trade-off between the acceptance of disciplined, soul-destroying monotony during the day and a relatively comfortable consumption after hours, the rigid separation between the death of alienated labour and the "life" of consumption. What needs to be emphasised, however, is not simply the oppressive nature of Fordist production but that the Ford contract was a striking acknowledgement of the dependence of capital upon labour and the attempt to reformulate the power of labour (ultimately, the power not to labour) as monetary demand for commodities. It was the innovatory acknowledgement and redefinition of the power of labour that made Ford "the most influential of all business leaders" (Schlesinger 1959, 173).

It was not just Ford and his followers who were introducing new styles of management. There were other voices of managerial change during the 1920s, as management sought to deal with the problems of high turnover and the informal resistance of the workers: many of the large corporations began to experiment during this period with more "liberal" ways of organising work and more systematic methods of organising production (Gordon et al. 1982, 172ff). All these methods sought ways of channelling the discontent of the workers into a form that would serve the interests of capital.

The changes at managerial level and the new views on the way that the state should develop were quite uncoordinated, although there were those who argued that what was needed was "a Taylor ... for the economic system as a whole" (Tugwell, quoted in Schlesinger 1959, 194) and others who saw connections between Taylor and Keynes (Schlesinger 1959, 201).

In the 1920s, however, the changes in management were still only beginning to spread, and "the old-world party" still reigned supreme in politics. In retrospect, the views of the conservatives are generally portrayed as simply reactionary and out of touch with the new reality of the postwar world. It can be argued, however, that the time had not yet come for the new strategy of domination. The old balance was broken, but it is not clear that the conditions yet existed for the establishment of any new equilibrium. In the immediate postwar world, the threat of revolution still loomed large in many parts of the world. It was only after the revolutionary

wave of struggles had been violently suppressed that the strategy of refor-
mulating working-class power became credible. It was only after the defeat
of the General Strike in Great Britain in 1926, for example, that there developed a new institutionalisation of working-class struggle that would later
provide the counterpart of Keynesian policy initiatives.

After the working class had been defeated on the streets and the
immediate threat of revolution had receded, the conditions were more
favourable for the institutional integration of working-class power, but
the urgency of change was less obvious. Only after the crash of 1929 and
the ensuing crisis did the pressure for change gain a new force.

The crash of 1929 was the final crash of the old order, the final breakdown of the established mode of domination. That the crash was a turning
point in historical development is generally undisputed, but it is usually
presented as an economic event external to the development of class relations. The immediate cause of the crash is generally seen as an overac-
cumulation of capital in relation to a limited market (see Clarke 1988, 217).
The boom in the U.S. economy during the 1920s had been based on the
rapid expansion of the new consumer durables industry, but the market
was narrow, being limited essentially to the middle class. An expansion
of credit allowed accumulation to continue after the market had been
exhausted, but this took the form of stock market speculation. The barrier
of the limited market finally asserted itself in the stock market collapse
of 1929.

The crash was more than that, however: it was the other face of the
October Revolution of 1917. On the surface there is no connection between
the two events: Negri asserts that "it would seem obvious that the events
of 1917 had no bearing on those of 1929" (1988, 22). In fact, the two dates
mark important aspects of the same crisis. The revolution of 1917 had been
the loudest declaration by the working class that the old relation between
capital and labour was at breaking point. The crash of 1929 brought home
to capital that this was indeed the case, despite all its attempts to recreate
the pre-war world.

But then why is the "inner connection" between 1917 and 1929 not
more obvious? If the crash of 1929 was the vindication of the claims made
by socialists about the intensity of the contradictions of capital and the
immanence of breakdown, why did it come too late, long after the revolutionary tide had already receded? If the crash of 1929 was simply the
most dramatic expression of the breakdown of the old pattern of relations

between capital and labour, if "the crisis of 1929 was actually a continuation of the unresolved economic crisis preceding World War 1," as Mattick puts it (1978, 116), then why did it not occur when the power of labour was at its greatest? What was the connection between the power of the working class, seen at its most dramatic in 1917, and the collapse of capitalism twelve years later? If crisis is the expression of the power of labour in-and-against capital, then why did crisis come when, on the face of it, labour had been decisively beaten?

Credit is the key to understanding the distance between 1917 and 1929, the key to the dislocation of the two faces of the crisis. The power of labour is refracted through the forms of the capital relation, especially through money and credit. As the prevailing pattern of exploitation comes up against its limits, as capital's pursuit of profit is obstructed by the established positions of labour, there is an expansion both in the demand for and in the provision of credit. On the one hand, capital seeks loans to tide itself over what it sees as a temporary difficulty. On the other, if capital finds it difficult to gain profit through production, it seeks to expand through the financial markets. Built into the existence of money as a form distinct from value is the possibility (or inevitability) of a temporal dislocation between the breakdown of the relation between capital and labour and its manifestation in the form of a fall in capitalist profitability.

Credit is always a gamble on the future. In borrowing, capital commits a portion of surplus value not yet produced. If the required surplus value is not produced, the capital will fall. If the conditions of production can be altered sufficiently to expand the production of surplus value by the requisite amount, then the gamble will have succeeded. Credit expansion, by postponing a fall in profitability, makes the restructuring of production relations objectively more urgent than ever. It also makes it more difficult, by maintaining the conditions in which the power of labour has developed.

This is essentially what happened in the 1920s. The restocking boom in the immediate aftermath of the war was over in Europe by 1921 (Clarke 1988, 197). In the United States, however, the boom continued through the 1920s, sustained at first by the restructuring of production that had taken place during the war (Mattick 1978, 116) and the development of the new automobile and consumer durable industries, and then increasingly through an enormous expansion of credit, both in the form of bank loans and through the creation of fictitious capital on the stock market (Mattick 1978, 119). Productivity rose sharply in the United States during the 1920s but not sharply enough to produce the surplus value required to sustain profitability. Eventually the gap between the surplus value actually produced and that which was being gambled upon in the stock market manifested itself in the crash of October 1929: "finally America, too, succumbed to the post-war realities," as Mattick puts it (1978, 116).

Even after the crash, however, there was no immediate recognition of the need for a new order, certainly not at the political level. In the United States, in Britain, and elsewhere, the government response was retrenchment. Pressure on the state to play a more active role in stimulating the economy and in providing welfare relief for the millions thrown out of work was answered by financial orthodoxy. The balanced budget became the symbol of the political defence of a world that no longer existed.

In the sphere of individual capital, change was forced more quickly. The collapse in profitability forced capital to reorganise its relation with labour in order to survive. The new systems of management that had slowly been making ground in the 1920s soon became a precondition for survival:

> Two effects of the Depression immediately focussed attention on the need for new systems of labour management. First, the collapse of profits itself pressured corporations to consider whatever methods were available which might restore profitability and improve their control over the labour process. Second, the Depression led fairly quickly to worker dissatisfaction—and ultimately, of course, to the emergence of industrial unions. The industrial union movement constituted a new force with which large employers had to contend, directly challenging some of the most important elements of both the drive system and the early explorations of more sophisticated policies. (Gordon et al. 1982, 176)

It was this new thrust of the power of labour that at last gave shape to capital's changing form of domination. In the United States, the dissatisfaction of labour and the protest against the power of money symbolised by the balanced budget had brought the defeat of Hoover in the elections of 1932 and the triumph of Roosevelt with his commitment to a "New Deal." The original New Deal was, however, vague and self-contradictory: it was only under the pressure of the industrial struggles of the 1930s and the rise of the new industrial unionism organised in the CIO that it acquired the shape that we associate with it today.

The new industrial unionism grew out of the new relations at work. The spread of Fordism meant the spread of a new type of mass unskilled worker in the large factories. The Fordist deal, the trade-off between boredom and pay, had made the wage the focus of struggle more clearly than ever before. When Ford announced his "five dollars a day" in 1915, it had been a unilateral act to stem the flight from intolerable working conditions. But once the wage had been made the focal point of the relation to such an exclusive extent, the workers were unlikely to wait for the fiat of management. Pressure for collective wage bargaining led to the mushrooming of a new industrial unionism in the early 1930s. The demand for recognition of the new unions as the representatives of labour in collective bargaining was increasingly accepted by companies throughout the 1930s. This was not without resistance, but there was also recognition by capital that the channelling of discontent into the wage demand was an important component in establishing a more orderly relation with labour. This was dramatically captured by the posters for the recruitment drive of the CIO: "President Roosevelt wants you to join the union." As Tronti points out, "The password 'organise the unorganised' was acceptable to both modern capitalism and the new union. In recent history there are these moments of elective affinity between the two classes when, each in its own camp, [they] find themselves internally divided and must simultaneously resolve problems of strategic location and of organisational restructuring" (1976, 117).

It was this drive that led to the labour policies of the Roosevelt administration and the enactment of the Wagner Act of 1935. Under immense social pressure and against often strong resistance from important sections of capital, a new relationship between capital and labour was forged in the United States in the 1930s, focussed on the recognition and attempted integration of the power of labour. The New Deal "implied the beginning of a fresh game but with the same players" (Mattick 1978, 129). The "fresh game" was what later became known as Keynesianism: "Lord Keynes," in Tronti's striking phrase, "is actually an American economist" (1976, 115). In the mid-1930s, however, the fresh game was still far from being established. For one thing, there were alternate competing models for the new game. In Germany, the crisis of the old pattern and the drive of labour had met with a different response. The violent suppression of the postwar revolutionary currents was not so cleanly separated from the institutional incorporation of the working-class movement, and the new corporatism took a particularly bloody form. In Russia too, the enormous power of labour's thrust in 1917 had given a very different form to the eventual containment of that power under Stalin.

It was not simply the existence of competing models that prevented the firm establishment of the new game. More crucial was the fact that the conditions had not yet been established for a firm restoration of capitalist profitability. The economic recovery of the early New Deal years proved to be short-lived. At the end of 1937, there was a new slump. Steel production, for example, declined from 80 per cent of capacity to 19 per cent. Despite the subsequent revival, there were still ten million unemployed in the United States in 1939, and private investments were still one-third below the level of 1929 (Mattick 1978, 138–39). Although the practices of the New Deal were given a new theoretical coherence by the publication of Keynes's *General Theory* in 1936, neither theoretical coherence nor government policies were sufficient to achieve the restructuring that was required to reestablish capitalism on a firm footing.

That restructuring was achieved through war. "Death, the greatest of all the Keynesians, now ruled the world once more" (Mattick 1978, 142). War succeeded where the New Deal, Nazism, and Stalinism had shown only possible lines of development. The war achieved a destruction and devaluation of constant capital even greater than that associated with the bankruptcies and depreciations of the Great Depression. At work, the managerial changes introduced after the crash of 1929 were carried further but in a new atmosphere of discipline: in the United States, for example, "many employers used the advantage of wartime discipline after 1941 to seek to regain some of the initiative and control they had surrendered to industrial unions at the end of the Depression" (Gordon et al. 1982, 182). In this, employers in all the major countries were helped considerably by the trade unions, which preached the subordination of class antagonism to the common goal of winning the war (see Gordon et al. 1982, 183; Middlemas 1979, 266ff). The changes in relations at work were accompanied by rapid change in the technology of production as governments poured resources into areas of technological development considered to be strategically important, so that there was rapid progress in areas such as electronics and petrochemicals. Unemployment was solved through the enlisting and killing of millions of people: a massive "scrapping of labour power" (Bonefeld 1988, 56).

The war was the culmination of the restructuring efforts of the interwar years. In an article in 1918, John Dewey, already one of the intellectual leaders of American liberalism, had pointed to "the social possibilities of war"—the use of technology for communal purposes, the subordination of production for profit to production for use, the organisation of the means for public control (Dewey 1918, cited in Schlesinger 1957, 39). The Taylorisation of society that Roosevelt's adviser Tugwell had looked for in the New Deal was given a new degree of reality in the war. The expansion of the state that New Dealers and Keynesians had long sought was realised to an unprecedented extent. The balanced budget so fiercely defended by the "old-world party" was forgotten. And with the end of the war and the establishment of one clearly hegemonic power, the United States, state intervention and monetary regulation could attain an international dimension quite impossible in the interwar period. Now at last, capital could deal again and, over the bodies of twenty million people, a fresh game could start.

For the first time in almost fifty years, the imminent collapse of capitalism, which had for so long been a preoccupation of both socialist and bourgeois thought, was no longer on the immediate agenda. From the turn of the century, the issue of the breakdown of capitalism had been at the centre of Marxist discussion: debate centred on the inevitability or otherwise of the breakdown, but for all concerned the question was one of immediate importance. For bourgeois thought too the war, the revolutionary wave, the crash and the Great Depression, fascism, rearmament and renewed war, shock upon shock to any notion of capitalist stability had made failure, collapse, and revolution the dominant preoccupations of thirty years.

The hopes and fears of revolution did not immediately disappear with the ending of the war in 1945. On the contrary, the immediate postwar period was a time of great ferment. But the balance of things had shifted. For the first time in nearly fifty years, capital had a basis on which it could pursue accumulation and exploitation with vigour, a basis on which it could build a new appearance of stability, hiding in a mist of amnesia and poppies the millions who had been slaughtered on the way.

II

The new game was broken up in the late 1960s and early 1970s. It had never been played without interruptions. Even after the turbulence of the immediate postwar period had been contained, even after the clear establishment of "Marshallism" in Europe and of U.S. domination throughout the world, anticolonial and revolutionary movements and industrial unrest rumbled throughout the 1950s and early 1960s. However, it was not until the late 1960s that the pattern of relations between capital and labour that had been established after the war began to disintegrate.

What is often referred to as the "crisis of Keynesianism" is not simply a crisis of economic theory, or of economic policymaking: these are manifestations of a crisis in the relation between capital and labour, a crisis in the particular pattern of the containment of the power of labour. Put like that, it is clear that the crisis can be understood neither in terms of the failure of the objective structures (or the working of the "objective laws of capital") nor simply in terms of the subjective drive of labour, or, even more clearly, in terms of tensions between capitalists or national capital groups. It was the relationship between capital and labour that broke down: there was a swelling and bursting of the tensions present in the relationship from the beginning. The antagonism contained by Keynesianism could be contained no longer.

The postwar pattern of domination had as its precondition the effective exploitation of labour. In the aftermath of the war, Fordist methods of mass production had become widely established not only in the United States but also in Europe. These brought a sharp rise in labour productivity but at a cost. Fordist production rested on an implicit trade-off between a high degree of alienation and boredom at work and rising consumption after hours: dissatisfaction was transformed into demand and regulated through annual pay bargaining. As this became established as the dominant pattern, its contradictions became clearer.

The fundamental contradiction of capitalist production is expressed as alienation, the contradiction between the potential of human creativity in the production of use values and the form imposed on that creativity under capitalism, the creation of value under the control of another: in short, the reduction of concrete work to abstract labour. Under Fordist production methods, with their unprecedented degree of unskilled repetitive labour, this contradiction reached a new level of intensity. Increasingly, it expressed itself not as a struggle against the abstraction of work (and for workers' control) but as a rebellion against labour as such. The deadening boredom of Fordist labour was met by revolts of all sorts aimed primarily at breaking the deadly repetition of meaningless tasks: there was a rise in sabotage, absenteeism, short "wildcat" stoppages, and so on that began to have a much more serious impact on productivity and profitability than the more widely publicised strikes over pay.

The revolt against labour was all the more effective for being embedded in a peculiarly rigid work organisation. The attack against the power of the skilled worker led by Taylor and subsequently by Ford, directed as it was against the flexibility and judgement of skill, had resulted in a very inflexible organisation of production. The fragmentation of work into minute, finely timed tasks and the subsequent integration of those tasks with machinery dedicated to a specific process, the same rigid fragmentation that initially served to break the power of the skilled worker became through struggle both a weapon in the revolt against labour and a limit on capital's right to command. The rigidity magnified the effect of any disruption of the flow of the labour process, since the nonperformance of one fragment of the process often made the performance of other fragments impossible: not just within a particular factory or company but between chains of suppliers and manufacturers. The rigidity also created defined positions that often became positions of power for the workers, from which they could fight to increase wages. Thus, work to rule and the demarcation dispute became common forms of industrial conflict, as workers used or defended rigidities originally imposed by capital.

In the face of rigidity and revolt, money was the great lubricant. Wages became the focus of both managerial change and worker discontent. Raising wages (or granting special bonuses) became the principal means by which management overcame its own rigidities and introduced changes in working practices: "payment for change" became established as a principle of trade union bargaining, at least in the better organised industries. Wage negotiations also became the principal focus of organised working-class protest; the trade unions became increasingly the "managers of discontent," in C. Wright Mills's phrase, channelling conflict into the form of a monetary demand to be fought over in the ritual process of pay-bargaining.

The monetisation of conflict became more and more problematic as the productive power of labour expressed itself in higher living standards. As the revolt against labour grew, the channelling of discontent became both less effective and more costly. On the one hand, rising real wages were often insufficient incentive to establish effective managerial control over the labour process. Complaints about loss of managerial control over the workplace became more and more common throughout the late 1960s and early 1970s (see Holloway 1987). At the same time, the difficulties in establishing effective control and the power of the resistance to the imposition of new working practices expressed themselves in growing wage demands, often accompanied by threatened or actual strike action to enforce them (see Armstrong et al. 1984). Wage control and the curbing of what was seen as trade union power became a dominant preoccupation of the period.

As the revolt against exploitation grew, both in its monetised and non-monetised forms, the extraction of surplus value became more and more difficult for capital. However, it is important not to overstate this. Despite the undoubted effectiveness of working-class struggle, the rate of exploitation did not decline: on the contrary, it continued to increase, as the growing mechanisation of the production process made labour more productive and the surplus value appropriated by capital continued to grow. What changed was not that the rate of exploitation declined but that exploitation became more costly for capital: in order to exploit a worker effectively, capital had to invest an ever-increasing amount in machinery and raw materials. This is indicated, for example, by the slowing in the growth of productivity in all the major economies between 1968 and 1973, despite growing investment in mechanisation (Armstrong et al. 1984, 249). Thus, the rate of profit declined in spite of the increasing rate of exploitation.

The key to the decline in the rate of profit (documented, for example, by Glyn and Sutcliffe 1972, and Armstrong et al. 1984) was thus the fact that exploitation was becoming more and more costly for capital. The rise in the cost of exploitation is what Marx referred to as a rise in the organic composition of capital: as capitalist production develops, there is a tendency for constant capital (the part of capital corresponding to dead labour embodied in machinery and raw materials) to rise in relation to variable capital (the part of capital corresponding to living labour power). Often the emphasis on the organic composition of capital is counterposed to explanations of the crisis in terms of the struggles of the working class (as in the debates between "Fundamentalists" and "Neo-Ricardians," for example). However, if the rising organic composition of capital is seen not as an economic law external to class struggle but as an expression of the rising costs of exploitation, the polarity between class struggle and the laws of capitalist development dissolves.

Why did it become more and more costly for capital to exploit labour effectively? The revolt against labour and the struggles for higher wages had an immediate effect, both in restraining and disrupting exploitation and in raising the costs. They also had a less immediate effect in prompting capital to circumvent the "refractory hand of labour" by introducing machinery to replace the unruly and unreliable workers. In this sense, the response of capital to the particular impetus of these struggles was simply part of its more general unceasing struggle to consolidate and intensify its domination by appropriating the products of labour and converting them as dead labour into means for intensifying the exploitation of living labour. Capital lives by turning labour's productive power against it (see Bonefeld 1990). Although the need to mechanise is imposed on individual capital in the form of the economic pressure of competition, mechanisation is not an "economic tendency" separate from class struggle but part of the unceasing struggle of capital to survive: the rising costs of exploitation express the difficulties of capitalist reproduction.

A historically new feature of the crisis of the rising cost of exploitation in the 1960s was the role played by what might be called the "indirect costs of exploitation." The expansion of the state, which was such a central feature of constructing an environment after the war for continued capital accumulation, brought with it major new costs for capital. Although changes in taxation form a significant part of the constant struggle by capital to reduce the costs of exploitation, state expenditure is in general paid for by capital, whatever the form of taxation, in the sense that it constitutes a deduction from the surplus value available for accumulation (see Bullock and Yaffe 1975). The development of the Keynesian welfare state after the war contributed much both to the effectiveness and the stability of exploitation, but it did so at a cost.

The costs of creating a stable state environment for accumulation increased as its effectiveness decreased. In the same way as wages became less and less effective as a means of channelling the revolt against labour, the state became less and less effective as a means of channelling social discontent. The socialisation of capital that was involved in the expansion of the state after the war brought with it an intensification of alienation in society. Just as Fordist production heightened the contradiction between the potential of human creativity and the alien form imposed on that creativity in capitalist value production, so the expansion of the state as welfare state heightened the contradiction between the potential for conscious social organisation and the form imposed on that potential under capitalism, the state. As the state penetrated more and more aspects of social life, there was a growing awareness of the contrast between social control and state control. The revolt against labour was complemented by a revolt against the state, often expressed quite simply in vandalism and crime, but also in the conscious pursuit of struggles in forms that were not easily integrated by the state: struggles over housing, education, health, transport, and so on (see, e.g., Cockburn, 1977; LEWRG, 1979). The interpenetration of factory struggles and struggles in society, dramatically illustrated by the May events in France in 1968 or Italy's "hot autumn" of 1969, was an important feature of the late 1960s and early 1970s in very many countries: this is what Negri (1988) refers to as the recomposition of the working class as social mass worker (operaio sociale).

The increasing difficulty of containing protest within the established channels of state conciliation expressed itself in the rising cost of 'demand management'. The institutionalisation of protest which was central to the Keynesian state was not simply based on bureaucratization through the trade unions, social democratic parties and institutions of the welfare state: its material support was the ability to grant limited but significant concessions to the pressures contained. As the pressures on the state grew, the costs of containing the pressures also grew and with them taxation and the indirect costs of exploitation.

By the late 1960s, it was becoming clear that the relatively stable expansion of the postwar years was coming to an end. Profits were declining in all the leading capitalist countries (Armstrong et al. 1984, pp. 245ff) and social unrest was increasing. Rising costs, particularly wage costs, were blamed for the fall in profits and increasing efforts were devoted to controlling the rise in wages, while increasing productivity. Initially, however, the basic postwar pattern of relations between capital and labour was not questioned. It was assumed that the attempt to control wages and raise productivity could be achieved only through the existing framework, that is, through the institutionalized recognition of the power of labour, through the trade unions. The efforts to control wages and raise productivity brought the trade unions even more crucially to the centre of the whole system of rule. This was true at the level of the company, where often significant changes in working practices or in technology could be achieved only through agreement with the trade unions (Holloway 1987). It was equally true where the state sought to control the rise in wages through some sort of incomes policy. It soon became clear that the only way in which a state incomes policy could succeed was with the active cooperation of the trade unions. Keynesianism-in-crisis made very explicit what underlay the whole postwar pattern of relations between capital and labour: the recognition and institutionalisation of the power of labour, and hence the central role of the trade unions.

The attempt to control wages made clear the contradictory position of the trade unions. While they could be drawn sufficiently into the state to make them the means of restraining wage demands, the only way in which the unions could at the same time retain the support of their members was by bargaining for other state concessions (on planning, employment policy or improvements in welfare state benefits) in return for wage restraint. The more the unions were drawn into the state, the more the state system rested on the granting of concessions: for capital, the restraint of the direct costs of exploitation (wages) had to be paid for by an increase in the indirect costs (rising state expenditure). The growing entrenchment of the unions at the heart of the system made everything more rigid: it was increasingly difficult to bring about major changes either in the organization of production or in the organisation of the state.

The increasing integration of the unions into the state made them appear more powerful. But their power was the institutionalised power of labour, and, as institutions, they increasingly stood outside and opposed to the power which they represented. The more powerful they appeared in terms of influence within the state, the less effective they became in either representing or restraining their members. Their power was increasingly a hollow power, an institutional power without substance. The same applied, in different degree, to social democratic parties. The central role of the trade unions in channelling the power of labour under the postwar mode of capitalist domination often gave a privileged position in the political system to those parties which had close links with the trade unions. Especially as the difficulties of accumulation became more obvious from the mid-to-late 1960s, social democratic parties were often favoured, even by organisations representing capital, as the only parties capable of controlling the demands of labour: a striking example was the "leaked" revelation by the Confederation of British Industry (CBI) just before the February 1974 election that they favoured a Labour victory. However, as the contradictory position of the trade unions became more evident, the contradictions within social democratic parties also became more intense, with increasingly sharp conflict between "left" and "right" wings and increasing loss of contact with the class they claimed to represent.

The growing difficulties of accumulation expressed themselves in a growing crisis of the institutional structures of Keynesianism, both at the level of the individual firm and at the level of the state. However, the predominant response of capital, even as the crisis deepened, still did not take the form of an outright attack on the established pattern of social relations. There was increasing emphasis on wage control, restraint on the expansion of public expenditure, and repression of non-institutionalised expressions of the power of labour; but the assumptions of Keynesianism were still widely accepted as the framework for economic and political development. The growing contradictions of the whole postwar pattern of domination and struggle were contained through the expansion of money.

The "old-world party" had of course warned of the dangers of inflation long before the war. When the Roosevelt administration took the United States off the gold standard in 1933, Bernard Baruch, a leading Democrat, had protested: "It can't be defended except as mob rule. Maybe the country doesn't know it yet, but I think we may find that we've been in a revolution more drastic than the French Revolution. The crowd has seized the seat of government and is trying to seize the wealth. Respect for law and order is gone" (quoted in Schlesinger 1959, 202).

There was a sense in which Baruch was right. Roosevelt's decision to abandon the gold standard was a move to unhinge the management of the national economy from the constraints of the world market in order to be able to respond to intense social pressure. But this was not an abandonment of the rule of money. On the contrary, the only way of saving the rule of money from the "mob" was through financial nationalism and unhinging national currencies from the international flow of value. "*Sauve qui peut*" became the motto of capital, faced in the different nation states with demands that could not be reconciled with the free operation of the international market. Abandoning the gold standard did not mean relinquishing the rule of money: it meant simply that the rule of money could respond more flexibly to social pressures in each national financial area.

The unhinging of the national currencies was not, of course, total. The international flow of capital continued in the form both of international finance and of international trade but less freely than before. Some degree of order was restored through the establishment of different currency areas and the Tripartite Agreement of 1936 between France, Britain, and the United States, under which the authorities agreed to intervene to maintain fixed exchange rates between the three major currency areas.

However, it was not until after the war that a new international monetary order was established by the Bretton Woods Agreement of 1944, which came into effect in 1947.

The Bretton Woods system sought to reconcile the rule of international money with the recognition of the power of labour. It did so by establishing a system built around the recognition of the dollar as the key international currency. This was made possible by the overwhelming strength of U.S. capital, clearly established by the end of the war. The dollar and gold were to be used interchangeably as international money, the dollar being convertible into gold at a fixed parity. National currencies were tied to the dollar by fixed exchange rates, which could be altered only in the case of fundamental disequilibrium; the new International Monetary Fund (IMF) was to provide money to overcome short-term imbalances (Burnham 1990; Bonefeld 1993b).

One effect of this system was to introduce the inflationary flexibility of the dollar into the international flow of money. As Mandel puts it, "at Bretton Woods the victorious imperialist powers of World War Two established an international monetary system that was designed to provide the basis for an international version of the inflationary credit expansion that had by now gained acceptance on the national scale" (1975, 462). The power of the "mob," which had forced Roosevelt to come off the gold standard in 1933, was now integrated into the international flow of capital. The Marshall Plan and other dollar-aid programmes after the war sought to achieve the Keynesian solution at an international level: the transformation of protest into demand through the creation of money (see Mandel 1975, 463).

A second element of the Bretton Woods system was the conservation of a degree of protection of national economies from the world market. The force of social pressures in the crisis of the 1930s had forced national governments to insulate their national economies from the destructive power of the world market by abandoning the gold standard and erecting tariff barriers. Some degree of insulation was preserved by the establishment of fixed exchange rates, which protected national currencies from short-term movements of money on the world market. The effect was not to isolate national economies from the international flow of capital but to create a series of valves designed to regulate that flow and preserve some degree of short-term protection. Just as abandoning the gold standard was an essential part of Roosevelt's New Deal, the preservation of these valves was an essential part of the Keynesian conception of active state intervention.

Both through the role of the dollar and the system of fixed exchange rates, the power of "the mob" was integrated into the international monetary system, where it reappeared as instability.

At the core of this instability was the expansion of credit, which has been a crucial element in the accumulation of capital since the war. The new international monetary order gave more scope to the expansion of credit at the national level and ensured through the dual role of the dollar as national and as international currency that credit inflation in the United States would enter into the international system as an element of instability.

The expansion of credit to maintain demand forced upon national governments by the intensity of social pressure during the 1930s had been given theoretical justification by Keynes as a permanent feature of economic policy. In practice, however, the main source of credit creation in the postwar period was not deficit financing by the state but the expansion of bank overdrafts granted by the banks to the private sector: both production credit to companies and consumer credit given to individuals, mainly for the purchase of houses and consumer durables. Mandel points out that in the United States, private indebtedness rose from 73.6 per cent to 140.0 per cent of the annual GNP between the years 1946 and 1974, while the public debt actually fell proportionally (Mandel 1975, 418). In other words, national governments exercised only indirect control over much of the expansion of credit, which was driven forward by the demand for credit both by productive capital and by consumers seeking a better standard of living, and by the supply of loanable capital seeking a more secure return than that which could be obtained from direct investment in production.

The lack of state control over the expansion of credit was greatly exacerbated by the development of a market in dollars outside the United States, the so-called Eurodollar market. This resulted from the position of the dollar as international currency. The recovery of the capitalist economies in other countries after the war gradually led to a relative decline in the superiority of the U.S. economy. The dollars that flooded the world markets, and which were initially used to buy commodities exported from the United States, were increasingly transformed into reserves in European banks (Bonefeld 1993b). Increasingly, these reserves were used as a source of credit both for public authorities and for private capital. Beginning in the early 1960s, there was the growth of an international financial market that existed outside all state control and alongside national regulated markets. By 1969, other capitalist countries held $40 billion (as compared with $11 billion in 1964), a figure that far exceeded the gold held in the U.S. reserves (Bonefeld 1990). Under those circumstances, the convertibility of the dollar into gold began to appear more and more fragile.

The fragility of the international monetary system became more apparent as the growing costs of exploiting labour effectively expressed themselves in falling profits and increasing social tension. The demand for credit increased as states sought to respond to social pressures and to maintain declining demand and companies sought loans as a way of tiding them over what they hoped would be temporary difficulties. The supply of credit also increased as capital sought outlets that were more profitable and more secure than productive investment.

An additional source of instability came from the changing position of national currencies, which were related to the dollar through fixed exchange rates under the Bretton Woods system. The fixed exchange rates insulated the national currencies from short-term speculation on the international money markets, but at the cost of possibly chronic balance of payments problems and intensified speculation as the necessity of a change in the fixed rates became apparent. The link between the world market and the national economy asserted itself in the form of a sharp currency crisis. This was the fate of sterling, when the decline of the British economy expressed itself in balance of payments problems, speculation, and finally the devaluation of the pound in 1967.

The devaluation of the pound, which was still an important currency in international transactions, further increased the fragility of the dollar, already stretched by the expansion of the Eurodollar market and the huge increase in public debt as a result of the vain attempt to quell the revolution in Vietnam. The impossibility of containing social tension, nationally and internationally, other than by the expansion of credit, expressed itself in growing monetary instability. Holders of dollars increasingly sought security by converting their dollars into gold. Faced with the enormous disparity between the number of dollars and the U.S. gold reserve, the Nixon administration announced in August 1971 that the convertibility of the dollar into gold was to be suspended indefinitely. A new system of fixed exchange rates was established by the Smithsonian Agreement of

December 1971, but this too was subjected to severe speculative pressure, and in March 1973 the principle of fixed exchange rates was abandoned (Bonefeld 1993b; Armstrong et al. 1984, 293).

To the extent that the system of fixed exchange rates had insulated national economies from the short-term speculative movement of capital, the final demise of the Bretton Woods system meant that that insulation no longer existed. State policies were again subordinated directly to the flow of money on the international markets. As Bonefeld (1993a, 58–59) put it, "The ultimate sanction for a domestically engineered management of accumulation that was in some way 'incompatible' with global accumulation was speculative pressure on its national currency. This pressure restricted national authority over money and credit-expansion and subordinated national policies to the international movement of money." This was not, however, a return to the gold standard, the realm of seemingly secure power so staunchly defended by the old-world party against Roosevelt and the Keynesians, against the depredations of the "mob." International money was no longer represented by gold but by the dollar, and its movement was now much faster and more volatile than it had ever been in the days of the gold standard.

The pressures on the old postwar pattern of social relations were mounting on all sides. Falling profits and mounting social unrest made a mockery of Keynesian claims to reconcile social conflict and ensure the harmonious, crisis-free development of capitalism. The breakdown of the international monetary system removed the insulation from the world market that was an essential element of the Keynesian conception of state intervention. These tensions found expression in the recession of 1974–75: production fell sharply in all the leading countries, inflation and unemployment soared (Mandel 1978, 14), and the flood of "petrodollars" into the Eurodollar markets increased the volatility of the world monetary system.

From all sides, the death of Keynesianism was proclaimed. In the debates of economists, Keynesianism rapidly lost ground to the newly fashionable monetarist economic theory. Conservative politicians in Britain, the United States, and elsewhere increasingly attacked the expansion of the state, the position of the trade unions, and the "politics of consensus," and turned to theorists such as Friedman and Hayek to justify their positions. Even social democratic parties, whose own position in the political system depended upon the recognition of the power of labour, began to denounce Keynesian solutions as no longer realistic. As British

Prime Minister James Callaghan put it at the Labour Party Conference in 1976:

> We used to think that you could spend your way out of a recession and increase employment by cutting taxes and boosting government spending. I tell you in all candour that that option no longer exists and that so far as it ever did exist, it only worked on each occasion since the war by injecting a bigger dose of inflation into the economy, followed by a higher level of unemployment at the next step.

The New Deal was over, the game was finished. Or so it seemed. But so far only one of the players had stood up from the table. The social forces that had imposed the recognition of the power of labour upon capital still existed, stronger than ever, and could not be abolished simply by the declarations of politicians. And if the Keynesian game was over, what were the new rules to be? Keynesianism had taken over thirty years of struggle and the deaths of millions of people to establish. After nearly thirty years of relative stability, capitalism was again in chaos. Could a new order be established simply by the will of the politicians, or would it again require the world to pass through destruction and misery? The abyss stood open.

References

Armstrong, Philip, Andrew Glyn, and John Harrison. *Capitalism since World War II*. London: Fontana, 1984.

Beynon, Huw. *Working for Ford*. Harmondsworth: Penguin Books, 1973.

Bonefeld, Werner. "Class Struggle and the Permanence of Primitive Accumulation." *Common Sense*, no. 6 (1988): 54–65.

Bonefeld, Werner. "The Global Money Power of Capital and the Crisis of Keynesianism." *Common Sense*, no. 13 (1993b): 54–62.

Bonefeld, Werner. *The Recomposition of the British State during the 1980s*. Aldershot: Dartmouth, 1993a.

Bonefeld, Werner. "The State Form and the Development of the State under Monetarism." PhD diss., University of Edinburgh, 1990.

Braverman, Harry. *Labor and Monopoly Capital*. New York: Monthly Review, 1974.

Bullock, Paul, and David Yaffe. "Inflation, the Crisis and the Post-war Boom." *Revolutionary Communist*, no. 3–4 (1975): 5–45.

Burnham, Peter. *The Political Economy of Postwar Reconstruction*. London: Macmillan, 1990.

Clarke, Simon. *Keynesianism, Monetarism and the Crisis of the State*. Aldershot: Edward Elgar, 1988.

Cockburn, Cynthia. *The Local State*. London: Pluto, 1977.

Coriat, Benjamin. *El Taller y el Cronometro*. Madrid: Siglo XXI, 1982.

Foster, William Trufant, and Waddill Catchings. *The Road to Plenty*. New York: Popular Edition, 1928.

Glyn, Andrew, and Robert Sutcliffe. *British Capitalism, Workers and the Profit Squeeze*. Harmondsworth: Penguin Books, 1972.

Gordon, David M., Richard Edwards, and Michael Reich. *Segmented Work, Divided Workers: The Historical Transformation of Labour in the United States*. Cambridge: Cambridge University Press, 1982.

Holloway, John. "The Red Rose of Nissan." *Capital and Class* 11, no. 2 (Summer 1987): 142–64.

Keynes, John Maynard. "Am I a Liberal?" *Collected Writings*, vol. 9. London: Macmillan, 1972.

Keynes, John Maynard. "The Economic Consequences of Peace." *Collected Writings*, vol. 2. London: Macmillan, 1971.

Keynes, John Maynard. *General Theory of Employment, Interest and Money*. London: Macmillan, 1936.

Lee, John R. "The So-Called Profit Sharing System in the Ford Plant." *Annals of the Academy of Political Science* 65 (1916): 297–310.

London Edinburgh Weekend Return Group (LEWRG): *In and Against the State*. London: CSE Books, 1979.

Mandel, Ernest. *Late Capitalism*. London: New Left Books, 1975.

Mandel, Ernest. *The Second Slump*. London: New Left Books, 1978.

Mattick, Paul. *Economics, Politics and the Age of Inflation*. London: Merlin, 1978.

Middlemas, Keith. *Politics in Industrial Society*. London: Andre Deutsch, 1979.

Negri, Antonio. *Revolution Retrieved: Selected Writings on Marx, Keynes, Capitalist Crisis and New Social Subjects 1967–1983*. London: Red Notes, 1988.

Schlesinger, Arthur. *The Age of Roosevelt: The Coming of the New Deal*. Cambridge, MA: Riverside, 1959.

Schlesinger, Arthur. *The Age of Roosevelt: The Crisis of the Old Order, 1919–1933*. Cambridge, MA: Riverside, 1957.

Tronti, Mario. "Workers and Capital." In *The Labour Process and Class Strategies*, CSE Pamphlet I. London: Stage 1, 1976.

SIX

Capital Moves

Capital moves. This statement is so obvious that there seems no point in writing it down, much less making it the title of an article. And yet...

In the obvious, commonsense interpretation, the phrase "capital moves" means that capital, normally in one place, gets up and moves. British capital is exported and invested in Africa. Japanese capital moves out of Japan and flows into the United States. Capital is understood as basically fixed but capable of motion. Capital is attached but capable of detaching itself. Thus Volkswagen, a German company, has a car factory in Puebla, but we know that it can close its factory and move its capital elsewhere. Capital is capable of movement, but it is defined first in terms of its attachment: attachment to a company (Volkswagen), attachment to a branch of industry (the automobile industry), and attachment to a place (Puebla or Germany). Thus, following the same reasoning, capital invested in the textile industry is often referred to as "textile capital," capital in the banking industry as "banking capital," capital owned by Mexicans as "Mexican capital," by U.S. Americans as "U.S. capital," etc. Although the capacity of capital to move or to detach itself from a particular owner or branch of economic activity is never put in question, the movement of capital is secondary to its initial definition in terms of attachment or fixity.

In all of these examples, capital is treated as a thing that can be owned; a thing that is normally attached to a particular place, company, or branch of economic activity; a thing that can be moved from place to place, from company to company, from one branch of activity to another.

All this is obvious, but once we try to deprive capital of its thinghood, it becomes less obvious. Why should we try to deprive capital of its thinghood? Why is the obvious analysis of the movement of capital not sufficient? The answer is surely that it depends on what we want to understand. If we want to understand capitalist development as economists or to understand the way that capital dominates society, then there is probably no reason to question the thinghood of capital. If, however, we want to understand not the domination and reproduction of capital but its vulnerability and rupture: if, in other words, we want to understand not how capitalism works but how it can be destroyed, then we need to open up the thinghood of capital, to break its facticity, to break the illusion/reality of the belief that capital is, capital moves, capital rules—that's the way things are. That is why Marx devoted much of his life to showing that capital is not a thing but a social relation that exists in the fetishised form of a thing.

If capital is understood as a social relation rather than a thing, then what does it mean to say that "capital moves"? The answer is now less obvious. How can a social relation move? The movement of capital can only refer to the mobility, or perhaps better, flux or fluidity of the social relations of capitalism, the relations of power under capitalism.

What the mobility of capitalist social relations means can best be seen by contrasting capitalism and feudalism. Under feudalism, the relation of domination/exploitation was a direct and personal one. A serf was bound to a particular lord, a lord was limited to exploiting the serf that he had inherited or could otherwise subjugate. Both sides of the class divide were bound: the serf was tied to the lord, the lord to a group of serfs. If the lord was cruel, the serf could not decide to go and work for another lord. If the serfs were lazy, unskilled, or otherwise insubordinate, the lord could discipline them but could not simply fire them. The relationship between serf and lord had a fixed, immobile character. The resulting discontent was expressed in revolt by the serfs, on the one hand, and the pursuit by the lords of other ways of expanding power and wealth, on the other. The personal, immobilised relationship of feudal bondage proved inadequate as a form of containing and exploiting the power of labour. Serfs fled to the towns, and the feudal lords accepted the monetisation of the relation of domination.

The transition from feudalism to capitalism was thus a movement of liberation *on both sides of the class divide*. Both sides fled from the other: the serfs from the lords (as stressed by liberal theory) but also the lords from the serfs, through the movement of their monetised wealth. Both sides fled from a relation that had proved inadequate as a form of domination. Both sides fled to freedom.

Flight to freedom is thus central to the transition from feudalism to capitalism. But there are, of course, two different and opposing senses of freedom here (a dualism that is the central contradiction of liberal theory). The flight of the serfs was a flight from subordination to the lord, the flight of those who, for one reason or another, no longer accepted the old subordination, the flight of the insubordinate. The flight of the lords was just the opposite: when they converted their wealth into money, it was a flight away from the inadequacy of subordination, a flight from insubordination. On the one side, the flight *of* insubordination, on the other side, the flight *from* insubordination: viewed from either side, it was the insubordination of labour that was the driving force of the new mobility of the class relation, of the mutual flight of serf and lord.

The flight of-and-from the insubordination of labour, the mutual repulsion of the two classes did not, of course, dissolve the class relation. For both serf and lord, the flight to freedom came up against the reassertion of the bond of mutual dependence. The freed serfs found that they were not free to stop work: since they did not control the means of production, they were forced to work for a master, someone who did control the means of production. To survive, they had to subordinate themselves again. However, this was not a return to the old relation: they were no longer tied to one particular master but were free to move, to leave one master and go and work for another. The transition from feudalism to capitalism involved the depersonalisation, disarticulation, or liquefaction of the relations of domination. The relation of exploitation was not abolished by the dissolution of the ties of personal bondage, but it underwent a fundamental change in form. The particular bond that tied the serf to one master was dissolved and replaced by a mobile, fluid, disarticulated relation of subordination to the capitalist class. The flight of insubordination entered into the very definition of the new class relation.

On the other side of society, the erstwhile lords who converted their wealth into money[1] also found that freedom was not all they had imagined,

---

1   In a helpful comment on the first draft of this essay, Chris Arthur remarks that "the paper virtually asserts that the capitalist is the lord with a new hat on. This is historical revisionism on a grand scale with no evidence given. He should at least concede to the usual story that a new mode of production

for they were still dependent on exploitation, and therefore on the subordination of the exploited, the workers, their former serfs. Flight from insubordination is no solution for the lords turned capitalists, for the expansion of their wealth depends on the subordination of labour. They are free to abandon the exploitation of any particular group of workers (for whatever reason—laziness, inappropriate skills) and either establish direct links of exploitation with another group of workers or simply participate through non-productive investment in the global exploitation of labour. Whatever form their particular relation to the exploitation of labour takes, the expansion of their wealth can be no more than a part of the total expansion of wealth produced by the workers. Whatever the form of class domination, labour remains the sole constitutive power. Just as in the case of their former serfs, flight to freedom turns out to be flight to a new form of dependence. Just as the serfs' flight from subordination leads them back to a new form of subordination, the lords' flight from insubordination leads them back to the need to confront that insubordination. The relation, however, has changed, for capital's flight from insubordination is central to its struggle to impose subordination (as, for example, in the

---

meant, at a minimum, the decline of the lord and the rise of the capitalist, at a maximum a sharp class struggle between the two, punctuated by episodes like the French Revolution." Chris is quite right: the argument of the essay is indeed that the capitalist is the lord transformed. What matters is not the question of personal continuity (present in some cases, absent in others) but the understanding of the transition from feudalism to capitalism as a change in the form of the relation of domination and struggle or, better, of the insubordination / subordination of labour. If class is understood not as a group of people (capitalists, lords) but as the pole of an antagonistic relation of domination (see Karl Marx, *Capital*; Richard Gunn, "Notes on Class," *Common Sense* No. 2 [1987]), then it is clearly wrong to see the struggle between capitalists and lords as a struggle between two classes. It was, rather, a struggle over the form of class domination, the form of subordinating insubordinate labour. For "historical revisionism" on a genuinely grand scale, see Heide Gerstenberger, who in *Die subjektlose Gewalt: Theorie der Entstehung bürgerlicher Staatsgewalt* (Münster: Verlag Westfälisches Dampfboot, 1990) supports a similar argument against the orthodoxy of Marxist historians with an impressive wealth of evidence. In English, see Heide Gerstenberger, "The Bourgeois State Form Revisited," in *Open Marxism*, vol. 1., eds. Werner Bonefeld, Richard Gunn, and Kosma Psychopedis (London: Pluto, 1992); John Holloway, "History and Open Marxism," *Common Sense*, no. 12 (1993); Heide Gerstenberger, "History and 'Open Marxism': A Reply to John Holloway," *Common Sense*, no. 14 (1993).

ever-present threat of factory closure or bankruptcy). The flight from insubordination has become a defining feature of the new class relation.

The insubordination of labour is thus the axis on which the definition of capital as capital turns. It is the mutual repulsion of the two classes, the flight of-and-from subordination, that distinguishes capitalism from previous class societies, that gives a peculiar form to the exploitation on which capitalism, like any class society, is based. The restlessness of insubordination enters into the class relation as the movement of labour and capital.

From the start, the new class relation between capitalists and workers (or, more accurately, since it is a depersonalised relation, between capital and labour) is a relation of mutual flight and dependence: flight of-and-from insubordination and dependence on re-subordination. Capital, by its very definition, flees from insubordinate labour in pursuit of more and more wealth but can never escape from its dependence upon the subordination of labour. Labour, from the start, flees from capital in pursuit of autonomy, ease, and humanity but can escape from its dependence upon and subordination to capital only by destroying it, by destroying the private appropriation of the products of labour. The relation between capital and labour is thus one of mutual flight and dependence, but it is not symmetrical: labour can escape, capital cannot. Capital is dependent on labour in a way in which labour is not dependent upon capital. Capital without labour ceases to exist: labour without capital becomes practical creativity, creative practice, humanity.

Both serf (now worker) and lord (now capitalist) remain as antagonistic poles of a relation of exploitation-and-struggle, but that relation is no longer the same. The insubordination of labour has entered into the definition of the relation as restlessness, mobility, liquidity, flux, fluidity, constant flight.[2] The class relation has become a constantly shift-

---

2   It follows that class antagonism cannot be understood simply in terms of production but in terms of the unity of circulation and production. The view of production as primary and circulation as secondary tends to lead to a view of the working class as the class of people subordinated in production, that is, the industrial proletariat. If capital is understood in terms of the unity of production and circulation (or the unity of the flight of-and-from insubordination and the imposition of subordination), then a different picture emerges. Capital lives by subordinating and then fleeing from the insubordination that is inseparable from subordination: it sucks in labour to exploit and then spits

ing, inherently mobile relation, in which all capitalists participate in the exploitation of all workers, all workers contribute to the reproduction of capital, and the patterns of exploitation are constantly changing, kaleidoscopically.

With the transition to capitalism, the dialectic of insubordination/subordination of labour that is the core of any class relation acquires a distinctive form—the antagonistic movement of the flight of-and-from the insubordination of labour to its renewed subordination. This peculiar historical form is expressed in the familiar categories of political economy: in the existence of labour power and the products of labour as commodities and of value, money, and capital. All of these categories express the indirect or disarticulated character of capitalist domination. All express the fact that the subordination of labour is mediated through the "freedom" of the worker and of the capitalist: in other words, the flight of-and-from insubordination. These categories, therefore, often taken to embody the law-bound character of capitalist development, are in reality expressions of the defining presence of the insubordination of labour within the capitalist relation of subordination, that is to say, of the chaos at the heart of capitalist domination.

This seems upside down. We are not accustomed to thinking of value in these terms. It is more common to think of value as establishing order (the "law" of value), as being the social bond in a society of autonomous producers. This is correct only if the emphasis is on the critique of liberal theory. The notion of the "law of value" says in effect: "despite appearances, the apparently autonomous producers of capitalist society are bound together by a social connection which operates behind their backs—the law of value." If, on the other hand, we start not from the appearance of fragmented individualism but from the historical irruption of the insubordination of labour into the very definition of subordination, then value expresses the fragmentation wreaked by this irruption upon the more cohesive domination of feudalism. The law of value is simultaneously the lawlessness of value, the loss of any social control over society's

---

it out as unpalatable. The antagonism that defines the working class is not one of subordination but of subordination/insubordination: the working class are not subordinate victims but the insubordinate from whom capital flees and who it must subordinate. If capital lives by sucking and spitting, the working class can accurately be defined as the unpalatable sucked and spat of the earth.

development and the presence of insubordination within subordination. Value is the political-economic expression of the presence of the contradictory flight of-and-from insubordination within subordination itself, just as freedom is its categorial expression in liberal political theory.

Value, in the form of money, is the new liquidity of the class relation. It is the fact that social relations come to be mediated through money that makes it possible for the worker to shift from one master to another, in each case selling his or her labour power in return for a certain amount of money. It is the fact that the lord-turned-capitalist can convert his wealth into money that makes it possible for him to abandon one group of workers and move to another and to participate in the global exploitation of labour.

Money not only liquefies the class relation, it also transforms or fetishises it. It gives its own colouring to the class relation, making subordination/insubordination appear as a relation between rich and poor, a relation of inequality between those with money and those without money, rather than one of antagonism. It transforms the antagonistic relation of subordination/insubordination into a relation of money, transforms the flight of-and-from subordination that defines the capital-labour relation into the movement of money or capital (understood as an economic phenomenon).

The banal phrase with which the article began, "capital moves," has now acquired a new meaning. It is a tautology. "Capital moves" does not mean that capital is normally still and now moves but that capital is inherently mobile.

Capital, then, is a social relation. But it is not simply a social relation of exploitation/subordination/domination. It is a social relation of subordination in which the defining presence of insubordination is expressed as unceasing restlessness and mobility. This mobility is both functional (as capital is metamorphosed from productive to commodity to money capital and back) and spatial (as capital flows/flees through the world in search of a means of self-expansion). The peculiar unity of subordination/insubordination that is the *differentia specifica* of capital is expressed in the unity of production and circulation or in the unity of the different functional forms of the circuit of capital (discussed by Marx in vol. 2 of *Capital*), or in the unity of the world as the locus of class struggle (the relation between insubordination and subordination). Conversely, the dislocations of production and circulation, or of the different functional forms of the circuit of capital or of the spatial flow/flight of capital can only be understood as the disunity-in-unity of insubordination and subordination, the constant inability of capital to contain labour, the constant overflowing of insubordination from subordination, the existence of labour against-and-in (and not just in-and-against) capital.

All this is just a rephrasing and development of what has been a central theme of debate in the Conference of Socialist Economists over the last twenty years and more—the critique of structuralism and of the separation of structure and struggle, which is, crucially, the separation of subordination and insubordination. It has been common in the mainstream (and overwhelmingly structuralist-functionalist) Marxist tradition to think of capitalism as a basically self-reproducing system of domination/subordination occasionally disrupted by class struggle (the open manifestation of insubordination) and as a self-reproducing economic system in which the exploited workers are victims except on the rare occasions on which they engage in open struggle. In this tradition, the labour theory of value is understood as the mechanism that explains the self-reproduction of capitalism: there is a peculiar blindness to the most obvious feature of the labour theory of value—namely, that it is a theory of capital's dependence upon labour, a theory therefore of class struggle. It is in the face of this stultifying and, above all, disempowering tradition of mainstream Marxism that it is important to reassert the unity of insubordination and subordination, the corrosive, destructive, chaotic presence of insubordination within the definition of subordination itself.

The way in which the notion of the mobility of capital is used in many current discussions of the "internationalisation" or "globalisation" of capital is one example of the separation of subordination and insubordination, structure and struggle. In such discussions, labour, if it features at all, appears only as a victim of the latest developments in capitalist domination. The actors in such discussions bear such designations as U.S. capital, Japanese capital, European capital, finance capital. Debate centres on the extension of the power of "finance capital," on the interimperialist rivalry between U.S. capital, Japanese capital, etc. All of these categories rest on the notion of capital as a thing, a notion that excludes the attempt to understand the restlessness of capital in terms of the power of insubordination. If current changes in capitalism are understood in terms of the conflict between different national capitals,[3] then class struggle, if it

---

3   The only possible justification for the notion of "national capital" would be an understanding of the national state as an obstacle to the equalisation of

appears at all, can only appear as a reaction to the changing form of domination not as the substance of the change. Everything is turned upside down: the "globalisation" of capital (which I take to refer to the enormous increase in the speed and scale of the flow or flight of capital in money form) is seen as an increase in the power of capital, rather than as a manifestation of capital's incapacity to subordinate labour.[4] The violence of money is a measure of capital's flight from the insubordination of labour and of the desperation of its need to re-subordinate.[5]

Marxism is a theory, not of the power of capital but of the power of insubordinate labour.

Acknowledgment

My thanks for their critical comments on the original draft of this essay to Ana Esther Ceceña, Andrés Barreda, and their seminar group in the UNAM, to Chris Arthur, Werner Bonefeld, and to Paul Stewart as coordinating editor for *Capital and Class*.

References

Bonefeld, Werner. *The Recomposition of the British State during the 1980s*. Aldershot: Dartmouth, 1993.

Bonefeld, Werner, and John Holloway. *Global Capital, the National State and the Politics of Money*. London: Macmillan, 1995.

---

the global rate of profit (see *Capital* vol. 3, chap. 10), but I have not seen such an argument made, and in any case it would have to be made in class terms. I see absolutely no reason for granting a priori validity to such questionable categories as "Britain," the "United States," "Mexico," "Ireland," "Japan," etc. Like any other category of social theory, these must be criticised.

4   For a development of some of the arguments in this essay, see Werner Bonefeld, *The Recomposition of the British State during the 1980s* (Aldershot: Dartmouth Pub. Co., 1993); Werner Bonefeld, and John Holloway, *Global Capital, the National State and the Politics of Money* (London: Macmillan, 1995).

5   This essay seems to float in the air, but it does not. Behind it lies the question of the relation between the Zapatista uprising in Chiapas and the devaluation of the Mexican peso, together with the upheavals on the world financial markets (the "systemic risk" to world capitalism) that the uprising has provoked. The understanding of the flight of capital from Mexico as an economic phenomenon quite distinct from the revolt in Chiapas (the separation of structure from struggle) makes it more difficult to establish the unity between the two forms of discontent, in the countryside of Chiapas and in the world's biggest city. The connecting fuse, once lit, could change the world.

Gerstenberger, Heide. "The Bourgeois State Form Revisited." In *Open Marxism*, vol. 1, edited by Werner Bonefeld, Richard Gunn, and Kosma Psychopedis. London: Pluto, 1992.

Gerstenberger, Heide. "History and 'Open Marxism': A reply to John Holloway." *Common Sense*, no. 14 (1993).

Gerstenberger, Heide. *Die subjektlose Gewalt: Theorie der Entstehung bürgerlicher Staatsgewalt*. Münster: Verlag Westfälisches Dampfboot, 1990.

Gunn, Richard. "Notes on Class." *Common Sense*, no. 2 (1987).

Holloway, John. "History and Open Marxism." *Common Sense*, no. 12 (1993).

Marx, K. *Capital*. London: Lawrence & Wishart, 1987.

SEVEN

Dignity's Revolt

I. Dignity Arose on the First Day of January 1994

The "Enough!" ("¡*Ya basta!*") proclaimed by the Zapatistas on the first day of 1994 was the cry of dignity. When they occupied San Cristóbal de las Casas and six other towns of Chiapas on that day, the wind they blew into the world, "this wind from below, the wind of rebellion, the wind of dignity," carried "a hope, the hope of the conversion of dignity and rebellion into freedom and dignity."[1] When the wind dies down, "when the storm abates, when the rain and the fire leave the earth in peace once again, the world will no longer be the world, but something better."[2]

A letter from the ruling body of the Zapatistas, the Comité Clandestino Revolucionario Indígena (CCRI),[3] addressed just a month later to another indigenous organisation, the Consejo 500 Años de Resistencia Indígena,[4] emphasises the central importance of dignity:

> Then that suffering that united us made us speak, and we recognised that in our words there was truth, we knew that not only pain and suffering lived in our tongue, we recognised that there is hope still in our hearts. We spoke with ourselves, we looked inside ourselves

---

1   EZLN, *La Palabra de los Armados de Verdad y Fuego*, vol. 1 (Mexico City: Editorial Fuenteovejuna, 1994), 31–32. The three volumes of this series are an invaluable source of EZLN interviews, letters, and communiqués from 1994. All translations of Spanish quotations are by the author.
2   EZLN, *La Palabra*, vol. 1, 35.
3   Clandestine Revolutionary Indigenous Committee.
4   The Council 500 Years of Indigenous Resistance.

and we looked at our history: we saw our most ancient fathers suffering and struggling, we saw our grandfathers struggling, we saw our fathers with fury in their hands, we saw that not everything had been taken away from us, that we had the most valuable, that which made us live, that which made our step rise above plants and animals, that which made the stone be beneath our feet, and we saw, brothers, that all that we had was *dignity*, and we saw that great was the shame of having forgotten it, and we saw that *dignity* was good for men to be men again, and dignity returned to live in our hearts, and we were new again, and the dead, our dead, saw that we were new again and they called us again to dignity, to struggle.[5]

Dignity, the refusal to accept humiliation and dehumanisation, the refusal to conform: dignity is the core of the Zapatista revolution of revolution. The idea of dignity was not invented by the Zapatistas, but they have given it a prominence that it has never before possessed in revolutionary thought. When the Zapatistas rose, they planted the flag of dignity not just in the centre of the uprising in Chiapas but in the centre of oppositional thought. Dignity is not peculiar to the indigenous peoples of the southeast of Mexico: the struggle to convert "dignity and rebellion into freedom and dignity" (an odd but important formulation) is the struggle of (and for) human existence in an oppressive society, as relevant to life in Edinburgh, Athens, Tokyo, Los Angeles, or Johannesburg as it is to the struggles of the peoples of the Lacandon Jungle.

The aim of this essay is to explore what it means to put dignity at the centre of oppositional thought. I should become clear why "Zapatismo" is not a movement restricted to Mexico but is central to the struggle of thousands of millions of people all over the world to live a human life against-and-in an increasingly inhuman society.

The essay aims not so much to give a historical account of the Zapatista movement as to provide a distillation of the most important themes, without at the same time concealing the ambiguities and contradictions of the movement. In order to distil a fragrant essence from roses, it is not necessary to conceal the existence of the thorns, but thorns do not

---

5   EZLN, *La Palabra*, vol. 1, 122; emphasis in the original. The continuing importance of this passage was underlined when it was quoted by Comandante Ramona in her speech to a meeting held in Mexico City on February 16, 1997, to protest against the government's failure to fulfil the Agreements of San Andrés.

enter into what one wants to extract. The purpose of trying to distil the theoretical themes of Zapatismo is similar to the purpose behind any distillation process: to separate those themes from the immediate historical development of the Zapatista movement, to extend the fragrance beyond the immediacy of the particular experience.

II. Dignity Was Wreaked in the Jungle

The uprising of January 1, 1994, was more than ten years in the preparation. The EZLN celebrates November 17, 1983, as the date of its foundation.[6] On that date a small group of revolutionaries established themselves in the mountains of the Lacandon Jungle—"a small group of men and women, three indigenous and three mestizos."[7]

According to the police version, the revolutionaries were members of the Fuerzas de Liberación Nacional (FLN),[8] a guerrilla organisation founded in 1969 in the city of Monterrey, one of a number of such organisations that flourished in Mexico in the late 1960s and early 1970s. Many of the members of the FLN had been killed or arrested, but the organisation had survived. Its statutes of 1980 describe the organisation as "a political-military organisation whose aim is the taking of political power by the workers of the countryside and of the cities of the Mexican Republic, in order to install a popular republic with a socialist system." The organisation was guided, according to its statutes, by "the science of history and society, Marxism-Leninism, which has demonstrated its validity in all the triumphant revolutions of this century."[9]

The supposed origins of the EZLN are used by the authorities to suggest the manipulation of the indigenous people by a group of hardcore professional revolutionaries from the city.[10] However, leaving aside

---

6   Ejército Zapatista de Liberación Nacional: Zapatista Army of National Liberation.

7   Subcomandante Insurgente Marcos, November 17, 1994: EZLN, *La Palabra*, vol. 3, 224. Marcos is the spokesperson and military leader of the EZLN. He is, however, subordinate to the CCRI, a popularly elected body. "Mestizos" are people of mixed indigenous and European origin—the vast majority of the Mexican population.

8   Forces of National Liberation.

9   Quoted in C. Tello Díaz, *La Rebelión de las Cañadas* (Mexico City: Cal y Arena, 1995), 97, 99.

10   The EZLN's reply to the government's claim is contained in a February 9, 1995, communiqué: "In relation to the connections of the EZLN with the organisation

the racist assumptions of such an argument, the supposed origin of the revolutionaries merely serves to underline the most important question: If, as is claimed, the small group of revolutionaries who set up the EZLN came from an orthodox Marxist-Leninist guerrilla group, how were they transformed into what eventually emerged from the jungle in the early hours of 1994? What was the path that led from the first encampment of November 17, 1983, to the proclamation of dignity in the town hall of San Cristóbal? For it is precisely the fact that they are not an orthodox guerrilla group that has confounded the state time and time again in its dealings with them. It is precisely the fact that they are not an orthodox group of revolutionaries that makes them theoretically and practically the most exciting development in oppositional politics in the world for many a long year.

What, then, was it that the original founders of the EZLN learned in the jungle? A letter written by Marcos speaks of the change in these terms: "We did not propose it. The only thing that we proposed to do was to change the world; everything else has been improvisation. Our square conception of the world and of revolution was badly dented in the confrontation with the indigenous realities of Chiapas. Out of those blows, something new (which does not necessarily mean 'good') emerged, that which today is known as 'neo-Zapatismo.'" [11]

The confrontation with the indigenous realities took place as the Zapatistas became immersed in the communities of the Lacandon Jungle. At first the group of revolutionaries kept to themselves, training in the mountains, slowly expanding in numbers. Then gradually they made

---

called 'Forces of National Liberation,' the EZLN has declared in interviews, letters, and communiqués that members of different armed organisations of the country came together in its origin, that the EZLN was born from that and, gradually, was appropriated by the indigenous communities to the point where they took over the political and military leadership of the EZLN. To the name of the 'Forces of National Liberation,' the government should add as the antecedents of the EZLN those of all the guerrilla organisations of the '70s and '80s, Arturo Gámiz, Lucio Cabañas, Genaro Vázquez Rojas, Emiliano Zapata, Francisco Villa, Vicente Guerrero, José María Morelos y Pavón, Miguel Hidalgo y Costilla, Benito Juárez, and many others whom they have already erased from the history books, because a people with memory is a rebel people" (La Jornada, February 13, 1995).

11 Subcomandante Insurgente Marcos, "Carta a Adolfo Gilly," Viento del Sur, no.4 (Summer 1995), 21–25, at 25.

contact with the local communities, initially through family contacts, then, from about 1985 onward, on a more open and organised basis.[12] Gradually, more and more of the communities sought out the Zapatistas to help them defend themselves from the police or the farmers' armed "white guards,"[13] more and more became Zapatista communities, some of their members joining the EZLN on a full-time basis, some forming part of the part-time militia, the rest of the community giving material support to the insurgents. Gradually, the EZLN was transformed from being a guerrilla group to being a community in arms.

The community in question is in some respects a special community. The communities of the Lacandon Jungle are of recent formation, most of them dating from the 1950s and 1960s, when the government encouraged colonisation of the jungle by landless peasants, most of whom moved from other areas of Chiapas, in many cases simply transplanting whole villages. There is a long tradition of struggle, both preceding the formation of the communities in the jungle, and then, very intensely, throughout the 1970s and 1980s, as the people fought to get enough land to ensure their own survival, as they tried to secure the legal basis of their landholdings, as they fought to maintain their existence against the expansion of the cattle ranches, as they resisted the threat to their survival posed by two government measures in particular, the Decree of the Lacandon Community,[14] which threatened to expropriate a large part of the Lacandon Jungle, and the 1992 reform of Article 27 of the Constitution, which, by opening the countryside up to private investment, threatened to undermine the system of collective landholding. The communities of the Lacandon Jungle are special in many respects, but arguably the rethinking of revolutionary theory and practice could have resulted from immersion in any community: what was important was probably not the specific characteristics of the Lacandon Jungle, so much as the transformation from being a group of dedicated young men and women into being an armed community of

---

12 See the account given by Tello (*La Rebelión*, 105) of the meeting between some of the insurgent leaders and the community of the *ejido* of San Francisco on September 23, 1985.

13 See the account given by Marcos in an interview with Radio UNAM, March 18, 1994 (EZLN, *La Palabra*, vol. 2, 69). The "white guards" are paid paramilitary groups who, often in collusion with the authorities, violently suppress protest and dissent.

14 Decree of the Lacandon Community, see Tello, *La Rebelión*, 59ff.

women, men, children, young, old, ill—all with their everyday struggles not just for survival but for humanity.

The Zapatistas learned the pain of the community: the poverty, the hunger, the constant threat of harassment by the authorities or the "white guards," the unnecessary deaths from curable diseases. When asked in an interview which death had affected him most, Marcos told how a girl of three or four years old, Paticha (her way of saying Patricia), had died in his arms in a village. She had started a fever at six o'clock in the evening, and by ten o'clock she was dead: there was no medicine in the village that could help to lower her fever. "And that happened many times, it was so everyday, so everyday that those births are not even taken into account. For example, Paticha never had a birth certificate, which means that for the country she never existed, for the statistical office (INEGI), there-fore her death never existed either. And like her, there were thousands, thousands and thousands, and as we grew in the communities, as we had more villages, more comrades died. Just because death was natural, now it started to be ours."[15] From such experiences arose the conviction that revolution was something that the Zapatistas owed to their children: "We, their fathers, their mothers, their brothers and sisters, did not want to bear anymore the guilt of doing nothing for our children."[16]

They learned the struggles of the people, both the struggles of the present and the struggles of the past, the continuing struggle of past and present. The culture of the people is a culture of struggle. Marcos tells of the storytelling by the campfire at night in the mountains—"stories of apparitions, of the dead, of earlier struggles, of things that have happened, all mixed together. It seems that they are talking of the revolution (of the Mexican Revolution, the past one not the one that is happening now) and at moments of now. It seems that is mixed up with the colonial period, and sometimes it seems that it is the pre-Hispanic period."[17] The culture of struggle permeates the Zapatista communiqués, often in the form of stories and myths: Marcos's stories of Old Antonio (el viejo Antonio) are a favourite way of passing on a culture impregnated with the wisdom of struggle.

---

15 Radio UNAM interview with Marcos, March 18, 1994, see EZLN, *La Palabra*, vol. 2, 69–70.

16 Marcos, Letter to children of a boarding school in Guadalajara, February 8, 1994, see EZLN, *La Palabra*, vol. 1, 179.

17 Radio UNAM interview with Marcos, March 18, 1994, EZLN, see *La Palabra*, vol. 2, 62.

And they learned to listen. "That is the great lesson that the indigenous communities teach to the original EZLN. The original EZLN, the one that is formed in 1983, is a political organisation in the sense that it speaks and what it says has to be done. The indigenous communities teach it to listen, and that is what we learn. The principal lesson that we learn from the indigenous people is that we have to learn to hear, to listen."[18] Learning to listen meant incorporating new perspectives and new concepts into their theory. Learning to listen meant learning to talk as well, not just explaining things in a different way but thinking them in a different way.

Above all, learning to listen meant turning everything upside down. The revolutionary tradition of talking is not just a bad habit. It has a long-established theoretical basis in the concepts of Marxism-Leninism. The tradition of talking derives, on the one hand, from the idea that theory (class consciousness) must be brought to the masses by the party and, on the other, from the idea that capitalism must be analysed from above, from the movement of capital rather than from the movement of anti-capitalist struggle. When the emphasis shifts to listening, both of these theoretical suppositions are undermined. The whole relation between theory and practice is thrown into question: theory can no longer be seen as being brought from outside but is obviously the product of everyday practice. And dignity takes the place of imperialism as the starting point of theoretical reflection.

Dignity was presumably not part of the conceptual baggage of the revolutionaries who went into the jungle. It is not a word that appears very much in the literature of the Marxist tradition.[19] It could only emerge as a revolutionary concept in the course of a revolution by a people steeped in the dignity of struggle.[20] But once it appears (consciously or uncon-

---

18 Marcos interview with Cristián Calónico Lucio, November 11, 1995, ms, 47. The interview is unpublished in written form but formed the basis of a video.

19 Ernst Bloch's *Naturrecht und Menschliche Würde* (Frankfurt: Suhrkamp, 1961) is a notable exception. Although theoretically very relevant, it probably did not exercise any influence on the Zapatistas.

20 In a recent interview, Marcos confirms that it was as a result of the integration of the revolutionaries with the indigenous communities that they started using the concept of dignity. "More than the redistribution of wealth or the expropriation of the means of production, revolution starts to be the possibility that human beings can have a space of dignity. Dignity begins to be a very

sciously) as a central concept, then it implies a rethinking of the whole
revolutionary project, both theoretically and in terms of organisation.
The whole conception of revolution becomes turned outward: revolution
becomes a question rather than an answer. *"Preguntando caminamos—*
asking we walk" becomes a central principle of the revolutionary movement, the radically democratic concept at the centre of the Zapatista call
for "freedom, democracy, and justice." The revolution advances by asking
not by telling; or perhaps even revolution *is* asking instead of telling, the
dissolution of power relations.

Here too the Zapatistas learned from (and developed) the tradition
of the indigenous communities. The idea and practice of their central
organisational principle, *"mandar obedeciendo"* ("to command obeying"),
derives from the practice of all important decisions being discussed by the
whole community until consensus is reached, with all holders of positions
of authority assumed to be immediately recallable if they do not satisfy
the community, if they do not command obeying the community. Thus the
decision to go to war was not taken by some central committee and then
handed down but was discussed by all the communities in village assemblies.[21] The whole organisation is structured along the same principle: the
ruling body, the CCRI is composed of recallable delegates chosen by the
different ethnic groups (Tzotzil, Tzeltal, Tojolabal, and Chol), and each
ethnic group and each region has its own committees chosen in assemblies
on the same principle.

The changes wreaked in those ten years of confrontation between the
received ideas of revolution and the reality of the indigenous peoples of
Chiapas were very deep. Marcos is quoted in one book as saying, "I think
that our only virtue as theorists was to have the humility to recognise
that our theoretical scheme did not work, that it was very limited, that
we had to adapt ourselves to the reality that was being imposed on us."[22]

---

strong word. It is not our contribution, it is not a contribution of the urban
element, it is the communities who contribute it. Such that revolution should
be the assurance that dignity be realised, be respected." Yvon Le Bot, *El Sueño
Zapatista* [The Zapatista Dream] (Mexico City: Plaza & Janés, 1997), 146.

21 See, for example, the Marcos's interview with correspondents from the *Proceso*,
El Financiero and the *New York Times*, February 1994, see EZLN, *La Palabra*, vol.
1, 204, at 216.

22 Guido Camú Urzúa and Dauno Tótoro Taulis, *EZLN: el ejército que salió de la
selva* (Mexico City: Editorial Planeta, 1994), 83.

However, the result was not that reality imposed itself on theory, as some argue,[23] but that the confrontation with reality gave rise to a whole new and immensely rich theorisation of revolutionary practice.

III. The Revolt of Dignity Is an Undefined Revolt

A revolution that listens, a revolution that takes as its starting point the dignity of those in revolt, is inevitably an undefined revolution, a revolution in which the distinction between rebellion and revolution loses meaning. The revolution is a moving outward rather than a moving toward.

There is no transitional programme, no definite goal. There is, of course, an aim: the achievement of a society based on dignity, or, in the words of the Zapatista slogan, "democracy, freedom, justice." But just what this means and what concrete steps need to be taken to achieve it is never spelled out. This has at times been criticised by those educated in the classical revolutionary traditions as a sign of the political immaturity of the Zapatistas or of their reformism, but it is the logical complement of putting dignity at the centre of the revolutionary project. If the revolution is built on the dignity of those in struggle, if a central principle is the idea of *"preguntando caminamos*—asking we walk," then it follows that it must be self-creative, a revolution created in the process of struggle. If the revolution is not only to achieve democracy as an end but is democratic in its struggle, then it is impossible to predefine its path, or indeed to think of a defined point of arrival. Whereas the concept of revolution that has predominated in this century has been overwhelmingly instrumentalist,[24] a conception of a means designed to achieve an end, this conception breaks down as soon as the starting point becomes the dignity of those in struggle. The revolt of dignity forces us to think of revolution in a new way, as a rebellion that cannot be defined or confined, a rebellion that overflows, a revolution that is by its very nature ambiguous and contradictory.

The Zapatista uprising is in the first place a revolt of the indigenous peoples of the Lacandon Jungle, of the Tzeltals, Tzotzils, Chols, and Tojolabals who live in that part of the state of Chiapas. For them, the conditions of living were (and are) such that the only choice, as they see it, is

---

23 Camú and Tótoro, EZLN.
24 The supreme example of the instrumentalist theory of revolution is, of course, Lenin's *What Is to Be Done?*

between dying an undignified death, the slow unsung death of misery suffered, and dying with dignity, the death of those fighting for their own dignity and the dignity of those around them. The government has consistently tried to define and confine the uprising in those terms, as a matter limited to the state of Chiapas, but the Zapatistas have always refused to accept this. This was, indeed, the main point over which the first dialogue, the dialogue of San Cristóbal, broke down.[25]

The Zapatista uprising is the assertion of indigenous dignity. The opening words of the Declaration of the Lacandon Jungle, read from the balcony of the town hall of San Cristóbal on the morning of January 1, 1994, were: "We are the product of 500 years of struggles."[26] The uprising came just over a year after the demonstrations throughout America that marked the 500th anniversary of Columbus's "discovery." On that occasion, October 12, 1992, the Zapatistas had already marched through San Cristóbal, when about ten thousand indigenous people, most of them Zapatistas under another guise, had taken the streets of the city.[27] January 1, 1994, made the Zapatistas the focus of the increasingly active indigenous movement in Mexico. When the EZLN began its dialogue with the government in April 1995, the dialogue of San Andrés Larrainzar, the first theme for discussion was indigenous rights and culture. The Zapatistas used the dialogue to give cohesion to the indigenous struggle, asking representatives of all the main indigenous organisations of the country to join them as consultants or guests in the workshops that were part of concluding that phase of the Indigenous Forum held in San Cristóbal in January 1996. The Indigenous Forum led in turn to the setting up of the Congreso Nacional Indígena,[28] which gives a national focus to previously dispersed indigenous struggles. The first phase of the dialogue of San Andrés also led to the signing of an agreement with the government designed to lead to changes in the constitution that would radically improve the legal position of indigenous peoples within the country, granting them important areas of autonomy.[29]

---

25 See the CCRI communiqué of June 10, 1994; and EZLN, *La Palabra*, vol. 2, 201.
26 EZLN, *La Palabra*, vol. 1, 5.
27 See the account given by Tello (*La Rebelión*, 151); see also Le Bot (*El Sueño*, 191).
28 National Indigenous Congress.
29 At the time of writing, the agreement still has not been implemented by the government.

The Zapatista movement, however, has never claimed to be just an indigenous movement.[30] Overwhelmingly indigenous in composition, the EZLN has always made clear that it is fighting for a broader cause. Its struggle is for all those "without voice, without face, without tomorrow," a category that stretches far beyond the indigenous peoples. The demands they make (work, land, housing, food, health, education, independence, freedom, democracy, justice, and peace . . .) are not demands limited to the indigenous: they are demands for all. The Zapatista movement is a movement for *national* liberation, a movement not just for the liberation of the indigenous but of all.

The fact that the EZLN is an Army of National Liberation seems to give a clear definition to the movement. There have been many other movements (and wars) of national liberation in different parts of the world (Vietnam, Angola, Mozambique, Cambodia, Nicaragua, etc). Here we have what appears to be a clearly defined and well-established framework: national liberation movements typically aim to liberate a national territory from foreign influence (the control of a colonial or neo-colonial power) and to establish a government of national liberation designed to introduce radical social changes and establish national economic autonomy. If the Zapatista movement were a national liberation movement in that sense, if the history of such movements is anything to go by, there would be little to get excited about: it might be worthy of support and solidarity, but there would be nothing radically new about it. This indeed has been the position of some critics on the Left.[31]

---

30 On the refusal of the Zapatistas to define their movement as an indigenous movement, see Le Bot, *El Sueño*, 206, where Marcos says in interview: "The principal preoccupation of the Committee [CCRI] and of the delegates was that the movement should not be reduced to the indigenous question. On the contrary, if it had been up to them, at least to that part of the committee [those who come from the areas with the strongest traditions] our discourse would have abandoned completely any reference to the indigenous."

31 The Zapatista use of national symbols, such as the Mexican flag and the national anthem, disconcerted some, especially among the European participants in the recent Intercontinental Gathering in Chiapas. For a critique of the alleged "nationalism" of the EZLN, see, for example, Sylvie Deneuve, Charles Reeve, and Marc Geoffroy, *Au-delà des passe-montagnes du Sud-Est mexicain* (Paris: Ab irato, 1996); and Katerina, "Mexico is not only Chiapas nor is the rebellion in Chiapas merely a Mexican affair," *Common Sense*, no. 22 (Winter 1997).

Looked at more closely, however, the apparent definition of "Army of National Liberation" begins to dissolve. In the context of the uprising, the term "national liberation" has more a sense of moving outward than of moving inward: "national" in the sense of "not just Chiapanecan" or "not just indigenous," rather than "national" in the sense of "not foreign."[32] "Nation" is also used in the Zapatista communiqués in the less clearly defined sense of "homeland" (*patria*): the place where we happen to live, a space to be defended not just against imperialists but also (and more directly) against the state. "Nation" is counterposed to the state, so that national liberation can even be understood as the liberation of Mexico from the Mexican state or the defence of Mexico (or indeed whatever territory) against the state. "Nation" in this sense refers to the idea of struggling wherever one happens to live, fighting against oppression, fighting for dignity. That the Zapatista movement is a movement of national liberation does not confine or restrict the movement to Mexico: it can be understood rather as meaning a movement of liberation, wherever you happen to be (and whatever you happen to do). The fight for dignity cannot be restricted to national frontiers: "dignity," in the wonderful expression used by Marcos in the invitation to the Intercontinental Gathering held in the Lacandon Jungle in July 1996, "is that homeland without nationality, that rainbow that is also a bridge, that murmur of the heart no matter what blood lives in it, that rebel irreverence that mocks frontiers, customs officials, and wars."[33] It is consistent with this interpretation of "national liberation" that one of the principal slogans of the Zapatistas recently has been the theme chosen for the Intercontinental Gathering, "for humanity and against neoliberalism."[34]

---

32 In this sense, for example, see the Third Declaration of the Lacandon Jungle (January 1, 1995): "The indigenous question will not be solved unless there is a *radical* transformation of the national pact. The only way to incorporate, with justice and dignity, the indigenous peoples into the nation is by recognising the peculiar characteristics of their social, cultural, and political organisation. The autonomies are not a separation but rather the integration of the most humiliated and forgotten minorities into contemporary Mexico. That is how the EZLN has understood it since its formation and that is how the indigenous bases that form the leadership of our organisation have directed. Today we repeat it: *our struggle is national*," see *La Jornada*, January 2, 1995, 5.

33 *La Jornada*, January 30, 1996, 12.

34 This is, of course, not the only interpretation possible. See, for example, Deneuve, Geoffroy, and Reeve, *Au-delà des passe-montagne.* Although it seems

The open-ended nature of the Zapatista movement is summed up in the idea that it is a revolution not a Revolution ("with small letters, to avoid polemics with the many vanguards and safeguards of *the revolution*").[35] It is a revolution, because the claim to dignity in a society built upon the negation of dignity can only be met through a radical transformation of society. But it is not a Revolution in the sense of having some grand plan, in the sense of a movement designed to bring about the Great Event that will change the world. Its revolutionary claim lies not in the preparation for the future Event but in the present inversion of perspective, in the consistent insistence on seeing the world in terms that are incompatible with the world as it is: human dignity. Revolution refers to present existence not to future instrumentality.

IV. The Revolt of Dignity Is a Revolt against Definition

The undefined, open-ended character of the Zapatista movement sometimes rouses the frustrations of those schooled in a harder-edged revolutionary tradition. Behind the lack of definition there is, however, a much sharper point. The lack of definition does not result from theoretical slackness: on the contrary, revolution is essentially anti-definitional.

The traditional Leninist concept of revolution is crucially definitional. At its centre is the idea that the struggles of the working class are inevitably limited in character, that they cannot rise above reformist demands, unless there is the intervention of a revolutionary party. The working class is a "they" who cannot go beyond certain limits without outside intervention. The self-emancipation of the proletariat is impossible.[36]

---

incorrect to interpret the Zapatista use of national liberation in the narrow, statist sense, there is no doubt that the term "national liberation" opens up an enormous and dangerous area of ambiguity, simply because the notion of "nation" and "state" have been so interwoven that it is difficult to disentangle them completely. It is argued below that the undoubted contradictions and tensions in the discourse of the Zapatistas are not the result of eclecticism but are the outcome of the consistent pursuit of the principle of dignity. They are not necessarily less serious for that. For a further discussion of Zapatista nationalism, see REDaktion, ed., *Chiapas und die Internationale der Hoffnung* (Cologne: Neuer ISP-Verlag, 1997), 178–84.

35 Subcomandante Insurgente Marcos, "México: La Luna entre los espejos de la noche y el cristal del día," *La Jornada*, June 11, 1995, 17.

36 This is most clearly elaborated in Lenin's *What Is to Be Done?* For example: "We said that there could not yet be Social-Democratic consciousness among

The emphasis on dignity puts the unlimited at the centre of picture, not just the undefined but the anti-definitional. Dignity, understood as a category of struggle, is a tension that points beyond itself. The assertion of dignity implies the present negation of dignity. Dignity, then, is the struggle against the denial of dignity, the struggle for the realisation of dignity. Dignity is and is not: it is the struggle against its own negation. If dignity were simply the assertion of something that already is, then it would be an absolutely flabby concept, an empty complacency. To simply assert human dignity as a principle (as in "all humans have dignity," or "all humans have a right to dignity") would be either so general as to be meaningless or, worse, so general as to obscure the fact that existing society is based on the negation of dignity.[37] Similarly, if dignity were simply the assertion of something that is not, then it would be an empty daydream or a religious wish. The concept of dignity only gains force if it is understood in its double dimension, as the struggle against its own denial. One is dignified, or true, only by struggling against present indignity, or untruth. Dignity implies a constant moving against the barriers of that which exists, a constant subversion and transcendence of definitions. Dignity, understood as a category of struggle, is a fundamentally anti-identitarian concept: not "my dignity as a Mexican . . ." but "our dignity is our struggle against the negation of that dignity."

---

the workers. This consciousness could only be brought to them from without. The history of all countries shows that the working class, exclusively by its own effort, is able to develop only trade union consciousness. . . . The theory of socialism, however, grew out of the philosophical, historical and economic theories that were elaborated by the educated representatives of the propertied classes, the intellectuals": V.I. Lenin, "What Is to Be Done," in *Essential Works of Lenin* (New York: Bantam Books, 1966), 74.

37 The notion of dignity is little used by mainstream political theory. Where it is used, it is often connected with notions of self-ownership (for example, Robert Nozick, *Anarchy, State and Utopia* [New York: Basic Books, 1981], 334) or self-possession (for example, Michael Walzer, *Spheres of Justice* [Oxford: Blackwell, 1983, 279]). The use of the term in mainstream political theory and philosophy differs crucially from the Zapatista concept in two respects: first, its primary point of reference is the individual; and, second, it refers to an abstract, indeterminate and idealised present in which it is assumed that people already have the "right" to dignity. At best, this is a sort of flabby wishful thinking that has little to do with the Zapatista concept of dignity as struggle against the denial of dignity, and is far removed indeed from seeing "our fathers with fury in their hands."

Dignity is neither characteristic of the indigenous of the southeast of Mexico nor to those overtly involved in revolutionary struggle. It is simply a characteristic of life in an oppressive society. It is the cry of "Enough!" (¡Ya basta!) that is inseparable from the experience of oppression. Oppression cannot be total; whatever its form, it is always a pressure that is confronted by a counter-pressure, dehumanisation confronted by humanity. Domination implies resistance and dignity.[38] Dignity is the other side, too often forgotten, too often stifled, of what Marx called alienation: it is the struggle of dis-alienation, of defetishisation.[39] It is the struggle for recognition but for the recognition of a self currently negated.

Dignity is the lived experience that the world is *not* so, that that is *not* the way things are. It is the lived rejection of positivism, of those forms of thought that start from the assumption that "that's the way things are." It is the cry of existence of that which has been silenced by "the world that is," the refusal to be shut out by Is-ness, the scream against being forgotten in the fragmentation of the world into the disciplines of social science that break reality and, in breaking, exclude, suppressing the suppressed. Dignity is the cry of "here we are!," the "here we are!" of the indigenous peoples forgotten by neoliberal modernisation, the "here we are!" of the growing numbers of poor who somehow do not show in the statistics of economic growth and the financial reports, the "here we are!" of the gay whose sexuality was for so long not recognised, the "here we are!" of the elderly shut away to die in the retirement homes of the richer countries, the "here we are!" of the women closed into the houses whose wives they are, the "here we are!" of the millions of illegal migrants[40] who are not where, officially, they should be, the "here we are!" of all those pleasures of human life excluded by the growing subjection of humanity to the market. Dignity is the cry of those who are not heard, the voice of those without voice. Dignity is the truth of truth denied.[41]

---

38 See, for example, James C. Scott, *Domination and the Arts of Resistance* (New Haven: Yale University Press, 1990).
39 This argument is developed in section V.
40 It is not surprising that the ¡*Ya basta*! of the Zapatistas has been strongly echoed by the "*sans papiers*," the movement of illegal immigrants in France.
41 The Zapatistas use truth and dignity as basically interchangeable concepts. The Zapatistas speak of what they say as the "word of those who are armed with truth and fire" ("*la palabra de los armados de verdad y fuego*"). The fire is there, but the truth comes first, not just as a moral attribute but as a weapon: they are

Us they forgot more and more, and history was no longer big enough for us to die just like that, forgotten and humiliated. Because dying does not hurt, what hurts is being forgotten. Then we discovered that we no longer existed, that those who govern had forgotten us in the euphoria of statistics and growth rates. A country which forgets itself is a sad country, a country which forgets its past cannot have a future. And then we seized our arms and went into the cities where we were animals. And we went and said to the powerful "here we are!" and to all the country we shouted "here we are!" and to all the world we shouted "here we are!" And see how odd things are because, for them to see us, we covered our faces; for them to name us, we gave up our name; we gambled the present to have a future; and to live . . . we died.[42]

This "here we are!" is not the "here we are!" of mere identity. It is a "here we are!" that derives its meaning from the denial of that presence. It is not a static "here we are!" but a movement, an assault on the barriers of exclusion. It is the breaking of barriers, the moving against separations, classifications, definitions, the assertion of unities that have been defined out of existence.

Dignity is an assault on the separation of morality and politics, and of the private and the public. Dignity cuts across those boundaries, asserts the unity of what has been sundered. The assertion of dignity is neither a moral nor a political claim: it is rather an attack on the separation of politics and morality that allows formally democratic regimes all over the world to co-exist with growing levels of poverty and social marginalisation. It is the "here we are!" not just of the marginalised but of the horror felt by all of us in the face of mass impoverishment and starvation. It is the "here we are!" not just of the growing numbers shut away in prisons, hospitals, and homes but also of the shame and disgust of all of us who, by living, participate in the bricking up of people in those prisons, hospitals, and homes. Dignity is an assault on the conventional definition of politics

---

armed with truth, and this is a more important weapon than the firepower of their guns. Although they are organised as an army, they aim to win by truth not by fire. Their truth is not just that they speak the truth about their situation or about the country, but that they are true to themselves, that they speak the truth of truth denied.

42 Communiqué of March 17, 1995, see *La Jornada*, March 22, 1995.

but equally on the acceptance of that definition in the instrumental conception of revolutionary politics that has for so long subordinated the personal to the political, with such disastrous results. Probably nothing has done more to undermine the "Left" in this century than this separation of the political and the personal, of the public and the private, and the dehumanisation that it entails.

Dignity encapsulates in one word the rejection of the separation of the personal and the political.[43] To a remarkable extent, this group of rebels in the jungle of the southeast of Mexico have crystallised and advanced the themes of oppositional thought and action that have been discussed throughout the world in recent years: the issues of gender, age, childhood, death, and the dead. All flow from understanding politics as a politics of dignity, a politics that recognises the particular oppression and respects the struggles of women, children, and the old. Respect for the struggles of the old is a constant theme of Marcos's stories, particularly through the figure of Old Antonio, but it was also forcefully underlined by the emergence of Comandante Trinidad as one of the leading figures in the dialogue of San Andrés. The way in which women have imposed recognition of their struggles on the Zapatista men is well known and can be seen, for example, in the Revolutionary Law for Women, issued on the first day of the uprising, or in the fact that it was a woman, Ana María, who led the most important military action undertaken by the Zapatistas, the occupation of the town hall in San Cristóbal on January 1, 1994. The question of childhood and the freedom to play is a constant theme in Marcos's letters. The stories, jokes, and poetry of the communiqués and the dances that punctuate all that the Zapatistas do are not embellishments of a revolutionary process but central to it.

The struggle of dignity is the "here we are!" of jokes, poetry, dancing, old age, childhood, games, death, love—of all those things excluded by serious bourgeois politics and serious revolutionary politics alike. As such, the struggle of dignity is opposed to the state. The Zapatista

---

43 The separation of personal and political, of private and public, is at the same time their mutual constitution. The point is not to conflate the personal and the political, the public and the private, but to abolish them (to abolish the separation that constitutes both). On this, see Karl Marx, "On the Jewish Question," Karl Marx and Frederick Engels, *Collected Works*, vol. 3 (Moscow: Progress Publishers, 1975). To that extent, the phrase "the personal is political" is misleading.

movement is an anti-state movement, not just in the obvious sense that the EZLN took up arms against the Mexican state but in the much more profound sense that their forms of organisation, action, and discourse are non-state, or, more precisely, anti-state forms.

The state defines and classifies and by so doing excludes. This is not by chance. The state, any state, embedded as it is in the global web of capitalist social relations, functions in such a way as to reproduce the capitalist status quo.[44] In its relation to us, and in our relation to it, there is a filtering out of anything that is not compatible with the reproduction of capitalist social relations. This may be a violent filtering, as in the repression of revolutionary or subversive activity, but it is also and above all a less perceptible filtering, a sidelining or suppression of passions, loves, hates, anger, laughter, dancing. Discontent is redefined as demands and demands are classified and defined, excluding all that is not reconcilable with the reproduction of capitalist social relations. The discontented are classified in the same way and the indigestible excluded with a greater or lesser degree of violence. The cry of dignity, the "here we are!" of the unpalatable and indigestible, can only be a revolt against classification, against definition as such.

The state is pure Is-ness, pure Identity. Power says, "I am who am, the eternal repetition."[45] The state is the great Classifier. Power says to the rebels: "Be ye not awkward, refuse not to be classified. All that cannot be classified counts not, exists not, is not."[46] The struggle of the state against the Zapatistas since the declaration of the ceasefire has been a struggle to define, to classify, to limit; the struggle of the Zapatistas against the state has been the struggle to break out, to break the barriers, to overflow, to refuse definition or to accept-and-transcend definition.

The dialogue between the government and the EZLN, first in San Cristóbal in March 1994, and then in San Andrés Larrainzar since April 1995, has been a constant double movement. The government has constantly

44 It is as a form of the capital relation that the state defines and classifies. The defining action of the state is one moment of the definition inherent in the alienation of labour, the containment of human creativity. For a development of the general argument, see John Holloway, "Global Capital and the National State," in *Global Capital, National State and the Politics of Money*, eds. Werner Bonefeld and John Holloway (London: Macmillan, 1995), 116–40.
45 Communiqué of May 1996, see *La Jornada*, June 10, 1996.
46 Ibid.

sought to define and limit the Zapatista movement, to "make it small," as one of the government representatives put it. It has constantly sought to define Zapatismo as a movement limited to Chiapas, with no right to discuss matters of wider importance. It did sign agreements on the question of indigenous rights and autonomy but apparently without having at the time any intention of implementing them.[47] In the section of the dialogue devoted to democracy and justice, however, the government representatives made no serious contribution and have apparently no intention of signing agreements. The Zapatistas, on the other hand, have constantly used the dialogue to break out, to overcome their geographical isolation in the Lacandon Jungle. They have done this partly through their daily press conferences during the sessions of the dialogue but also by negotiating the procedural right to invite advisers and guests, and then inviting hundreds of them to participate in the sessions on indigenous rights and culture and on democracy and justice: advisers from a very wide range of indigenous and community organisations, complemented by a wide range of academics. Each of the two topics also provided the basis for organising a Forum in San Cristóbal, first on Indigenous Rights and Culture in January 1996, and then on the Reform of the State in July of the same year, both attended by a very large number of activists from all over the country.

On the one hand, the government's drive to limit, define, make small, on the other, the (generally very successful) Zapatista push to break the cordon. On the one hand, a politics of definition, on the other, a politics of overflowing. This does not mean that the Zapatistas have not sought to define: on the contrary, defining constitutional reforms on indigenous autonomy is seen by them as an important achievement. But it has been a definition that overflows, thematically and politically. The definition of indigenous rights is seen not as an endpoint but as a start, as a basis for moving on to other areas of change but also as a basis for taking the movement forward, a basis for breaking out.

The difference in approach between the two sides of the dialogue has at times resulted in incidents that reflect not only the arrogance of the government negotiators but also the lack of understanding derived from their perspective as representatives of the state. This has even been expressed in how time is understood. Given the bad conditions of communication

---

47 At the time of writing (February 1997), the agreement still has not been implemented by the government.

in the Lacandon Jungle and the need to discuss everything thoroughly, the Zapatista principle of "*mandar obedeciendo*" ("to command obeying") means that decisions take time. When the government representatives insisted on rapid replies, the Zapatistas replied that they did not understand the indigenous clock. As recounted by Comandante David afterwards, the Zapatistas explained: "We, as Indians, have rhythms, forms of understanding, of deciding, of reaching agreements. And when we told them that, they replied by making fun of us. 'Well then,' they said, 'we don't understand why you say that, because we see that you have Japanese watches, so how do you say that you use the indigenous clock, that's from Japan.'"[48] And Comandante Tacho commented: "They haven't learned. They understand us backwards. We use time, not the clock."[49]

Even more fundamentally, the state representatives have been unable to understand the concept of dignity. In one of the press conferences held during the dialogue of San Andrés, Comandante Tacho recounts that the government negotiators "told us that they are studying what dignity means, that they are consulting and making studies on dignity. That what they understood was that dignity is service to others. And they asked us to tell them what we understand by dignity. We told them to continue with their research. It makes us laugh, and we laughed in front of them. They asked us why, and we told them that they have big research centres and big studies in schools of a high standard and that it would be a shame if they do not accept that. We told them that if we sign the peace, then we will tell them at the end what dignity means for us."[50]

The Zapatista sense of satire and their refusal to be defined is turned not only against the state but also against the more traditional "definitional" Left. In a letter dated February 20, 1995, when the Zapatistas were retreating from the army after the military intervention of February 9, Marcos imagines an interrogation by the state prosecutor consisting of the accusations and his responses:

> The whites accuse you of being black: Guilty.
> The blacks accuse you of being white: Guilty.
> The machos accuse you of being feminist: Guilty.
> The feminists accuse you of being macho: Guilty.

---

48 *La Jornada*, May 17, 1995.
49 *La Jornada*, May 18, 1995.
50 *La Jornada*, June 10, 1995.

The communists accuse you of being an anarchist: Guilty.
The anarchists accuse you of being orthodox: Guilty.
The reformists accuse you of being an extremist: Guilty.
The "historical vanguard" accuses you of appealing to civil society
    and not to the proletariat: Guilty.
Civil society accuses you of disturbing its tranquillity: Guilty.
The stock market accuses you of spoiling their lunch: Guilty.
The serious people accuse you of being a joker: Guilty.
The jokers accuse you of being serious: Guilty.
The adults accuse you of being a child: Guilty.
The children accuse you of being an adult: Guilty.
The orthodox leftists accuse you for not condemning homosexuals
    and lesbians: Guilty.
The theorists accuse you for being practical: Guilty.
The practitioners accuse you for being theoretical: Guilty.
Everybody accuses you for everything bad that happens to them:
    Guilty.[51]

Dignity's revolt mocks classification. As it must, because dignity makes sense only if understood as being-and-not-being, and therefore defying definition or classification. Dignity is that which pushes from itself toward itself, and cannot be reduced to a simple "is." The state, any state, on the other hand, is. The state, as its name suggests, imposes a state, an Is-ness, upon that which pushes beyond existing social relations. Dignity is a moving outward, an overflowing, a fountain; the state is a moving inward, a containment, a cistern.[52] The failure to understand dignity is not peculiar to the Mexican state: it is simply that statehood and dignity are incompatible. There is no fit between them.

Dignity's revolt, therefore, cannot aim at winning state power. From the beginning, the Zapatistas made it clear that they did not want to win power, and they have repeated it ever since. Many on the more traditional "definitional" Left were scandalised with the more concrete repudiation of winning power in the Fourth Declaration of the Lacandon Jungle at

---

51 *La Jornada*, March 5, 1995.
52 "The cistern contains; the fountain overflows." William Blake, "Proverbs of Heaven and Hell," in, for example, Jacob Bronowski, ed., *William Blake: A Selection of Poems and Letters* (Harmondsworth: Penguin Books, 1958), 97.

the beginning of 1996, when the Zapatistas launched the formation of the Zapatista Front of National Liberation (FZLN) and made rejection of all ambition to hold state office a condition of membership.[53] The repudiation of state power is, however, simply an extension of the idea of dignity. The state, any state, is so bound into the web of global capitalist social relations that it has no option, whatever the composition of the government, but to promote the reproduction of those relations, and that means defining and degrading. To assume state power would inevitably be to abandon dignity. The revolt of dignity can only aim at abolishing the state or, more immediately, at developing alternative forms of social organisation and strengthening anti-state power. "It is not necessary to conquer the world. It is enough to make it anew."[54]

The central principles on which the Zapatistas have insisted in developing alternative forms of social organisation are those of "*mandar obedeciendo*" ("to command obeying") and "*preguntando caminamos*" ("asking we walk"). They have emphasised time and again the importance of making all important decisions through a collective process of discussion, and that the way forward cannot be a question of their imposing their line but of opening up spaces for discussion and democratic decision where their view would only be one among many. In relation to the state (and assuming that the state still exists), they have said many times that they do not want to hold state office, that it does not matter which party holds state office as long as those in authority "command obeying." The problem of revolutionary politics is not to win power but to develop forms of political articulation that would force those in office to obey the people (so that, fully developed, the separation between state and society would be overcome and the state effectively abolished). Just what this would mean has not been spelled out by the EZLN,[55] apart from the obvious principle that

---

53 "A political force whose members do not hold or aspire to hold popularly elected offices nor governmental posts at any level. A political force that does not aspire to take power. A force that is not a political party," see La Jornada, January 2, 1996.
54 First Declaration of La Realidad, January 1996, see La Jornada, January 30, 1996.
55 They have often mentioned the idea of plebiscites or referendums as a necessary part of a new political system. It is clear, however, from the experience of other states that plebiscites and referendums are quite inadequate as a form of articulating popular decision-making and are in no sense comparable to the communal discussions that are central to the Zapatistas' own practice.

the president or any other office-holder should be instantly recallable if they fail to obey the people's wishes, as is the case with all members of the EZLN's ruling body, the CCRI.[56]

Although the details are not clear and cannot be, since they could only be developed in struggle, the central point is that the focus of revolutionary struggle is shifted from the *what* to the *how* of politics. All the initiatives of the Zapatistas (the Convención Nacional Democrática, the "consultation" on the future of the EZLN, the invitation of advisers to the dialogue with the government, the organisation of the forum on indigenous rights and culture and on the reform of the state, the intercontinental meeting for humanity and against neoliberalism, among others) have been directed at promoting a different way of thinking about political activity. Similarly, all the contacts with the state and even the proposals for the "reform" of the state have in fact been anti-state initiatives in the sense of trying to develop new political forms, forms of action that articulate dignity, forms that do not fit with the state. The principal problem for a revolutionary movement is not to elaborate a programme to say *what* the revolutionary government will do (although the EZLN has its sixteen demands as the basis for such a programme); the principal problem is rather *how* to articulate dignities, how to develop a form of struggle and a form of social organisation based upon the recognition of dignity. Only the articulation of dignities can provide the answer to what should be done: a self-determining society must determine itself.

V. Dignities Unite

The Zapatistas rose up on January 1, 1994, to change Mexico and to make the world anew. Their base was in the Lacandon Jungle, far from any important urban centre. They were not part of an effective international or even national organisation.[57] Since the declaration of the ceasefire

---

56 "And we demand that the authorities should be able to be removed just as soon as the communities decide it and come to an agreement. It could be through a referendum or some other similar mechanism. And we want to transmit this experience to every level: when the president of the Republic is no use any more he should be automatically removed. As simple as that." Press Conference given by Subcomandante Marcos, February 26, 1994, see EZLN, *La Palabra*, vol. 1, 244.

57 If indeed they are part of the FLN, as the state maintains, it has remained remarkably ineffective.

on January 12, 1994, they have remained physically cordoned within the Lacandon Jungle.

Cut off in the jungle, how could the EZLN transform Mexico or, indeed, change the world? Alone there was little that they could do to change the world, or even to defend themselves. "Do not leave us alone" ("*no nos dejen solos*") was an oft-repeated call during the first months of the ceasefire. The effectiveness of the EZLN depended (and depends) inevitably on their ability to break the cordon and overcome their isolation. The revolt of dignity derives its strength from the uniting of dignities.

But how could this uniting of dignities come about when the EZLN itself was cornered in the jungle and there was no institutional structure to support them? Marcos suggests a powerful image in a radio interview in the early months of the uprising:

> Marcos, whoever Marcos is, who is in the mountains, had his twins, or his comrades, or his accomplices (not in the organic sense but in terms of how to see the world, the necessity of changing it or seeing it in a different way) in the media, for example, in the newspapers, in the radio, in the television, in the journals, but also in the trade unions, in the schools, among the teachers, among the students, in groups of workers, in peasant organisations and all that. There were many accomplices or, to use a radio term, there were many people tuned in to the same frequency, but nobody turned the radio on.... Suddenly they [the comrades of the EZLN] turn it on, and we discover that there are others on the same radio frequency—I'm talking of radio *communication* not *listening* to the radio—and we begin to talk and to communicate and to realise that there are things in common, that it seems there are more things in common than differences.[58]

The idea suggested by Marcos for thinking about the unity of struggles is one of frequencies, of being tuned in, of wavelengths, vibrations, echoes. Dignity resonates. As it vibrates, it sets off vibrations in other dignities, an unstructured, possibly discordant resonance.

There is no doubt of the extraordinary resonance of the Zapatista uprising throughout the world, as evidenced by the participation of over

58   Radio UNAM interview with Marcos, March 18, 1994, EZLN, see *La Palabra*, vol. 2, 97.

three thousand people from forty-three countries in the Intercontinental Meeting organised by the EZLN in July 1996. "What is happening in the mountains of the Mexican southeast that finds an echo and a mirror in the streets of Europe, the suburbs of Asia, the countryside of America, the towns of Africa, and the houses of Oceania?"[59] And equally, of course, what is happening in the streets of Europe, the suburbs of Asia, the countryside of America, the towns of Africa, and the houses of Oceania that resonates so strongly with the Zapatista uprising?

The notion of resonance or echo or radio frequency may seem a very vague one. It is not so. The EZLN have engaged in a constant struggle over the past few years to break through the cordon, to overcome their isola-tion, to forge the unity of dignities on which their future depends. They have fought in many different ways. They have fought with enormous success by letters and communiqués, by jokes and stories, by the use of symbolism, and by the theatre of their events. They have fought by the construction of their "Aguascalientes," the meeting place constructed for the National Democratic Convention (Convención Nacional Democrática) in July 1994, and by the construction of a series of new Aguascalientes in the jungle after the first one was destroyed by the army in February 1995. They have fought too by the creative organisation of a whole series of events that have been important catalysts for the opposition in Mexico and (increasingly) beyond. The first important event was the National Democratic Convention, organised immediately after the EZLN had rejected the proposals made by the government in the Dialogue of San Cristóbal and held just weeks before the presidential elections of August 1994: an event that brought more than six thousand activists into the heart of the jungle only months after the fighting had finished. The following year, the EZLN built on the popular reaction to the February 1995 military intervention to organise a consultation throughout the country on what the future of the EZLN should be, an event attended by over a million people. As previously mentioned, the new dialogue with the government, which began in April 1995, provided the basis for inviting hundreds of activists and specialists to take part as advisers and for organising the forums on Indigenous rights and culture (January 1996) and on the reform of the state (July 1996). The same year also saw the organisation of the

---

59 Closing speech by Marcos to the Intercontinental Meeting in La Realidad, see
    Chiapas, no. 3, 106–16, at 107.

Intercontinental Meeting for Humanity and against Neoliberalism, held within the Zapatista territory at the end of July. In each case, these were events that seemed impossible at the time of their announcement and that stirred up enormous enthusiasm in their realisation.

The communiqués and events have also been accompanied by more orthodox attempts to establish lasting organisational structures. The National Democratic Convention (CND) established a standing organisation of the same name, with the aim of coordinating the (non-military) Zapatista struggle for democracy, freedom, and justice throughout the country. After internal conflicts had rendered the CND ineffective, the Third Declaration of the Lacandon Jungle, in January 1995, proposed the creation of a Movement for National Liberation, an organisation that was stillborn. The Fourth Declaration of the Lacandon Jungle, a year later, launched the Frente Zapatista de Liberación Nacional (the Zapatista National Liberation Front—FZLN) to organise the civilian struggle. Although it has provided an important point of organisational support for the Zapatistas, it has stirred up none of the enthusiasm aroused by the EZLN itself.

The relative failure of the institutional attempts to extend the Zapatista struggle lends weight to the argument that the real force of the Zapatista uniting of dignities has to be understood in terms of the much less structured notion of resonance, which is indeed the counterpart of the idea of "*preguntando caminamos*" ("asking we walk"). We advance by asking not by telling: by suggesting, arguing, proposing, inviting, looking for links with the other struggles that are the same struggle, looking for responses, listening for echoes. If those echoes are not there, we can only propose again, argue again, probe again, ask again: we cannot create echoes where they do not exist.

This does not mean that organisation is not important, that it is all just a matter of vibrations and spontaneous combustion. On the contrary, the whole Zapatista uprising shows the importance of profound and careful organisation. It does suggest, however, a different, less structured and more experimental way of thinking about organisation. The concept of organisation must be experimental in a double sense: experimental because there is no pregiven model of revolutionary organisation but also experimental in the sense that the notion of dignity and its corollary, "asking we walk," mean that revolutionary organisation must be seen as a constant experiment, a constant asking. The notion of dignity does not imply an appeal to spontaneity, the idea that revolt will simply explode without prior organisation; but it does imply thinking in terms of a multitude of different forms of organisation and, above all, thinking of organisation as a constant experiment, a constant probing, a constant asking, a constant searching: not just to see if together we can find some way out of here, but because the asking is in itself the antithesis of Power.[60]

Yet there is obviously a tension here implied in the very notion of the "uniting of dignities." The Zapatistas speak not just of "dignity" but of "dignities." Clearly, then, it is not a question of imposing one dignity or of finding what "true dignity" really means. It is a question rather of recognising the validity of different forms of struggle and different opinions of what realizing dignity means. This does not mean a complete relativism in which all opinions, even fascist ones, are granted equal validity. Conflicts between different dignities are inevitable: it is clear, for example, that the Zapatista women's understanding of the dignity of their struggle sometimes conflicts with the men's understanding of their dignity. What the concept of dignity points to is not the correctness of any particular solution to such conflicts, but rather a way of resolving such conflicts in which the particular dignities are recognised and articulated. Even here, the Zapatistas argue that

---

60 The question of what sort of organisation should develop out of the Intercontinental Meeting of the summer of 1996 was addressed by Marcos in his closing speech: "What follows? A new number in the useless enumeration of numerous internationals? A new scheme that will give tranquillity and relief to those anguished by the lack of recipes? A world programme for world revolution? A theorisation of utopia that will allow us to maintain a prudent distance from the reality that torments us? An organigram that will secure us all a post, a responsibility, a name and no work? What follows is the echo, the reflected image of the possible and the forgotten: the possibility and necessity of talking and listening. . . . The echo of this rebel voice transforming itself and renewing itself in other voices. An echo that converts itself into many voices, into a network of voices that, in the face of the deafness of Power, chooses to speak to itself, knowing itself to be one and many, knowing itself to be equal in its aspiration to listen and make itself heard, recognising itself to be different in the tonalities and levels of the voices that form it. . . . A network that covers the five continents and helps to resist the death promised to us by Power. There follows a great bag of voices, sounds that seek their place fitting with others. . . . There follows the reproduction of resistances, the I do not conform, the I rebel. There follows the world with many worlds that the world needs. There follows humanity recognising itself to be plural, different, inclusive, tolerant of itself, with hope. There follows the human and rebel voice consulted in the five continents to make itself a network of voices and resistances" (closing speech by Marcos to the Intercontinental Meeting in La Realidad, see *Chiapas*, no. 3, 106–16, at 112).

there is not just one correct way of articulating dignities: while they themselves organise their discussions on the basis of village assemblies, they recognise that this may not be the best form of articulating dignities in all cases. What form the articulation of dignities might take in a big city, for example, is very much an open question, although there are obviously precedents[61] and, in some cases, deep-rooted traditions of forms of direct democracy. The struggle to unite dignities in a world that is based on the denial and fragmentation of dignities is not an easy one.

VI. Dignity Is the Revolutionary Subject
Dignity is a class concept not a humanistic one.

The EZLN do not use the concept of "class" or "class struggle" in their discourse, in spite of the fact that Marxist theory has clearly played an important part in their formation. They have preferred instead to develop a new language, to speak of the struggle of truth and dignity. "We saw that the old words had become so worn out that they had become harmful for those that used them."[62] In looking for support, or in forming links with other struggles, they have appealed not to the working class or the proletariat but to "civil society." By "civil society" they seem to mean "society in struggle" in the broadest sense: all those groups and initiatives engaged in latent or overt struggles to assert some sort of control over their future, without aspiring to hold governmental office.[63] In Mexico, the initial reference point is often the forms of autonomous social organisation that arose in Mexico City in response to the earthquake of 1985 and the state's incapacity to deal with the emergency.

It is not difficult to see why the Zapatistas chose to turn their back on the old words. That does not mean, however, that all the problems connected with these words are thereby erased. The Zapatistas have been criticised by some adherents of the traditional orthodox Marxist Left for not using the concept of class. It is argued that because they do not use the traditional

---

61 Obvious precedents are, for example, Marx's discussion of the Paris Commune in the *Civil War in France* or Pannekoek's discussion of workers' councils in the early years of this century.

62 *La Jornada*, August 27, 1995.

63 "Civil society, those people without party who do not aspire to be in a political party in the sense that they do not aspire to be the government, what they want is that the government should keep its word, should do its work": Marcos interview with Cristián Calónico Lucio, November 11, 1995, MS, 39.

triad of class struggle, revolution, and socialism, preferring instead to speak of dignity, truth, freedom, democracy, and justice, their struggle is a liberal one, an armed reformism that has little possibility of leading to radical change. An extreme form of this sort of application of a class analysis is the argument that the Zapatista uprising is just a peasant movement and, while it should be supported, the proletariat can have little confidence in it.

The orthodox Marxist tradition works with a definitional concept of class. The working class may be defined in various ways: most commonly as those who sell their labour power in order to survive; or as those who produce surplus value and are directly exploited. The important point here is that the working class is defined.

In this approach, any definition of the working class is based on its subordination to capital: it is because it is subordinated to capital (as wage workers or as producers of surplus value) that it is defined as working class. Capitalism, in this approach, is understood as a world of predefined social relations that are firmly fixed or fetishised.[64] The fixity of social relations is taken as the starting point for the discussion of class. Thus, working-class struggle is understood as starting from the pre-constituted subordination of labour to capital. Any sort of struggle that does not fall within this definition is then seen as nonclass struggle (raising problems about how it should be defined).

The definitional approach to class raises two problems. First, it inevitably raises the question of who is and who is not part of the working class. Are intellectuals like Marx and Lenin part of the working class? Are those of us who work in the universities part of the working class? Are the rebels of Chiapas part of the working class? Are feminists part of the working class? Are those active in the gay movement part of the working class? In each case, there is a concept of a predefined working class to which these people do or do not belong.[65]

---

64 On the dialectic of constituting and constituted, see the article by Werner Bonefeld, "Capital as Subject and the Existence of Labour," in *Open Marxism* vol. 3, eds. Werner Bonefeld, Richard Gunn, John Holloway, and Kosmas Psychopedis (London: Pluto, 1995), 182–212; see also John Holloway, "The State and Everyday Struggle," in *The State Debate*, ed. Simon Clarke (London: Macmillan, 1991).

65 The understanding of the working class as a defined group has been extended ad infinitum to discussions about the class definition of those who do not fall within this group as new petty bourgeoisie, salariat, etc.

The second and more serious consequence of defining class is the definition of struggles that follows. The classification of the people involved leads to certain conclusions about the struggles in which they are involved. Those who define the Zapatista rebels as not working-class draw certain conclusions about the nature and limitations of the uprising. From the definition of the class position of the participants there follows a definition of their struggles: class defines the antagonism that the definer accepts as valid. This leads to a blinkering of the perception of social antagonism. In some cases, for example, the definition of the working class as the urban proletariat directly exploited in factories combined with evidence of the decreasing proportion of the population who fall within this definition has led people to the conclusion that class struggle is no longer relevant for understanding social change. In other cases, the definition of the working class and working-class struggle in a certain way has led to an incapacity to relate to the development of new forms of struggle (the student movement, feminism, environmentalism, and so on). The definitional understanding of class has done much in recent years to create the situation in which "the old words had become so worn out that they had become harmful for those that used them."

The notion of dignity detonates the *definition* of class but does not thereby cease to be a class concept. It does so because the starting point is no longer a relation of subordination but a relation of struggle, a relation of insubordination/subordination. The starting point of dignity is the negation of humiliation, the struggle against subordination. From this perspective there does not exist a settled, fixed world of subordination upon which definitions can be constructed. Just the contrary: the notion of dignity points to the fact that we are not just subordinated or exploited, that our existence within capitalist society cannot be understood simply in terms of subordination. Dignity points to the fact that subordination cannot be conceived without its opposite, the struggle against subordination, or insubordination. A world of subordination is a world in which subordination is constantly at issue. The forms of social relations in capitalist society cannot be understood simply as fetishised, constituted forms but only as forms that are always in question and that are imposed only through the unceasing struggle of capital to reproduce itself. Once the starting point is dignity, once the starting point is the struggle to convert "dignity and rebellion into freedom and dignity," then all that was fixed becomes shaky, all that appeared to be defined becomes blurred.

From the perspective of dignity, class cannot be understood as a defined group of people. This is quite consistent with Marx's approach. His understanding of capitalism was based not on the antagonism between two groups of people but on the antagonism in the way in which human social practice is organised. Existence in capitalist society is conflictual and antagonistic. Although this antagonism appears as a vast multiplicity of conflicts, it can be argued (and was argued by Marx) that the key to understanding this antagonism and its development is the fact that present society is built upon an antagonism in the way that the distinctive character of humanity, namely creative activity (work in its broadest sense) is organised. In capitalist society, work is turned against itself, alienated from itself; we lose control over our creative activity. This negation of human creativity takes place through the subjection of human activity to the market. This subjection to the market takes place fully when the capacity to work creatively (labour power) becomes a commodity to be sold on the market to those with the capital to buy it. The antagonism between human creativity and its negation thus becomes focused in the antagonism between those who have to sell their creativity and those who appropriate that creativity and exploit it, and in so doing transform that creativity into labour. In shorthand, the antagonism between creativity and its negation can be referred to as the conflict between labour and capital, but this conflict (as Marx makes clear) is not a conflict between two external forces but between work (human creativity) and work alienated.

Social antagonism is not in the first place a conflict between two groups of people: it is a conflict between creative social practice and its negation, in other words, between humanity and its negation, between the transcending of limits (creation) and the imposition of limits (definition). In this interpretation, the conflict does not take place after subordination has been established, after the fetishised forms of social relations have been constituted: rather it is a conflict *about* the subordination of social practice, *about* the fetishisation of social relations.[66] The conflict is between subordination and insubordination, and it is this that allows us to speak of insubordination (or dignity) as a central feature of capitalism.

---

66 What Marx calls primitive accumulation is thus a permanent and central feature of capitalism not a historical phase. On this, see Werner Bonefeld, "Class Struggle and the Permanence of Primitive Accumulation," *Common Sense*, no. 6 (1988).

Class struggle does not take place within the constituted forms of capitalist social relations: rather the constitution of those forms is itself class struggle. This leads to a much richer concept of class struggle in which the whole of social practice is at issue. *All* social practice is an unceasing antagonism between the subjection of practice to the fetishised and perverted defining forms of capitalism and the attempt to live against-and-beyond those forms. There can thus be no question of the existence of nonclass forms of struggle.

Class struggle, in this view, is a conflict that permeates the whole of human existence. We all exist within that conflict, just as the conflict exists within all of us. It is a polar antagonism that we cannot escape. We do not "belong" to one class or another: rather, the class antagonism exists in us, tearing us apart. The antagonism (the class divide) traverses all of us.[67] Nevertheless, it clearly does so in very different ways. Some, the very small minority, participate directly in and/or benefit directly from the appropriation and exploitation of the work of others. Others, the vast majority, are, directly or indirectly the objects of that appropriation and exploitation. The polar nature of the antagonism is thus reflected in a polarisation of the two classes,[68] but the antagonism is prior to not subsequent to the classes: classes are constituted through the antagonism.

Since classes are constituted through the antagonism between work and its alienation, and since this antagonism is constantly changing, it follows that classes cannot be defined. The concept of class is essentially non-definitional. More than that, since definition imposes limits, closes openness, and negates creativity, it is possible to say that the capitalist class, even if it cannot be defined, is the class that defines, identifies, and classifies. Labour (the working class that exists in antagonism to capital) is not only incapable of definition but essentially anti-definitional. It is

---

67 For a development of this point, see Richard Gunn's article, "Notes on Class," *Common Sense*, no. 2 (1987); Werner Bonefeld, "Capital, Labour and Primitive Accumulation: Notes on Class and Constitution," unpublished MS (1997).

68 Thus, for Marx, capitalists are the personification of capital, as he repeatedly points out in *Capital*. The proletariat too first makes its appearance in his work not as a definable group but as the pole of an antagonistic relation: "a class . . . which . . . is the *complete loss* of man and hence can win itself only through the *complete rewinning of man*": Karl Marx, "Contribution to the Critique of Hegel's Philosophy of Law: Introduction," in Marx and Engels, *Collected Works*, vol. 3 (London: Lawrence and Wishart, 1975), 186.

constituted by its repressed creativity: that is to say, by its resistance to the (ultimately impossible) attempt to define it. Not only is it mistaken to try to identify the working class (are the Zapatistas working class?), but class struggle itself is the struggle between definition and anti-definition. Capital says, "I am, you are"; labour says, "We are not, but we are becoming; you are, but you will not be," or, "We are/are not, we struggle to create ourselves."

Class struggle is the unceasing daily antagonism (perceived or not) between alienation and dis-alienation, between definition and anti-definition, between fetishisation and de-fetishisation. The trouble with all these terms is that *our* side of the struggle is presented negatively: as dis-alienation, anti-definition, de-fetishisation. The Zapatistas are right when they say that we need a new language not just because the "old words" are "worn out," but because the Marxist tradition has been so focused on domination that it has not developed adequate words to talk about resistance.[69] Dignity is the term that turns this around, that expresses positively that which is suppressed, that for which we are fighting. Dignity is that which knows no Is-ness, no objective structures. Dignity is that which rises against humiliation, dehumanisation, marginalisation. Dignity is that which says, "We are here, we are human, and we struggle for the humanity that is denied to us." Dignity is the struggle against capital.

Dignity is the revolutionary subject. Where it is repressed most fiercely, where the antagonism is most intense, and where there is a tradition of communal organisation, it will fight most strongly, as in the factory, as in the jungle. But class struggle, the struggle of dignity, the struggle for humanity against its destruction, is not the privilege of any defined group: we exist in it, just as it exists in us, inescapably. Dignity does not exist in a pure form any more than the working class exists in a pure form. It is that in us that resists, that rebels, that does not conform. Constantly undermined, constantly smothered and suffocated by the myriad forms of alienation and fetishisation, constantly overlaid and distorted, constantly

---

69 The autonomist concept of self-valorisation is perhaps the closest that the Marxist tradition comes to a concept that expresses positively the struggle against-and-beyond capital, but the term is clumsy and obscure. On self-valorisation, see, for example, Harry Cleaver, "The Inversion of Class Perspective in Marxian Theory: From Valorisation to Self-Valorisation," in *Open Marxism*, vol. 2, eds. Werner Bonefeld, Richard Gunn, and Kosmas Psychopedis (London: Pluto, 1992), 106–45.

repressed, fragmented, and corrupted by money and the state, constantly in danger of being extinguished, snuffed out, it is the indestructible (or maybe just the not yet destroyed) NO that makes us human. That is why the resonance of the Zapatistas goes so deep: "as more and more rebel communiqués were issued, we realised that in reality the revolt came from the depths of ourselves."[70] The power of the Zapatistas is the power of the ¡Ya basta!, the negation of oppression that exists in the depths of all of us, the only hope for humanity.

VII. Dignity's Revolution Is Uncertain, Ambiguous, and Contradictory

Uncertainty permeates the whole Zapatista undertaking. There is none of the sense of the historical inevitability that has so often been a feature of past revolutionary movements. There is no certainty about the arrival at the Promised Land, nor any certainty about what this Promised Land might look like. It is a revolution that walks asking—not answering.

Revolution in the Zapatista sense is a moving outward rather than a moving toward. But how can such a movement be revolutionary? How can such a movement bring about a radical social transformation? The very idea of social revolution is already greatly discredited at the end of the twentieth century: How does the Zapatista uprising help us to find a way forward?

There is a problem at the heart of any concept of revolution. How could it be possible for those who are currently alienated (or humiliated) to create a world of non-alienation (or dignity)? If we are all permeated by the conditions of social oppression in which we live, and if our perceptions are constrained by those conditions, shall we not always reproduce those conditions in everything we do? If our existence is traversed by relations of power, how can we possibly create a society that is not characterised by power relations?

The simplest way out of this problem is to bring in a saviour, a deus ex machina. If there is some figure who has broken free of alienation and come to a true understanding, then that figure can perhaps lead the masses out of the present alienated society. This is essentially the idea of

---

70 Antonio García de León in his prologue to an edition of the Zapatista communiqués: EZLN, *Documentos y Comunicados: 1° de enero/8 de agosto de 1994* (Mexico City: Ediciones Era, 1994), 14.

the vanguard party proposed by Lenin:[71] a group of people who by virtue of their theoretical and practical experience can see beyond the confines of existing society, and who for that reason can lead the masses in a revolutionary break. There are, however, two basic problems. How is it possible for anyone, no matter what their training, to so lift themselves above existing society that they do not reproduce in their own action the concepts and faults of that society? Even more fundamental: How is it possible to create a self-creative society other than through the self-emancipation of society? The experience of revolution in the twentieth century suggests that these are very grave problems indeed.

However, if the notion of a vanguard is discarded, and with it the notion of a revolutionary programme that depends on the existence of such a vanguard, then what are we left with? The Leninist solution may have been wrong, but it was an attempt to solve a perceived problem: the problem of how you bring about a radical transformation of society when the mass of people are so imbued with contemporary values that self-emancipation seems impossible. For many, the failure of the Leninist solution proves the impossibility of social revolution and the inevitability of conforming.

The Zapatista answer is focused on the notion of dignity, which points to the contradictory nature of existence. We are humiliated but have the dignity to struggle against the humiliation to realise our dignity. We are imbued with capitalist values but also live a daily antagonism toward those values. We are alienated but still have sufficient humanity to struggle against alienation and for a non-alienated world. Alienation is but is not, because dis-alienation is not but also is. Oppression exists, but it exists as struggle. It is the present existence of dignity (as struggle) that makes it possible to conceive of revolution without a vanguard party. The society based on dignity already exists in the form of the struggle against the negation of dignity.[72] Dignity implies self-emancipation.

---

71 The deus ex machina idea stretches far beyond Leninism, of course. It can be seen also in those theories that privilege the revolutionary role of the intellectuals. On a quite different plane, the same notions are reflected in the state's understanding of the Zapatista movement and its racist assumption that the real protagonists of the movement are urban white or mestizo intellectuals, such as Marcos.

72 "Alienation could not even be seen and condemned of robbing people of their freedom and depriving the world of its soul if there did not exist some measure

The consistent pursuit of dignity in a society based on the denial of dignity is in itself revolutionary. But it implies a different concept of revolution from the "storming the Winter Palace" concept that we have grown up with. There is no building the revolutionary party, no strategy for world revolution, no transitional programme. Revolution is simply the constant, uncompromising struggle for what cannot be achieved under capitalism: dignity and control over our own lives.

Revolution can only be thought of in this scheme as the cumulative uniting of dignities, the snowballing of struggles, the refusal of more and more people to subordinate their humanity to the degradations of capitalism. This implies a more open concept of revolution: the snowballing of struggles cannot be programmed or predicted. Revolution is not just a future event but the complete inversion of the relation between dignity and degradation in the present, the cumulative assertion of power over our own lives, the progressive construction of autonomy. As long as capitalism exists (and as long as money exists), the degradation of dignity, the exploitation of work, the dehumanisation and immiseration of existence will continue: the assertion of dignity clearly comes into immediate conflict with the reproduction of capitalism. This conflict could only be resolved by the complete destruction of capitalism. What form this might take and how the cumulative uniting of dignities could lead to the abolition of capitalism is not clear. It cannot be clear if it is to be a self-creative process. What is clear is that the experience of the last hundred years suggests that social transformation cannot be brought about by the conquest (be it "democratic" or "undemocratic") of state power.

This notion is not reformist, if reformism means that social transformation can be achieved through the accretion of state-sponsored reforms. Anti-reformism is not a question of the clarity of future goals but of the strength with which those forms (especially the state) that reproduce capitalist social relations are rejected in the present. It is a question not of a future programme but of present organisation.

An uncertain revolution is, however, an ambiguous and contradictory revolution. Openness and uncertainty are built in to the Zapatista concept of revolution. And that openness also means contradictions and

of its opposite, of that possible coming-to-oneself, being-with-oneself, against which alienation can be measured": Ernst Bloch, *Tübinger Einleitung in die Philosophie* (Frankfurt: Suhrkamp, 1963), vol. 2, 113. Dignity, in other words.

ambiguities. At times it looks as if the EZLN might accept a settlement that falls far short of their dreams, at times the presentation of their aims is more limited, apparently more containable. Certainly, both the direction and the appeal of the uprising would be strengthened if it were made explicit that exploitation is central to the systematic negation of dignity, and that dignity's struggle is a struggle against exploitation in all its forms. The very nature of the Zapatista concept of revolution means that the movement is particularly open to the charge of ambiguity. Yet historical experience suggests that ambiguities and contradictions are deep-rooted in any revolutionary process, no matter how clearly defined the line of the leadership. Rather than deny the contradictions, it seems better to focus on the forms of articulation and political experiment that might resolve those contradictions. It is better to recognise, as Tacho does, that in undertaking revolution, the Zapatistas are "going to classes in a school that does not exist."[73]

But what does the EZLN want? What is their dream of the future? Clearly, there are many dreams of the future: "For one it can be that there should be land for everybody to work, which for the peasant is the central problem, no? In reality they are very clear that all the other problems turn on the question of land: housing, health, schools, services. Everything that makes them leave the land is bad and everything that lets them stay on it is good. To stay with dignity."[74] That is a dream of the future, a simple dream perhaps, but its realisation would require enormous changes in the organisation of society.

Or again, in another interview, Marcos explains the Zapatista dream in these terms:

> In our dream the children are children and their work is to be children. Here no, in reality, in the reality of Chiapas, the work of the children is to be adults from the time they are born, and that is not right; we say that that is not right.... My dream is not of agricultural redistribution, the great mobilisations, the fall of the government and elections and a party of the left wins, whatever. In my dream, I dream of the children, and I see them being children. If we achieve that, that the children in any part of Mexico are children and nothing

---

73 Le Bot, *El Sueño*, 191.
74 Radio UNAM interview with Marcos, March 18, 1994, EZLN, see *La Palabra*, vol. 2, 89.

else, we've won. Whatever it costs, that is worth it. It doesn't matter what social regime is in power, or what political party is in government, or what the exchange rate between the peso and the dollar is, or how the stock market is doing, or whatever. If a child of five years can be a child, as children of five years should be, with that we are on the other side. . . . We, the Zapatista children, think that our work as children is to play and learn. And the children here do not play, they work.[75]

Again, a simple dream, possibly to some a reformist dream, but one that is totally incompatible with the current direction of the world, in which the exploitation of children (child labour, child prostitution, child pornography, for example) is growing at an alarming rate. This dream of children being children is a good example of the power of the notion of dignity: the consistent pursuit of the dream would require a complete transformation of society.

A society based on dignity would be one based on mutual recognition, in which people "do not have to use a mask . . . in order to relate with other people."[76] It would also be an absolutely self-creative society. In an interview for the Venice Film Festival, in response to the standard question, "What is it that the EZLN wants?" Marcos answered, "We want life to be like a cinema poster from which we can choose a different film each day. Now we have risen in arms, because for more than 500 years they have forced us to watch the same film every day."[77]

There are no five-year plans here, no blueprint for the new society, no predefined utopia. There are no guarantees.

There are no guarantees, no certainties. Openness and uncertainty are built in to the Zapatista concept of revolution. And that openness also means contradictions and ambiguities. These contradictions and ambiguities are part and parcel of the Zapatista concept of revolution, of the idea of a revolution that walks asking. Inevitably, the contradictions and ambiguities are part of the development of the movement, and undoubtedly it is possible to sustain interpretations of Zapatismo that are more

---

75 Ibid.
76 Marcos interview with Cristián Calónico Lucio, November 11, 1995, MS, 61. This would of course mean a society without power relations.
77 *La Jornada*, August 25, 1996.

restricted than the one offered here. The argument here is an attempt to distil rather than to analyse. Our question is not "What will happen to the EZLN?" but "What will happen to us?" Or rather not "happen to," since the whole point is that we are not "happened to": How will *we* (not "*they*") change the world? How can we change a world in which capitalism starves thousands of people to death each day, in which the systematic killing of street children in certain cities is organised as the only way of upholding the concept of private property, in which the unleashed horrors of neoliberalism are hurtling humanity toward self-destruction?

And what if they fail? There is no guarantee that the EZLN will still exist when this is published. It may be that the Mexican government will have launched an open military assault (already tried on February 9, 1995, and an always present threat): the army could be more successful than the last time they tried it. It is also possible that the EZLN will become exhausted: that they will be drawn by tiredness, by their own ambiguities, or by the simple lack of response from civil society into limiting their demands and settling for definitions. These are all possibilities. The important point, though, is that the Zapatistas are not "they": they are "we"—we are "we." When the huge crowds who demonstrated in Mexico City and elsewhere after the army intervention of February 9 chanted, "We are all Marcos," they were not announcing an intention to join the EZLN. They were saying that the struggle of the Zapatistas is the life-struggle of all of us, that we are all part of their struggle and their struggle is part of us, wherever we are. As Major Ana-María put it in the opening speech of the Intercontinental Meeting:

> Behind us are the we that are you.[78] Behind our balaclavas is the face of all the excluded women. Of all the forgotten indigenous people. Of all the persecuted homosexuals. Of all the despised youth. Of all the beaten migrants. Of all those imprisoned for their word and thought. Of all the humiliated workers. Of all those who have died from being forgotten. Of all the simple and ordinary men and women who do not count, who are not seen, who are not named, who have no tomorrow.[79]

---

78 This is clumsy but is the best translation I could find for the more elegant "*Detrás de nosotros estamos ustedes.*"

79 "Discurso inaugural de la mayor Ana María," *Chiapas* no. 3, 101–5, at 103.

We are all Zapatistas. The Zapatistas of Chiapas have lit a flame, but the struggle to convert "dignity and rebellion into freedom and dignity" is ours.

EIGHT

Zapata in Wall Street

It was in the early hours of December 19, 1994, that Zapata rode into Wall Street on his white stallion, cartridge belts crossed on her chest, the flash of dignity in her eyes. In the days that followed, there was consternation in Wall Street, panic on the world's financial markets. The stock markets shook, the political leaders confabulated. The volcano Popocatépetl started to belch forth smoke and ashes from its snowy peak.

"We have made the Power of Money tremble," Zapata of the balaclava remarked some time later. "It has realised there is something it cannot buy or sell, that dignity is starting to unite. The Power of Money is afraid, because the uniting of dignities signifies its downfall,[1] its rapid transition to part of a nightmare that is coming to an end, the conclusion of a historical phase ruled by arrogance and stupidity."[2]

I

In the early morning of December 19, 1994, the EZLN (Ejército Zapatista de Liberación Nacional—Zapatista Army of National Liberation) announced that they had broken through the military cordon that had encircled them for almost a year and had undertaken actions in thirty-eight

---

1   On the concept of dignity, see John Holloway, "Dignity's Revolt," in *Zapatista! Reinventing Revolution in Mexico*, eds. John Holloway and Eloína Peláez (London: Pluto, 1998).

2   Communiqué of September 29, 1995. Note that this remark was made in another context not in direct reference to the events following December 19.

municipalities of the state of Chiapas, in southeast Mexico.[3] Not a shot was fired and nobody was hurt.[4]

The reaction of the financial markets was immediate. Capital fled. The prices of Mexican shares fell both in Mexico City and in Wall Street, as investors sold their stock. In the money markets, there was a flight of capital from the Mexican peso to dollars.[5] On the following day the Mexican government announced a 15.3 per cent devaluation of the peso in relation to the dollar and blamed the devaluation on the Zapatistas.[6] In spite of the devaluation, the flight of capital from the peso continued and on December 22 the government decided to let the peso float freely on the market. The peso fell and within a few days it had lost 40 per cent of its pre-December 19 value.[7]

In the weeks and months that followed, the impact of the Mexican devaluation and of the flight of capital from Mexico was felt throughout the world. For several years Mexico had been regarded as a neoliberal success story, the star of the "emerging markets,"[8] the poor country that

---

3   *La Jornada*, December 20, 1994.
4   The IMF report on the devaluation of the peso quite wrongly refers to this event as "violence in Chiapas" (International Monetary Fund, 1995, 53–54).
5   *El Financiero*, December 23, 1994, calculates the outflow of capital in the first three weeks of December at $7.5 billion.
6   This does not mean, of course, that the Zapatistas were "to blame" nor that they "caused" the devaluation. There is little doubt, however, that it was the Zapatista action that triggered the flight of capital that led to the devaluation.
7   Investors who did not get their capital out fast enough lost heavily. According to the *Financial Times*: "US institutions which have become big investors in emerging markets—and especially in Mexico—are estimated to have lost up to 20% of their holdings in the country this week"; and "Investors who hold Mexican assets have lost billions of dollars in a couple of days, as big currency losses have compounded market downturns" (December 23, 1994). Some weeks later, the estimates were even more drastic: "The Mexican crisis which has seen dollar-based equity investors lose more than 40% in less than a month": *Financial Times*, January 12, 1995.
8   The term "emerging markets" refers to the financial markets outside the main financial centres. These had seen a very rapid development in the previous few years, and Mexico had played a leading role. An emerging market is defined by the International Finance Corporation, an arm of the World Bank, as a country with gross national product per head of less than $8,355. According to Baring Securities, the broker, some $200bn of emerging market equities were held by foreign investors at the end of 1993, compared with just $2.1bn in 1986. Emerging markets grew rapidly in the early 1990s, when U.S. interest

had succeeded in constructing the North American Free Trade Agreement with its rich neighbours and in becoming a member (in April 1994) of the Organisation for Economic Cooperation and Development (OECD). When the peso fell, it seemed to many of the investors who had taken part in the enormous flow of capital to the emerging markets in the years 1990 to 1994 that none of these markets was secure. There was a "flight to quality" as capital flowed to the more firmly established markets[9] and fled from those considered risky, threatening the stability of currencies and stock markets not only in Latin America (especially Argentina and Brazil) but also in Thailand, Hong Kong, Hungary, Sweden, Spain, Portugal, Pakistan, South Africa, Italy, Indonesia, Poland, Nigeria, Canada, and other countries.[10]

In the middle of January, the president of the United States declared that his government would give a loan of $40 billion to stabilise the Mexican peso. When this proposal encountered strong opposition in Congress, Clinton announced the creation of an international package of support totalling more than $50 billion, then by far the biggest intervention of this type in the history of the world's financial markets.[11] The announcement succeeded in stabilising the peso but the dollar fell as a result. The resulting rise in the price of the yen in relation to the dollar caused an increase in unemployment in Japan and protest marches in Tokyo. In Europe the financial turbulence gave rise to new tensions in the process of monetary integration.

---

rates were low: "Overseas investment by US equity investors doubled from 42.3bn in 1992 to 84.8bn in 1993, according to Baring Securities." Phillip Coggan, *Financial Times*, January 7, 1995.

9   Quality was identified especially with Germany, Switzerland, and Japan; see *Financial Times*, January 12, 1995.

10 This is reflected in the headlines of the contemporary financial press. See, for example, the *Financial Times*, January 13, 1995: "Currency turmoil hits dollar: Pressure on European and Asian markets as 'flight to quality' continues"; and "HK interest rates rise to defend dollar: Fallout from peso collapse in Mexico hits Asia."

11 The $17.8 billion contributed by the IMF was "three and a half times as much as the IMF has ever lent to any other country," see *Financial Times*, May 16, 1995. As Alexander Cockburn and Ken Silverstein ("War and Peso," *New Statesman and Society*, February 1995, 20) point out, this "should not be seen so much as a 'rescue' in any sense of restoring the Mexican economy to health, but as a way of keeping Mexico 'in play.'" As the *Financial Times*, February 1, 1995, put it, the purpose of the credit was to "reassure investors that the [Mexican] government would not renege on its foreign obligations."

When the political and economic leaders of the world came together in Davos in January 1995, Mexico was the principal topic of discussion; when the Group of Seven met in Toronto in February, Mexico was the principal topic; when the International Monetary Fund met at the end of April, Mexico was still one of the principal topics. There was much talk of the risk of a "systemic crisis" of world finance, even of "global financial apocalypse."[12] The argument advanced by the U.S. government to defend its original proposal and to justify the international financial package was that the collapse of the peso was not just a Mexican or an American concern, but that it put at risk the stability of the international financial system as a whole.

II

The world financial system did not collapse and has not collapsed. Popocatépetl did not erupt and has not erupted.

Yet the incursion of Zapata into Wall Street remains important. It immediately connects the most important revolutionary uprising of recent years and the chronic financial instability that is a central feature of contemporary capitalism. It is the sharp confrontation of two worlds. On the one hand, the naked, undisguised power of money, of capital in movement, of the states and all their energies brought to focus on ensuring the reproduction of capital. On the other hand, a beautifully executed piece of mischief, a mockery, a cry of dignity, the "Here we are!" of a world that refuses to be extinguished, of a world that does not yet exist. The confrontation throws light on both sides—on the nature of the financial instability of capitalism and on the problems of revolution.

The argument here is not that the Zapatistas were the sole cause of world financial turmoil. What is important is that they precipitated the financial upheaval. The fact that the action of a few thousand rebels in the jungle of southeast Mexico could precipitate a world financial crisis tells us a lot about the fragility of the financial system in contemporary capitalism and the power of insubordination in these circumstances. As the director of the Banque de France is reported to have commented at the time, "The international system is now so fragile that a handful of Indians in a corner of Mexico can put it in danger."[13]

---

12 Cockburn and Silverstein, "War and the Peso," 18, quoting the *New York Times*, nd.
13 Quoted in Yvon Le Bot, *El Sueño Zapatista* (Mexico City: Plaza y Janés, 1997), 255.

What has made the international financial system so fragile, and what is its relation to the explosion of insubordination in the southeast of Mexico?

III

That the international financial system is fragile can hardly be doubted after the recent East Asian, Russian, and Brazilian financial crises. The fear of systemic crisis has become endemic to contemporary capitalism. Since the announcement of the Mexican government in August 1982 that it would have trouble maintaining interest payments on its debts, the world has seen a series of major financial crises, each one of which was seen as the potential harbinger of financial disaster: the Latin American debt crisis of the early 1980s, the stock market crash of 1987, the savings and loans and junk bond crises of the late 1980s, the property market crashes of the early 1990s in Japan, Britain, the U.S., and elsewhere, the "tequila crisis" that followed the Zapatista action of December 19, 1994, and then the East Asian, Russian, and Brazilian crises in 1997, 1998, 1999. In each case total financial collapse was avoided, but in each case it was a genuine fear. Disaster was avoided but at the cost of introducing new elements of instability. The threat of systemic crisis has become almost routine in the world's financial markets.

The key to the growing financial instability of capitalism is the chronic expansion of debt, in other words, the chronic and growing separation between productive and financial accumulation.

Debt is of course a normal feature of capitalist development. The separation between real accumulation and monetary accumulation can be seen as part of the cycle of capitalist reproduction. As a period of rapid accumulation approaches its end (with the deterioration of conditions for accumulation),[14] more and more productive capitalists seek to overcome their difficulties by borrowing. More capital is also made available for lending, as the conditions no longer exist for profitable expansion through direct investment in production. Accumulation, in other words, becomes more and more fictitious: the monetary representation of value becomes more and more detached from the value actually produced. This reaches a point where borrowers are no longer able to repay their loans,

---

14 Note that credit does not explain the crisis. The crisis must be explained in terms of the deterioration of the conditions of accumulation.

or even the interest on their loans: borrowers go bankrupt, creditors collapse, and there is a massive destruction of fictitious capital. The crisis that is unleashed destroys inefficient capitals, drives up unemployment, drives down wages, increases social discipline, and generally restores the conditions of profitable exploitation and accumulation that permit the cycle to begin again. Such a destruction of fictitious capital can be seen, for example, in the stock market crash of 1929.

For capital, the problems begin to arise when this "normal" cycle of the expansion and destruction of credit is blocked. This is essentially what has happened in postwar capitalism. In the wake of the miseries and unrest caused by the crash of 1929, of the horrors of fascism and the Second World War, and in the wake of the Russian Revolution, it became acceptable for the state to intervene and to regulate or avoid as far as possible the destruction of fictitious capital. Keynesianism was the theoretical and practical recognition of the untold destruction that a repetition of the "normal" cycle of capital would involve. In order to avoid the horrors of such destruction and the concomitant threat to the survival of capitalism, the expansion of credit became a permanent rather than cyclical feature of capitalism,[15] a permanent attempt to postpone crisis.

The problems that arise for capital from this type of development became clear in the 1960s and early 1970s. The constant expansion of credit implies above all a weakening of the discipline of the market and of the social discipline imposed by the law of value. By postponing or modifying crisis, it makes possible the survival of inefficient capitals and, even worse from the point of view of capital, of inefficient workers. It also implies the autonomisation of financial markets from commodity markets. Credit feeds on credit. In order to avoid defaulting in the repayment of loans and interest, debtors need to borrow more. An increasing proportion of credit granted is recycling credit granted just for the purpose of repaying loans (or, often, the interest on loans). The more elaborate the structure of credit becomes, the more difficult it is to maintain but also the more difficult to undo. A full-scale "credit crunch" (the destruction of fictitious capital)

---

15 See, for example, Werner Bonefeld, Alice Brown, and Peter Burnham, A Major Crisis (London: Dartmouth, 1995), 39: "From the late 1960s depressed rates of accumulation and depressed rates of profit coincided with rapid monetary expansion. There has been a persistent growth in the imbalance between the expansion of money and the creation of assets against which to charge the expansion of money."

would not only cause massive social hardship but would also threaten the existence of the banking system and, with it, the existing structure of capitalism.

The criticisms that had been voiced by the opponents of Keynes in the 1920s and 1930s arose with force again in the 1970s, when they formed the basis of the monetarist assault on the assumptions of the postwar development of capitalism. The monetarist critique of Keynesianism was directed against the fictitious character of capitalist development (funny money, as they called it) and against the social indiscipline that the modification of the market promoted. However, the attempt by the United States, British, and other governments, to impose market discipline through tightening the money supply (that is, restricting the expansion of credit) from 1979 to 1982, not only caused considerable social hardship and economic destruction but also threatened to destroy the international banking system. The restriction of credit by raising interest rates in the United States created a situation in which it became extremely difficult for some of the biggest debtors (such as the Mexican, Argentine, and Brazilian governments) to repay their debts or even to pay the interest due. When the Mexican government threatened in 1982 to default on its payments, thus precipitating the so-called "debt crisis" of the 1980s, it became clear that the attempt to eliminate the expansion of credit threatened the survival not only of the debtors but also of the creditors, in this case the world's major banks.

The attempt to precipitate the massive destruction of fictitious capital through tight monetary policies had proved impossible to implement. The reproduction of capital required a new and massive expansion of credit. The problem for capital was how to provide the credit needed to reproduce capital without allowing this credit expansion to undermine the discipline needed for the exploitation of labour. The solution attempted was the so-called "supply-side" economics of the 1980s: the combination of measures to discipline labour and an unprecedented expansion of credit.[16] The dangers involved in such a development were signalled by a number

---

16 For a discussion of this, see Werner Bonefeld, "Monetarism and Crisis," in *Global Capital, National State and the Politics of Money*, eds. Werner Bonefeld and John Holloway (London: Macmillan, 1995); Werner Bonefeld and John Holloway [1995a], "Conclusion: Money and Class Struggle," in *Global Capital, National State and the Politics of Money*, eds. Werner Bonefeld and John Holloway (London: Macmillan, 1995), 210–27.

of critics of this "voodoo economics" in the mid-1980s.[17] Although the critics were correct in pointing to the instability entailed by the expansion of debt, the stock market crash of 1987, of which they had warned, simply increased the pressures to expand credit in order to avoid a worse crisis. The response of the governments was the same: the expansion of credit and the introduction of measures to avoid at all costs a massive destruction of fictitious capital.[18]

The response to the recession of the early 1990s was the same "Keynesian" response, especially on the part of the United States and Japanese governments: reducing interest rates to stimulate borrowing and to create money through credit. In this case, however, a lot of the money borrowed in the United States (on the basis of the 3 per cent interest rate set by the Federal Reserve)[19] was not invested in the U.S. but in the international money markets, and especially in the so-called emerging markets where there were high profits to be won.[20] The most important of the emerging markets was Mexico, where the inflow of capital in the form of money contributed to opening up a huge abyss between the reality

---

17 See, for example, Henry Kaufman, *Interest Rates, the Markets, and the New Financial World* (London: Tauris, 1986); Tim Congdon, *The Debt Threat* (Oxford: Blackwell 1988); Harry Magdoff and Paul M. Sweezy, *Stagnation and the Financial Explosion* (New York: Monthly Review, 1987).

18 See Bonefeld, Brown, and Burnham, *A Major Crisis*, 66–68: "The crash did not result in a meltdown of the stock market. This was prevented by a huge reflation package that included lowering of interest rates, relaxing controls on the money supply, and financial support for banks and other financial institutions. The reflation package helped to sustain the credit-based boom. Samuel Brittan's advice was well observed: 'When a slump is threatening, we need helicopters dropping currency notes from the sky. This means easier lending policies and, if that is not enough, some mixture of lower taxes and higher government spending.' ... By the end of the 1980s bank loans in the US had more than doubled and in Japan they were three times their level at the beginning of the decade."

19 For a discussion of this, see, for example, James Grant, *The Trouble with Prosperity* (New York: Times Books, 1996).

20 See, for example, John Plender, the *Financial Times*, February 13, 1995: "US investors' urge to buy $27.5 bn of emerging market equities between 1990 and the first half of 1994, compared with only $1.2 bn in the previous 10 years, partly reflected the new fashion for diversification. But it was more a *speculative spillover from the loose monetary policy that was required to deal with the problems of the banks.*"

of the process of accumulation and its appearance, the abyss that was revealed in the devaluation of the peso.[21]

The result of the constant postponement of crisis through the expansion of debt has been an ever-growing separation between productive and monetary accumulation. Money has been expanding at a far faster rate than the value it represents. In other words, despite the very real restructuring of the productive process that has taken place over the last twenty years or so, the survival of capitalism is based on an ever-increasing expansion of debt. Many statistics can be used to tell what is basically the same story. Public debt, which was the central theme of the monetarist attack against Keynesianism, continues to expand: the OECD calculates that the net public debt of its member states increased from 21 per cent of the gross domestic product in 1978 to 42 per cent in 1994.[22] The net debt of the European governments grew from less than 25 per cent of GDP in 1980 to more than 55 per cent in 1994.[23] According to IMF figures for the member states of the Group of Seven, domestic credit as a proportion of gross domestic product rose from 44.48 per cent in 1955 to 104.54 per cent in 1994. The world bond market (which is closely tied to the financing of government budget deficits) tripled in size between 1986 and 1997.[24] The growth in world money transactions has been far faster than the growth in world trade: while yearly transactions in the London Eurodollar market

---

21 Grant (1996) wonders why the speculative boom in the United States had not led to a recession. The answer is surely that the "Mexican" crisis was in part the collapse of the U.S. bubble, as were later the East Asian, Russian, and Brazilian crises.

22 *Financial Times*, October 31, 1994.

23 *Financial Times*, January 16, 1995; see also Andrew Walter, *World Power and World Money* (London: Harvester Wheatsheaf, 1993), 215: "Between 1976 and mid-1987, aggregate US debt rose from $2.5 trillion to nearly $8 trillion, and the ratio of total debt to GDP rose from 136 per cent to 178 per cent. . . . [T]he indebtedness of the private sector in Japan has risen substantially in recent years: the indebtedness of non-financial companies increased from 94 per cent of GDP in 1975 to 135 per cent of GDP in 1990, while that of households increased from 45 per cent to 96 per cent of disposable income over the same period." Between 1985 and 1997, total U.S. household debt as a percentage of disposable personal income rose from just over 60 per cent to almost 85 per cent (*Financial Times*, January 2, 1998).

24 Peter Warburton, *Debt and Delusion* (London: Penguin Books, 1999), 3. Also: "The world bond market has grown from less than $1 trillion in 1970 to more than $23 trillion in 1997."

represented six times the value of world trade in 1979, by 1986 it had risen to about twenty-five times the value of world trade and eighteen times the value of the world's largest economy.[25] Well over a trillion dollars are exchanged daily on the world's foreign exchange markets, and this figure has been increasing about 30 per cent a year in the 1990s. The late 1980s and the 1990s have seen a massive rise in the expansion of debt through securitisation—the development of new forms of property in debt, particularly the so-called derivatives: the derivatives markets grew at the rate of 140 per cent a year from 1986 to 1994.[26] In Wall Street, price-earning ratios on shares are at record highs.[27]

The separation between real and monetary accumulation is crucial for understanding the instability, volatility, fragility, and unpredictability of capitalism today. Since the whole financial structure of capitalism is so heavily based on credit and debt, any default or threat of default by a major debtor (such as Mexico) can cause great upheaval in the financial markets: the urgency with which the international package to support the peso was put together was related to fears that the Mexican government could default on the payment of its debt. More generally, the autonomisation of the financial markets that the non-destruction of fictitious capital supports implies the possibility of creating ever more sophisticated financial instruments of doubtful validity; it also implies the increasingly rapid movement of greater and greater quantities of money on the world's financial markets, and therefore a radical change in the relation between individual states and world capital.[28]

All this does not mean that world financial collapse is imminent. It does, however, mean that a chronic financial instability has become a

---

25 Walter, *World Power*, 197.

26 See International Monetary Fund, *International Capital Markets: Developments, Prospects and Policy Issues* (Washington, DC: IMF, 1995), 18.

27 For a detailed discussion of the expansion of debt in the 1990s and the dangers of financial collapse, see Warburton, *Debt and Delusion*.

28 It is calculated that in 1992 daily world foreign exchange turnover averaged about $1 trillion. Total "central bank reserves are less than the equivalent of *two days* turnover in the world's foreign exchange markets, which indicates that one central bank or even a number of central banks intervening together in exchange markets cannot hope to oppose a concerted onslaught on a particular currency or currencies by the exchange markets": Walter, *World Power*, 199. On the changing relation between money and the state, see Bonefeld and Holloway, *Global Capital*.

central feature of contemporary capitalism, and that the possibility of a world financial collapse has become a structural characteristic of capitalism, even in periods of rapid accumulation. It may or may not be that the leading capitalist states and banks can continue to manage this instability in such a way as to avoid global financial collapse, but this instability management involves all the violence, arbitrariness, and discrimination that debt collection and administration always involve: the discriminatory and (regionally) selective imposition of crisis.

This was the world into which Zapata rode on December 19, 1994: a fragile world of false appearances, growing insecurity, and the violence and authoritarianism inherent in crisis and debt administration.

IV

When the Zapatistas brought their insubordination into the world's financial markets, they brought it into a world that had already been shaped by insubordination. The extent to which the reproduction of capitalism now depends on the constant expansion of debt is the clearest indication of capital's incapacity to adequately subordinate labour. The insubordination of labour has entered into the very core of capital as chronic financial instability.

The point was made clearly by the U.S. politician Bernard Baruch when Roosevelt abandoned the gold standard in 1933 to meet social pressures for more flexible economic and social policies: "It can't be defended except as mob rule. Maybe the country doesn't know it yet, but I think we may find we've been in a revolution more drastic than the French Revolution. The crowd has seized the seat of government and is trying to seize the wealth. Respect for law and order is gone."[29] The mob had been allowed into the very heart of capital. The government had given in to social discontent by adopting policies that would undermine the stability of the currency.

That was the essence of the debates of the interwar period surrounding the restoration and then the abandonment of the gold standard. While Keynes and those of like mind argued that it was necessary to adapt capitalist rule to incorporate the new strength of labour by accepting a new, expanded role for the state and more flexible monetary policies, their

---

29 Quoted in Arthur M. Schlesinger, *The Age of Roosevelt: The Coming of the New Deal* (Cambridge, MA: Riverside; 1959), 202.

opponents argued that to do so would undermine the long-term stability of money and therefore of capitalism.[30] Baruch and his friends (the "old-world party," as Keynes called them) were, of course, right, but in the short term they lost the argument: the mob was allowed into the heart of money and, as we have seen, monetary stability was undermined.

The same argument arose again in the 1970s when the crisis of Keynesianism became manifest. Now it took the form of an argument about the need to limit democracy (and the role of the state): the undermining of monetary stability was discussed in terms of the "economic consequences of democracy."[31] More recently, the argument has taken the form of advocating greater independence for central banks from government (and therefore formal-democratic) influence. In each case, the struggle of capital has been to get the mob out of money. In each case, it has failed, simply because, as we have seen, the integration of labour through the expansion of debt and the avoidance of crisis has taken such proportions that the measures required to restore capitalism to financial stability would be so drastic as to threaten the existence of capitalism itself.

What is at issue in the current financial instability of capitalism is capital's absolute dependence on the subordination of labour and its incapacity to overcome that dependence. Marx suggests in his discussion of value that there is a fundamental weakness at the core of capitalist strength, a contradiction that constantly subverts capital's presentation of reality, a dependence that undermines its domination. That contradiction is constituted by the fact that labour is the only source of value, in other words, that capital depends on labour for its own production and reproduction.[32] Capital will be reproduced only if it succeeds in subordinating labour. All that Marx says about the contradictions of capitalism stems from this simple relation of dependence.

---

30 For a full discussion of this argument, see John Holloway, "The Abyss Opens: The Rise and Fall of Keynesianism," in *Global Capital*, eds. Bonefeld and Holloway.

31 See Samuel Brittan, *The Economic Consequences of Democracy* (London: Temple Smith, 1977).

32 For a fuller discussion of this argument, see, for example, John Holloway, "From Scream of Refusal to Scream of Power: The Centrality of Work," in *Open Marxism*, vol. 2, eds., Werner Bonefeld, Richard Gunn, and Kosmas Psychopedis (London: Pluto, 1992), 155–81.

The subordination of labour clearly involves the direct control of wage labour and all that follows from that in terms of the organisation of the labour process and the development of technology. The notion of wage labour, however, already presupposes subordination: it presupposes in large part, therefore, the resolution of capital's problem and provides the basis for a very narrow concept of class and class struggle. If the central problem for capital is its dependence on the subordination of labour, then we must cast our gaze far wider than simply asking how capital makes the subordination of labour effective. Workers do not come prepackaged, as the materialisation of pre-subordinated labour. Capital's reproduction depends not just on the effective exploitation of pre-subordinated labour but on the constantly renewed transformation of social practice into subordinate labour, the constantly renewed metamorphosis of human creativity into exploited labour, the constantly renewed subjection of creativity to the demands of valorisation. What aggravates the dependence of capital upon labour is not just the struggle of wage labour for higher wages or better conditions but the five-billion-headed struggle against the subordination of social practice to value. If capital's struggle is to alienate, fetishise, and degrade humanity (the creativity that makes people human) into subordinate labour, then anti-capitalist struggle is simply the struggle against dehumanisation and for humanity, dignity, in other words, the everyday stuff of life.[33]

When the Zapatista action of December 19, 1994, sparked off an international financial crisis, it was not an intrusion into a financial world that just happened to be going through a moment of fragility. It was rather a new act of insubordination that was added to years and years of insubordination and non-subordination that had already undermined the stability of the financial system. Such insubordination or non-subordination takes many forms: it may be the classical working-class struggles against employers or overt rebellion, as in the case of the Zapatista uprising, or it may simply be the grinding, corrosive non-subordination of life to the command of capital: all of those types of insubordination make more desperate the struggle of capital to achieve the subordination of labour on

---

33 The so-called tendency of the rate of profit to fall can be seen, therefore, as meaning simply that as capitalism progresses, there is a tendency for the contradiction or relation of dependence to grow more intense, that capital is driven to subordinate social practice more and more intensely.

which its existence depends.[34] The inherent incapacity of capital to free itself from its dependence on labour constitutes its fragility. It is this that makes it not a mountain but a volcano. Monetary instability is the smoke that shows us the intensity of the volcanic activity.

V

The Zapatista uprising took place in a world characterised by financial instability. The question is not whether the Zapatista action "caused" or did not "cause" the devaluation. The point is rather that the fragility of the capitalist financial system is such that the Zapatista action did precipitate a flight of capital that led to the devaluation of the peso, with dramatic consequences for the finances of the whole world.

Mexico was probably the most concentrated expression of the world fiction of a capitalism increasingly based on debt. In the previous years Mexico had become an important focal point of the world tension between value and its monetary representation, between the reality and appearance of accumulation. The huge inflow of (speculative) money capital into Mexico in the years prior to 1994 had bolstered an exchange rate that did not reflect the generation of profits in the country (i.e., the level of exploitation of the workers in Mexico). This inflow, however, cannot be seen as a peculiarly Mexican phenomenon: rather it was just one expression of the separation between money and production at the world level. The separation between money and production means precisely that: that the money will flow to the part of the world where it has good prospects for rapid expansion, irrespective of the productive base. The autonomisation of the financial markets implies that the gap between money and production will be concentrated with particular intensity in one part of the world (or one particular currency) or another. The fictional basis of capital accumulation is worldwide, but its geographical impact is constantly shifting with the spatial flow of capital. In the years before the devaluation, Mexico had become one of the most important centres in the world of the tension implied in the fictional base of accumulation. The bubble bursting

---

34 There seems little reason to draw sharp distinctions between the different forms, calling one class struggle and another not. Clearly there are differences in the extent to which different forms of insubordination affect the reproduction of capital, but these differences are neither abrupt nor evident.

in Mexico does not mean an end to that tension but simply that it moves on to somewhere else (East Asia, for example).

The fact that the country that was one of the most fragile points in the world financial system was also the location of one of the most important revolutionary movements in recent years is not mere chance. The Mexican state's policy of encouraging the inflow of capital in whatever form was part of its attempt to overcome its declining legitimacy. The more manifest the instability of the political regime, particularly after January 1, 1994, the more desperate the measures taken by the state to maintain the flow of capital into the country.[35] In other words, although it is not necessarily the case, the rise of political insubordination, far from frightening capital away in the first place, may generate, through state policies, conditions that are particularly favourable for the short-term expansion of capital. The more unstable a political system, the greater the lengths to which it will go to attract the inflow of capital necessary to bolster its position; the more desperate capital is to find a means of self-expansion, the more likely it is to rush into risky situations, in the hope that it will be able to get out again before the crash comes. In a capitalist system increasingly dependent on the expansion of credit (and on the autonomisation of the financial system that such a development implies), there will be a tendency—at least—for radical insubordination (or revolutionary activity) and the most vulnerable points of the world financial system to coincide. The link between the Zapatista action of December 19 and the "systemic risk" to world capitalism is not just a one-off event but suggests a growing interconnection between rebellious or revolutionary activity, on the one hand, and the financial instability not just of particular countries but of world capitalism, on the other.[36]

---

35 Both the instability of the regime and the inflationary creation of money were also greatly increased as a result of the assassination of the ruling party's presidential candidate, Luis Donaldo Colosio, on March 23, 1994.

36 Marxist debate in the early part of the century was much concerned with the relation between revolution and what was seen as capitalism's tendency toward collapse. In the events of December 19–20, 1994, and their sequel, the two seem to come together in a remarkably clear fashion: on the one hand, the well-planned action of a revolutionary group, on the other, a wave of turbulence that illustrates the fragility of the existing structure of world capitalism. Revolutionary action and capitalist instability come together, but it is not clear what can be learned from all this about the possibility of revolution (or the collapse of capitalism).

What are the implications of this coming together of revolutionary activity and monetary instability? The link between the Zapatista action and the monetary instability can be understood in two quite different ways. It can be seen as a remarkable display of the power of insubordination: the action of rebels in the jungles of Chiapas leads to political instability in Japan, and so on. It can also be seen as a remarkable display of the power of capital: money and its turbulent movement appears to impose severe limits on what can be achieved within any national (or otherwise territorially defined) area. Both understandings are correct: both moments are present, the power of insubordination and the power of capital. Since the future of the world (and in this moment the future of Mexico) lies in the interplay of these two moments, it is worth focusing on each of them before returning to the question of their interrelation.

VI

The Zapatistas frightened capital away. Capitalists do not like insubordination. They do not like struggles that put the security of their investments at risk. When profits are threatened by insubordination, capital flees. When the government linked the devaluation of the peso to the action of the Zapatistas, this was not simply a ploy to discredit the Zapatistas: its basis was the fundamental and obvious point that human dignity and capital are mutually incompatible. The devaluation resulted from the fact that capital fled from the Zapatistas' dramatic act of insubordination.

Capital might not have fled from Mexico if conditions otherwise had been such as to offer good prospects of profit. The flight of capital from the Zapatistas revealed that there was a more general problem for capital in Mexico, namely that labour in Mexico was not productive enough to generate the sort of profits that would entice capital to stay in spite of the Zapatistas. The flight of capital laid bare the inadequacy of the exploitation of labour in Mexico, the inadequacy of the subordination of labour. The flight of capital made clear the continuity between the open subordination of the Zapatistas (and others) and the inadequacy of the subordination of workers more generally in Mexico to the demands of capital. (Hence the importance of parties and dancing in the Zapatista discourse: parties as the symbol that we are still human, that we have not yet been reduced by capital to total subordination).

Capital was frightened away by the Zapatistas, but it was fleeing from the combination of the insubordination and non-subordination of labour in Mexico: its flight expressed the unity of the antagonism (overt and latent) of labour (in its broadest sense) to capital. It "recomposed" labour, brought together resistances to capital that had appeared to be separate.[37]

This recomposition took place in the first instance in the area defined by the currency, the Mexican state. However, the flight of capital quickly became a much more general flight from countries in which the conditions of profitable expansion did not seem sufficiently secure. The specific fright of capital provoked by the Zapatistas became a much more general and ill-defined fright. Capital fled toward "quality," and away from all those areas in which the combination of insubordination and non-subordination appeared to threaten the security of profits. In many cases the condition of budgetary deficits was taken as the measure of the stability of capitalist control. In the case of Sweden, for example, the flight of capital was prompted by the government's inability to reduce its budgetary deficit, which in turn reflected the strength of popular resistance to cuts in welfare provision. The worldwide "flight to quality" provoked by the Zapatista action was a flight from all those countries in which the combination of insubordination and non-subordination (real or suspected) put the expansion of capital at risk. The recomposition of labour, or bringing together of resistances to capital that had appeared separate, took place not just within Mexico but throughout the world. The devaluation of the Swedish krona, for example, resulted not just from the struggle of workers and welfare recipients in Sweden against the cuts in the welfare budget but from the coming together of these struggles with the flight of capital provoked by the Zapatistas. The financial crisis in Sweden thus expressed the unity of the struggles of the Zapatistas in the Lacandon Jungle and those of single parents (say) in Stockholm.

The relation between the Zapatista action and the turbulence of the world's financial markets is not an external one. It is not that the *subjective*

---

37 In an interview published recently, Marcos comments on the financial crisis: "I believe that our actions opened something like a hole in a pressure cooker, that's why it explodes. But in Mexico, in concrete, things are overturned because the poverty of the indigenous comes to be shared by millions of Mexicans. Everything is generalised. The government really had a focus of unrest that it had to wipe out. Or rather, the indigenous were no longer simply people to sympathise with; now they could become comrades in struggle for many people who now started to have the same standard of living, in the same conditions of poverty": Le Bot, *El Sueño*, 256.

action of the Zapatistas takes place in an *objectively* unstable structure. Rather, the extent of the turbulence and financial instability indicates the extent of insubordination and non-subordination throughout the world.[38] The Zapatista action punctured the fiction of subordination not only in Mexico but across the planet.

The puncturing of a fiction, in a world in which capital accumulation is increasingly based upon a fiction, is central to the "uniting of dignities," to any recomposition of labour. The idea of exposing a fiction, of attacking an untruth, has been central to the Zapatista discourse from the beginning. Dignity and truth have been put forward as the central values of the rebellion. The word of the EZLN is, they say, the word of those "armed with truth and fire." Wearing a mask is a way of making themselves seen and drawing attention to the fact that it is the other side, the side of Power, that hides behind a mask of falsehood. The lesson that the technocrat-politicians have learned in their postgraduate studies abroad is always the same: "'Pretend that you know what you are doing.' 'This is the fundamental axiom of the politics of power in neoliberalism,' their master has told them."[39]

The wave of monetary turbulence set off by the Zapatista action is thus the integration of the Zapatista insubordination into the insubordination (and non-subordination) of the world. That this wave of insubordination

---

38 Non-subordination and insubordination can, of course, be understood only in relation to the changing subordination demanded by capital.

39 In a communiqué of July 17, 1995, Durito, the beetle, tells Marcos: "Let us suppose now that a young generation of 'junior politicians' has studied abroad how to 'save' this country in the only form in which they can conceive of its salvation, that is to say, ignoring its history and attaching it to the tail of the express train of human brutality and imbecility, capitalism. Let us suppose that we gain access to the notebooks of these students without a homeland. What do we find? Nothing! Absolutely nothing! Are they bad students? Not at all! They are good, fast students. But it turns out that they have learned only one single lesson in each of the courses they have taken. The lesson is always the same: 'Pretend that you know what you are doing.' 'This is the fundamental axiom of the politics of power in neoliberalism,' their master has told them. They ask 'And what is neoliberalism, dear teacher?' The master does not respond, but I can deduce from his perplexed look, his reddened eyes, the saliva dribbling though the cracks in his lips, and the obvious wear of his right sole, that the master does not dare tell his pupils the truth. And the truth is, as I discovered, that neoliberalism is the chaotic theory of economic chaos, the stupid exaltation of social stupidity, and the catastrophic political implementation of catastrophe": *La Jornada*, July 20, 1995.

was seen as creating a "systemic risk" at a moment when anti-capitalist struggle is so often proclaimed to be dead is eloquent testimony to the fact that insubordination is very much alive and shaping the world far beyond the confines of the Lacandon Jungle. The monetary resonance of the Zapatistas is just part of the extraordinary resonance of their cry of "¡Ya basta!"

The most important thing about the world financial instability that flowed from the Zapatista action of December 19 is that it was a dramatic illustration of the enormous power of insubordination (and non-subordination) of labour (human dignity, in other words) throughout the world. This should be shouted from the rooftops, again and again and again.

VII

The Zapatistas shook the financial world. But nobody shouted "Bravo! Bravo! More! More!" Why not? Because the flight of capital from the Zapatistas was simultaneously a counterattack by capital. The same instability that shows the power of insubordination also shows the power of subordination. If insubordination showed its power by frightening capital away, capital showed its power by fleeing.

In some ways the flight of capital has been a more effective display of the power of capital against insubordination than any military intervention.[40] Rates of exploitation have risen sharply. It is hard to know how many people have died as a result of the flight of capital but presumably more than have been killed by direct military action against the Zapatistas since the beginning of 1994. The movement of money has acted with particular ruthlessness as capital's "police force."[41]

The flight of capital makes clear the reality of a society in which the production of material wealth is based on the subordination of labour. In such a society, insubordination brings material costs. In a society based on the crushing of dignity, the proclamation of human dignity means

---

40 The flight of capital from the Zapatistas and from the general inadequacy of the subordination of labour in Mexico had a dramatic effect on the living standards of most people in the country. Unemployment rose sharply, the purchasing power of wages fell equally sharply, supermarket sales fell by about 30 per cent in a year, indices of suicides and violence rose, as did the numbers of people living in extreme poverty.

41 On money as capital's police force, see Bonefeld, Brown, and Burnham, *A Major Crisis*.

material loss. It is not so much administrative action that imposes these costs as the simple movement of money: money moves away from insubordination, away from the proclamation of dignity. This is what makes a national revolution, or indeed "national liberation," very difficult to imagine. Either the state in question tries to make itself attractive to capital, in which case there is no revolution or liberation at all, or else considerable material loss results. The only way in which the antagonism between money and liberation could be overcome would be through the liberation of the entire world, that is, the abolition of money.

It is now clear why nobody shouted "More! More!" when the Zapatistas frightened capital away. The movement of money confronts the Zapatistas with two major obstacles. First, it would be very difficult for them or their supporters to say openly that their action had brought material loss to the people of Mexico. Second, it is difficult for a movement that presents itself as one of national liberation to say that national liberation is a chimera, that the only possibility is world liberation (although their political practice has become increasingly oriented toward world liberation). However, if it is not said that the flight of capital is the expression of the power of insubordination, then there is a danger that the movement of capital appears as an unavoidable necessity, a law of nature to which one must submit. The wave of monetary turbulence in the world then appears not as the monetary expression of a wave of insubordination but as a series of national problems, the result in each case of mistaken economic policies or the weakness of governments in conceding too much to social pressures. If the movement of money is not confronted as the expression of the world power of the enemy, capital, then the only possibility is to bow to the great principle of capitalist rule in the 1980s and 1990s: There Is No Alternative.

The world monetary turbulence not only recomposes labour: it simultaneously decomposes it. Like a great flash of lightning, it shows the interconnections and then leaves us in a more profound darkness than ever. The flight of capital to "quality" establishes a unity between struggles in different parts of the world, but it does so in a form that simultaneously conceals (or fetishises) that unity. While it is certainly true that the devaluation of the Swedish krona results from the combined impact of the action of the Zapatistas and the struggles of welfare recipients in Sweden, the form in which the unity of action is established simultaneously makes the connection invisible. Money divides in the process of uniting. Within Mexico too, the devaluation is the combined result of the insubordination of the Zapatistas and the insubordination and non-subordination of labour in general, but it does not appear as such. On the contrary, the devaluation presents itself as the intervention of a cruel reality, which must be accepted, making struggle pointless.

The monetary response to the Zapatista action is at least as violent as a direct military response. The political effect, however, is very different. Money is a far more effective weapon for capital than brute force. Where the open military intervention of the first days of January 1994 and of February 9, 1995 had the effect of stimulating struggle against the Mexican government in Mexico and throughout the world, the effect of the monetary assault has been, tendentially at least, to weaken struggle. Money has always been the principal form of capitalist rule, military force its uncouth henchman. But that is now truer than ever. Neoliberalism is the naked rule of money, a rule so effective, so violent, that military dictatorships have become increasingly redundant: the violence of the everyday "democratic" policing to enforce respect for the increasingly obscene rule of money is sufficient.[42] To attack neoliberalism (not a policy but the capitalism of the late twentieth century) is to attack the rule of money: not of the banks, not of a group of finance capitalists or of a political party or clique, but of money. Until money (capital) is attacked, no seizure of power, no electoral victory will eliminate its violence. Until money itself is attacked, no liberation, either national or otherwise, is possible.

VIII

Where does all this leave us? Any reflection on the world today seems at moments to be filled with hope but more often to be full of horror. Those of us who insist on hoping, who insist on thinking that there must be some way of getting away from the horrors that confront us on every side, some

---

42 The unity of money and violence is illustrated by the Mexican government's military intervention against the Zapatistas on February 9, in response (in part at least) to the anxieties of bankers after the devaluation of December 1994. The pressures to which it was responding are illustrated by a January 13, 1995, internal memorandum of the Chase Manhattan Bank that said, "While Chiapas, in our opinion, does not pose a fundamental threat to Mexican political stability, it is perceived to be so by many in the investment community. The government will need to eliminate the Zapatistas to demonstrate effective control of the national territory and security policy," quoted by Cockburn and Silverstein, "War and the Peso," 18.

way of creating a radically different world, often feel that we are screaming in a padded cell, insane and without echo. To know that we are, rather,
the fire in the volcano, gives us no certainty but it does give substance to
our hope.

The reality of capitalism today is an increasingly vicious reality,
within which political (i.e., state-oriented) options are more and more
restricted and more and more tightly policed by the movement of money.
The reality of capitalism is, however, at the same time a volcanic, fragile
reality. Its fragility is concentrated in the fragility of the world monetary
system: a fragility that is grounded in the increasingly fictitious character
of capital accumulation. Lipietz poses the issue strikingly in terms of an
"image which has been haunting me since the crisis began—the image
of a cartoon character who has gone over the edge of a cliff and carries
on walking on thin air. This seemed to me to illustrate the position of
the world economy, which continues to work 'on credit' while the actual
ground on which postwar growth has been based . . . crumbles beneath
it." Lipietz himself is concerned to ensure that the character does not go
"crashing into the abyss." Certainly that has been the main preoccupation
of international economic policy coordination over the last twenty years
at least. At times the salvation of the cartoon character has been envisaged in terms of setting his "feet back on solid ground."[43] That was what
was attempted by the pursuit of tight monetary policies before the "debt
crisis" of 1982. This caused both enormous hardship and almost sent the
character into the abyss. More often, salvation has been understood as
keeping the character afloat through the increased expansion of credit.
The international bailout of the peso with $50 billion (and, more recently,
the international packages of "support" for the East Asian economies)
is an example of this policy. The problem with this approach is that it
reproduces the fragility and volatility of capitalism on an expanded scale,
together with all the misery and starvation that accompanies it. The so-
called discipline of the market is increasingly mediated through the arbi-
trary (and corrupt) state regulation of punishment, as states choose which
debtors should suffer annihilation (either as companies or as physical

---

43 Alain Lipietz, *The Enchanted World: Inflation, Credit and World Crisis* (London:
Verso, 1985), 5–7.

people) and which must be saved in the interests of keeping the cartoon character afloat, in accord with the "too big to fail doctrine."[44]

But what do *we* want to do with the cartoon character, we who hope for a different world, we who are screamed at by the horrors of the present? Do we put its feet on the ground, keep it afloat, or send it crashing into the abyss?

Push it into the abyss.

There is no other way to imagine the end of capitalism and the beginnings of a society in which human existence is not ruled by the god of money. Movements that aim to transform society radically will *always* provoke monetary upheaval as capital flees and counterattacks-by-fleeing. Revolutionary attacks on capital will *always* provoke tremors that appear to be internal to capital. The only possible way of thinking about a revolution is in terms of capitalism being eaten from the inside as it is eaten from the outside: monetary instability joining with overt revolutionary action to produce change.

But would monetary collapse not bring about the barbarism of which socialists have always warned? Is the barbarism of collapse the only alternative to the barbarism of capitalism?

The quotation that stands at the beginning of this essay suggests another option. Marcos suggests there that it is the "uniting of dignities" that has the capacity to bring about the downfall of money, "its rapid transition to part of a nightmare that is coming to an end, the conclusion of a historical phase ruled by arrogance and stupidity." The argument in this essay has been that it is indeed the "uniting of dignities," in other words, the coming together of the insubordination and non-subordination of labour, that is behind the instability of money. It is this uniting of dignities that makes it possible to conceive that the cartoon character, Money, crashing into the abyss would be the liberation rather than the damnation

---

44 See, for example, John Plender in the *Financial Times*, February 13, 1995: "The US banking system is uniquely prone to moral hazard as a result of excessively generous deposit insurance and a 'too big to fail' doctrine for dealing with troubled banks. The urge to extend safety nets to all-comers has now been extended to foreign bond fund investors on the implausible argument that a Mexican default would have threatened the whole financial system. What better way could there be to encourage fiscal profligacy and more trouble in banking with sovereign borrowers."

of humanity, the liberation of the human potential to solve the world's problems rather than its annihilation.

The uniting of dignities has not taken the form of the development of a world revolutionary party, as envisaged by revolutionaries in the earlier part of the century. It is now clear that the myriad ways in which people fight for their humanity cannot so easily defined, and that the "uniting" of their dignities is a far less structured and far less visible uniting than had previously been foreseen. Rather than the discipline that a party requires, it seems far more realistic to think of the "uniting of dignities" as a "network of voices that, in the face of the deafness of Power, chooses to speak to itself, knowing itself to be one and many, knowing itself to be equal in its aspiration to listen and make itself heard, recognising itself to be different in the tonalities and levels of the voices which form it."[45]

This may seem insane, as it always has to politicians and their theorists, just as the totally absurd uprising of the Zapatistas on January 1, 1994, was insane.

Yet they made the Power of Money tremble.

Yet they made the volcano belch forth smoke and ashes.

References

Bonefeld, Werner. "Monetarism and Crisis." In *Global Capital, National State and the Politics of Money*, edited by Werner Bonefeld and John Holloway, 35–68. London: Macmillan, 1995.

Bonefeld, Werner, Alice Brown, and Peter Burnham. *A Major Crisis*. London: Dartmouth, 1995.

Bonefeld, Werner, Richard Gunn, John Holloway, and Kosmas Psychopedis, eds. *Open Marxism*, vol. 3. London: Pluto, 1995.

Bonefeld, Werner, and John Holloway, eds. *Global Capital, National State and the Politics of Money*. London: Macmillan, 1995.

Bonefeld, Werner, and John Holloway [1995a]. "Conclusion: Money and Class Struggle." In *Global Capital, National State and the Politics of Money*, edited by Werner Bonefeld and John Holloway, 210–27. London: Macmillan, 1995.

Brittan, Samuel. *The Economic Consequences of Democracy*. London: Temple Smith, 1977.

Cockburn, Alexander, and Ken Silverstein. "War and Peso." *New Statesman and Society*, February 1995, 24.

---

45 Closing speech by Marcos to the Intercontinental Meeting in La Realidad, July 1996: Subcomandante Marcos, "Discurso de clausura, Encuentro Intercontinental por la Humanidad y Contra el Neoliberalismo," *Chiapas*, no. 3 (1996), 106–16.

Congdon, Tim. *The Debt Threat.* Oxford: Blackwell, 1988.

Financial Times. October 31 1994; December 23, 1994; January 7, 1995; January 12. 1995; January 13, 1995; January 16, 1995; February 1, 1995; February 13, 1995; May 16, 1995, January 2, 1998.

El Financiero, December 23, 1994.

Grant, James. *The Trouble with Prosperity: A Contrarian's Tale of Boom, Bust, and Speculation.* New York: Times Books, 1996.

Harman, Chris. "Where Is Capitalism Going?" *International Socialism* No. 58 (1993).

Holloway, John. "The Abyss Opens: The Rise and Fall of Keynesianism." In *Global Capital, National State and the Politics of Money,* edited by Werner Bonefeld and John Holloway, 7–34. London: Macmillan, 1995.

Holloway, John. "Dignity's Revolt." In *Zapatista! Reinventing Revolution in Mexico,* edited by John Holloway and Eloína Peláez, 159–98. London: Pluto, 1998.

Holloway, John. "From Scream of Refusal to Scream of Power: The Centrality of Work." In *Open Marxism,* vol. 3, edited by Werner Bonefeld, Richard Gunn, John Holloway, and Kosmas Psychopedis, 155–81. London: Pluto, 1995a.

Holloway, John, and Eloína Peláez, eds. *Zapatista! Reinventing Revolution in Mexico.* London: Pluto, 1998.

International Monetary Fund. *International Capital Markets: Developments, Prospects and Policy Issues.* Washington, DC: IMF, 1995.

La Jornada, December 20, 1994; July 20, 1995.

Kaufman, Henry. *Interest Rates, the Markets, and the new Financial World.* London: Tauris, 1986.

Le Bot, Yvon. *El Sueño Zapatista.* Mexico City: Plaza y Janés, 1997.

Lipietz, Alain. *The Enchanted World.* London: Verso, 1985.

Magdoff, Harry, and Paul M. Sweezy. *Stagnation and the Financial Explosion.* New York: Monthly Review, 1987.

Marcos, Subcomandante. "Discurso de clausura, Encuentro Intercontinental por la Humanidad y Contra el Neoliberalismo." *Chiapas,* no. 3 (1996): 106–16.

Schlesinger, Arthur M. *The Age of Roosevelt: The Coming of the New Deal.* Cambridge, MA: Riverside, 1959.

Walter, Andrew. *World Power and World Money.* London: Harvester Wheatsheaf, 1993.

Warburton, Peter. *Debt and Delusion.* London: Penguin Books, 1999.

NINE

Where Is Class Struggle?

Where Is Class Struggle Today?

Perhaps the biggest argument against Marxist theory today is not that it is wrong in its criticism of capitalism but that it is wrong in insisting on the importance of class struggle. The evils of capitalism are plain for all to see, but where is the class struggle that Marxists keep talking about? Struggle certainly, struggle there is: the struggles of the antiglobalisation movement from Seattle to Genoa, the struggles of the Zapatistas in Mexico or of the landless peasants in Brazil, the struggles of women and gays against discrimination, the struggles to protect the environment, even the spectacular protest of the people who flew the planes into the World Trade Centre. Struggle is easy to see, but is it class struggle? Where has the labour movement been in the last twenty or thirty years? Certainly not leading the revolution. Is it not better then to stop talking about class struggle and to speak of new social actors or simply of "the multitude"?

This chapter will argue that class struggle has probably never been so vicious and violent as it is today.

The Existence of Capital Is Class Struggle

But no, we must go back before that. Why start with capital, why not with racism or patriarchy? Are there not lots of different types of oppression?

Let's not start with capital, then. Let's start with ourselves. We want to change the world. We want to change the world because it stinks, because it is obscenely unjust, because it is violent, because the way society is organised at the moment it looks as if humanity will probably destroy itself before very long. (If you don't want to change the world, go and read a different book.)

Changing the world implies doing. If we want to change society, then we must think of society not as-it-is but as something that people have made and that people can change. We must think of ourselves as doers not as beings. This is sometimes referred to as materialism, or even dialectical materialism: what Marx means by materialism is basically understanding society in terms of human doing, "sensuous human activity, practice" (First Thesis on Feuerbach, 1976, 3).

Doing is central to any revolutionary project, to any project of changing the world. That is why revolutionary thought means thinking of society in terms of doing. This is not just a call to action, to rushing out in the street and doing something. It means first trying to understand society (and our own repudiation of present society) in terms of the way that human doing, human activity, is organised.

When we think of our doing, our activity, one of the first things that strikes us is that it is social. It is difficult to think of any activity that does not depend on the doing of others, either now or in the past. I sit here writing and think of it perhaps as my great individual act, but I know that without the doing of the people who made the computer, installed the electricity, built the building, made the desk, wrote all those other books that have influenced me, I could not be writing what I am writing. The doing of others is always the precondition of our own doing, the means of our doing; and our doing becomes the means of the doing of others. Our doing is always part of a social flow of doing.

Our doing is not only social, it is also projective. An aspect of our doing is the aim to change, to make things other than they are. Our doing includes a projection beyond that which is. This projection-beyond is fundamental to any idea of changing the world. For Marx, it was also the characteristic that distinguished humans from animals—or from machines, we might add. In a famous passage in *Capital*, he contrasts the architect and the bee: "A spider conducts operations that resemble those of a weaver, and a bee puts to shame many an architect in the construction of her cells. But what distinguishes the worst architect from the best of bees is this, that the architect raises his structure in imagination before he erects it in reality. At the end of every labour-process, we get a result that already existed in the imagination of the labourer at its commencement. He not only effects a change of form in the material on which he works, but he also realises a purpose of his own" (1965, 178).

What happens to doing in capitalism? Somebody comes along, takes what we have done and says, "This is mine." The capitalist (and the feudal lord and the slave-owner before him, but let us focus on the capitalist) appropriates that which we have done, the product of our work.

This shatters doing. The capitalist, by appropriating the product, shatters the social flow of doing. (Oh, he may conceivably be a very nice man, or possibly woman, and this is not a very nice thing to do, but if he doesn't do it, he won't be a capitalist: that's what Marx means by talking of capitalists as the "personifications of capital.") What we have done becomes his property. He now owns the means of doing of others—the means of production, in other words. In order for others to do (and to survive) they must get access to the means of production: this they do by selling their labour power (their capacity to do) to the owner of the means of production. Their doing is now converted into labour at the command of the capitalist, labour that produces commodities that are, of course, the capitalist's property and that he can sell on the market.

The direct connection between our doing and the doing of others is broken. Of course, our doing is still part of a social flow of doing, but it does not appear that way. Now my writing appears as an individual act in which I use a number of *things* (computer, electricity, desk, and so on), for which I have paid money, commodities that I buy on the market. Our doing is social—but indirectly social.

The social flow of doing is broken, and so too is the projective character of doing. It is now the capitalist, the owner of the means of production to whom the worker sells her labour power, who decides what the worker will do. The conception or projection is now the activity of the capitalist, the execution is left to the worker. With that, the worker is reduced to the status of a bee, having been deprived of the projection that is the distinctive character of humans. This does not just happen once, it is a repeated process. Since the capitalist appropriates the product of the labour, the worker leaves the labour process just as poor as she entered, just as dependent on the kindness of the capitalist in employing her the next day. The capitalist, on the other hand, gets richer and richer, since the product produced by the worker is worth more than what the capitalist has paid her for her labour power. The capitalist, in other words, exploits the worker, extracts more value from the worker than he pays her.

So What?

We started with interesting things like the Zapatistas and the World Trade Center, and now the argument seems to be dragging us into the factory, dragging us toward some sort of economic theory of society. That's the problem with Marxism, isn't it?

No, you didn't understand. Or perhaps I didn't explain. Doing is not in itself economic. It is lying in bed, making dinner, eating, writing articles, doing essays, making love, going on a demonstration, making a chair, producing electricity, making a car, whatever. It is the existence of capitalism that defines a major part of our doing as labour, as an "economic" activity. It is the fact that our only access to the means of survival is through money and our only way of getting money is by selling our labour power and turning a big part of our daily doing into labour at the command of others—that is what puts "economics" at the centre of our lives. But the critique of capitalism is not an economic critique, it is necessarily a critique of economics. That is why Marx in *Capital* did not develop an alternative economics but a critique of economics (or a critique of political economy). The struggle is to emancipate doing from labour, life from economics. That is why our analysis cannot start from labour but must begin with doing, "sensuous human activity, practice."

Doing in capitalism is a shattered, fragmented, separated process. "Separation," says Marx, is the "real generation process of capital" (1972, 422). Capital is the separation of the vast majority of people from the means of doing (means of production), the separation of the product from the producers, the separation of people from purposive social activity (their "species-being," as Marx puts it in the 1844 *Manuscripts*), the separation of people from one another, the separation of "labour" from other forms of activity. This separation affects absolutely every aspect of our lives. The doing that is separated off from labour is affected, for it is defined as leisure, as secondary, as not very serious—"I don't do anything, I'm just a housewife," or "I don't do anything at the moment, I'm unemployed." The doing that creates the conditions for the doing of others is now seen as producing "things" for others to buy. The relations between people thus become refracted through things; they become reified or fetishised, as Marx puts it in the first chapter of *Capital*. The way in which we relate to the doing of others is through the exchange of things. Social relations acquire the form of things (such as money, commodities, capital, the state) that we neither recognise as forms of social relations nor as the product of our own doing. Fetishism does not refer just to the economic, to the appearance of social relations in economic forms, but to every aspect of society, every aspect of the way in which we see our own lives and our relations to others. Every aspect of our doing is transformed by that fundamental rupture of the social flow of doing, the separation process that is capital.

And how does the separation take place? Through struggle, of course. It does not take place automatically. Think of what the capitalist says to us each day. He says, "All of these wonderful things that you see around you, all these things that you would like to have in order to survive, all these things that you would like to enjoy, all of that is private property, all that is mine. If you want to enjoy any of these things, you can do so by earning money. But in order to get money, you must give up any idea of spending your days doing what you like: you must come and labour for me, and if you do what I tell you, I shall give you money so that you can buy some of these things. But, mind you, I shall only give you enough money to keep you going for a short time, tomorrow you must come back and labour for me again. And of course I shall employ you only as long as I manage to exploit you successfully and make a profit from employing you." He says all this as though it were obvious, but of course it is not. Think of the poor capitalist. In order to carry through his existence as a capitalist, he must persuade or force us to accept it when he says, "This is mine"; he must force us to respect his private property. This is not done easily: it requires the services of millions of police and security guards, not to mention teachers, social workers, and parents. Then he must persuade or force us to accept the horrifying, absurd idea that we should turn our daily doing into labour under his command. In general terms, he does this by protecting his private property, but he still has to get us up early in the morning (never an easy task, especially when the prospect is going to work at the command of others) and convince us to go to work, do what he commands, and do it efficiently (more efficiently than his fellow capitalists, with whom he has to compete).

All this is not easy. It is made more complicated by the fact that we are not slaves or serfs. We are free. "Ha ha!" you laugh, "free to obey the command of the capitalist." Yes, certainly, but also, as a result of the struggles of slaves and serfs, really free in a way that is sometimes inconvenient for the capitalist. He cannot stop us from going and selling our labour power to a different capitalist if we get tired of him. He also cannot (usually) shoot us or flog us if we do not obey his commands at work. In other words, unlike feudal lords, capitalists require the support of an apparently external instance in order to apply the sort of violence that is required to maintain a system of exploitation. This is the state. The separation of state and society, the political and the economic, is another, very important aspect of the separation process that is capital. The state, as part of the process of separation, regulates the process of separation as best it can: it protects the separation of done from doing, the "this is mine!" of private property that ruptures everything. All systems of exploitation are armed robbery; what is peculiar about capitalism is that the person who holds the arms is distinct from the person who does the robbing.

All of this is struggle. Of course it is. It is struggle over what we think, how we act, over how we get up in the morning, and therefore over what time we go to bed and what we do in bed; it is the struggle of the alarm clock, as we throw it at the wall, and then still get up to go and sell our labour power. It is an extremely violent struggle in which thousands and thousands of people die each day, because they are cut off from the flow of doing and starve, because of the repression against those who do not accept the "this is mine!" proclaimed by the capitalists, because what they are commanded to do by capital is dangerous. It is a struggle that comes in the first place from them, from the capitalists. If it were up to us, we would lie in bed or potter about all day or dedicate ourselves with passion to whatever we like to do. It is they who do not leave us in peace. It is they who say, "Get up out of bed and come to labour for us—or starve, if you prefer." The struggle, then, is between two ways of doing, two forms of social relations. Capital is the imposition on our lives of a certain form of doing, a certain form of relating to one another. Capital is the struggle both to transform our doing into labour and also, once we are in the workplace, to get us to work as capital commands.

And of course we struggle back. We struggle back because we are not yet machines. We struggle back by throwing the alarm clock at the wall, by going to bed late, even when we know it will impair our efficiency at work the next day. We struggle back by giving higher priority to playing with our children than to producing profit. We struggle back by fighting for higher wages at work or by fighting for more acceptable conditions.

We struggle back when we demonstrate against the misery created by the imposition of private property. We struggle back by projecting beyond capitalism, by dreaming of a better society, a society in which we ourselves will decide what we do. We struggle in the workplace and outside the workplace. We struggle for a different way of doing, a different form of social relations.

This, Then, Is Class Struggle

It is class struggle not because we wear cloth caps. It is class struggle not because we think of ourselves as being left wing, but because we live and want to live: if class struggle were exclusive to the Left or the consciously militant, there would be no hope. It is class struggle not because we want to be the working class, but because we don't want to be working class. On our part, it is struggle not for being a class but against being a class. It is capital that classifies us. It is capital that says to us each day, "You are without property, you must come and work for us; and then you will go home without property and come back the next day, and so on for the rest of your life, and so on for the lives of your children and of their children." It is capital that ensures that each day what is produced in the factory is not just commodities but two classes. As Marx puts it, "capitalist production, therefore, under its aspect of a continuous connected process, of a process of reproduction, produces not only commodities, not only surplus-value, but it also produces and reproduces the capitalist relation; on the one side the capitalist, on the other the wage-labourer" (1965, 578). Capitalist production produces classes, imposes discipline and regimentation, forces our doing into the narrow band of labour that produces profit for the capitalist (or labour that supports capitalist profitability, in the case of state employment). Capital is grey. We are the rainbow, fighting for a world in which doing becomes free, liberated from the bonds of value production, from the chains of profit.

The existence of capital is class struggle: the daily repeated separation of people from the social flow of doing; the daily repeated enforcement of private property; the daily repeated transformation of doing into labour at the command of capital; the daily repeated seizure of the products of that labour. It is class struggle, but it does not appear as such. It does not appear to be class struggle (or indeed struggle at all) because of the very nature of the struggle itself. Capital's struggle is to separate doers from the social flow of doing, but that very separation means that people no longer understand themselves as doers or as social. The separation means that people appear as individuals and as beings rather than as doers. The more successful capitalist class struggle is, the more invisible it becomes: people are transformed from doers bound together by the community of their doing into free and equal individuals tied together by external institutions such as the state. Capitalist class struggle takes place through apparently neutral forms, such as property, money, law, and the state. These are all ways in which capital as a form of doing is imposed upon our lives. Capital does not say, "We are going to exploit you, we are going to force you to labour for us until you crawl home exhausted at the end of the day, and then we are going to force you to come back and back for the rest of your life." No, capital simply says a number of key words: "Respect private property, the money, the law." When it says, "Respect private property," it means, "Stand aside while we separate you from the means of doing and of survival." "Respect money" means, "Just let us get on with shattering all social relations, with mediating all relations between people through money." And respecting the law means that we should give up all idea of shaping our own doing, that all activity must be made to conform with the acceptance of private property, that we must bow to an external force. Capitalist class struggle comes clothed in liberal theory.

Capital cannot stand still. Under feudalism, the relations of exploitation were more or less stable: what the lord demanded of his serfs did not vary very much over time. It is different with capital. Capital is driven forward constantly by its "were-wolf's hunger for surplus-labour" (Marx 1965, 243). The fact that capital is fragmented into many distinct capitalist units (companies), each in competition with the other, each depending for its survival on being able to exploit its workers more effectively than the other, means that capital can never stand still, that it is constantly driven forward to intensify the exploitation of labour. Intensifying exploitation means not only imposing tighter discipline in the factory but creating the conditions in society (that is, the world) that make this exploitation easier. This means subordinating every aspect of life more and more tightly to the aims of value production. More and more intensely, every aspect of life becomes a battleground for the imposition of capital, a battleground on which we resist and try to defend and develop what we consider to be human or emancipatory. In education, for example, recent years have seen a huge assault in all parts of the world to bring teaching into line with the requirements of the market (that is, capital). Sometimes this takes the form of outright privatisation, allowing the content of education to be dictated directly by the market, sometimes it means the introduction of various forms of control within the state system of education to achieve the same end. Of course that assault meets constant resistance, either in the form of student strikes or, far less dramatically, in the form of teachers and students pushing beyond market requirements in the attempt to develop an honest and critical understanding. Sometimes it takes the form of teachers writing or recommending and students reading books like this one and suddenly finding that, just when they thought that class struggle was dead, they are in the middle of it.

Capital Has Been Particularly Violent in Recent Years

The violence stems from the curse that strikes all who try to dominate and exploit: they depend absolutely upon those whom they exploit and dominate. Capital depends for its existence on its capacity to transform doing into labour and to exploit that labour. Not just that: it depends for its existence, as we have just seen, not just on being able to maintain exploitation but on being able to constantly intensify it. It needs not just to subordinate society but to subordinate it more and more and more. If it cannot do so, it falls into crisis. The crisis tells capital that in order to survive, it must intensify subordination. In the 1970s, capital was manifestly in crisis, socially and economically. The weakness of subordination was obvious in society from the late 1960s: strikes, demonstrations, student movements, and revolutionary movements in many parts of the world. The failure to subordinate became economically manifest in the worldwide crisis that broke in 1973–74. The response of capital came in various forms (emphasis on a return to traditional family values and increasing police and in some cases military action), but above all it took the form of money and property.

Money has been central to class struggle over the last twenty-five years or so. First, in the early years of Reagan and Thatcher, tight monetary policies were applied as a means of reducing debt and imposing the discipline of the market. When this strategy threatened to destroy the world financial system, a more flexible approach to debt was adopted, allowing more spending to those (basically big companies, rich people, and rich states) whose well-being was considered essential to the health of capitalism, while using debt as a means of disciplining those who required discipline (basically the poor) or were simply disposable (a large part of the world's population is not an "industrial reserve army" for capital in any sense but simply a nuisance).

The extension of property has also been important to capital's struggle. Just as in the early days of capitalism landowners pushed the peasants off the land, enclosed it, and said, "This is mine," so capital is now enclosing more and more areas of human activity and saying, "This is my property—this is mine." The development of the concept of "intellectual property" has been crucial. Capital spends enormous sums of money on trying to assert its property rights over music, software, pharmaceutical discoveries, genes, and so on. In many parts of the world this extension of property rights has been carried out with a remarkable violence, as the traditional agricultural or medicinal knowledge of communities has been appropriated by capitalist enterprises that patent that knowledge without compensation, and then enforce their property rights against all comers, including the communities themselves.

Money and property are very violent forms of struggle. They have undoubtedly caused far more deaths in the last twenty years than all the wars fought in the last hundred. Thirty-five thousand children die each day simply because property and money separate them from what they need to survive. But they are also remarkably vulnerable forms of struggle. Money, especially in the form of debt, is contested all the time, both by those who will not pay and by those who point to the enormous destruction of human lives that the enforcement of debt involves. Property, especially intellectual property, is also contested almost universally—both by those who habitually copy software, videos, and CDs, and by those who campaign against the misery caused to AIDS sufferers, for example, by the protection of pharmaceutical patents. Both of these issues have been important features of the anti-capitalist movement of recent years.

Is this class struggle? Of course it is. Why not refer to it just as a multiplicity of struggles by new social actors or by the "multitude"? Because the concept of class points to the fact that behind the particular issues (AIDS in Africa, copying music from the internet, student loans, poverty in Latin America) there is a single struggle: the struggle by capital for profit, that is, the struggle by capital to exploit, to convert doing into labour and impose its form of social relations, and the struggle by us for a different form of doing, for a society based on the recognition of human dignity. Class points to that underlying unity in a way that the other categories do not. It also points to something else that is fundamental: there is no certainty that we shall win, that humanity will survive the attacks of capital, but the concept of class gives us hope, for it shows that capital depends upon us for its existence, that we are the only subjects.

References

Marx, Karl. *Capital*, vol. 1. Moscow: Progress Publishers, 1965.
Marx, Karl. *Theories of Surplus Value*, Part III. London: Lawrence and Wishart, 1972.
Marx, Karl. "Theses on Feuerbach," In Karl Marx and Frederick Engels, *Collected Works*, vol. 5. London: Lawrence and Wishart, 1976.

TEN

Zapatismo and the Social Sciences

Perhaps the saddest legacy that the twentieth century leaves us is disillusionment, loss of hope.[1]

If we look back at the debates of a hundred years ago, what is striking about them is their optimism. Look, for example, at the debate between Rosa Luxemburg and Eduard Bernstein on the question of reform or revolution: both sides in the debate took it for granted that of course the world could be made a better place, that a society based on justice could be created. The only question was how this should be done.

And then came the slaughter of two world wars, Stalin and Auschwitz and Hiroshima, Pol Pot, and the final blow for even the blindest of optimists, the collapse of the Soviet Union. Here in Latin America, the death of optimism has perhaps been even more bitter. All the enthusiasm of the revolutionary struggles of the 1960s and 1970s, where has it led? To a poor, isolated, and bureaucratic state in Cuba, and in the rest of Latin America to tragedy, to the slaughter of thousands of enthusiastic militants and innocent victims. True, the military dictatorships have gone, but what is left is not much better: corruption, poverty, and social inequality get worse all the time. All of that enthusiasm, for what? Why so many struggles? Why so many dead? We are here, of course, but what of our friends,

---

1   This is the text of a talk presented to the congress of SCOLAS (Southwest Council of Latin American Studies) in Puebla, Mexico, in March 2000. Many of the ideas presented here are developed in more general form in my book *Change the World without Taking Power* (London: Pluto, 2002), to be published shortly in Turkish by Iletsim.

what of the people we admired? While fortunately this is not part of the personal experience of most Europeans of my generation, it is for many Latin Americans. And for what?

For many, hope has evaporated from their lives, giving way to a bitter reconciliation with reality. It will not be possible to create the free and just society we hoped for, but at least we can vote for a centre or left-of-centre party, knowing quite well that it will not make any difference, but at least that way we will have some sort of outlet for our frustration.

We narrow our horizons and our expectations. Hope goes out of our lives, our work, even the way we think. "Revolution," even "emancipation," become ridiculous words. Well, of course, we are getting old. But that is not the problem. The problem is that the young too are old, many of them even older than the old. The problem is that the world is getting old.

The bitterness of history: that is what we have to live with. Like a thin grey mist, it penetrates everywhere. As social scientists, or academics in general, we are particularly affected. Disillusionment seeps into the core of the way we think, into the categories we use and the theories we espouse.

Foucault makes the point clearly in the first volume of his *History of Sexuality*, when he says, "The fear of ridicule or the bitterness of history prevents most of us from bringing together revolution and happiness . . . or revolution and pleasure."[2] And he makes fun of those who would speak of sex in terms of repression for constructing a discourse "in which the ardour of knowledge, the will to change the law and the expected garden of delights are joined together."

The bitterness of history and the fear of ridicule are two sides of the same process. Expectations are scaled down. The bitterness of history teaches us that it is now ridiculous to maintain the grand narrative of human emancipation, the grand narrative of hope for a society based on human dignity. The best we can do is think in terms of particular narratives, the struggle of particular identities for better conditions; the struggle of women, of blacks, of gays, of the indigenous but no longer the struggle of humanity for humanity. The fragmented worldview of post-modernism is a coming to terms with disillusionment.

---

2   Michel Foucault, *Histoire de la sexualité, vol. 1, La volonté de savoir* (Paris: Gallimard, 1976), 13.

Postmodernism is, of course, not the only way in which social scientists accept the bitterness of history. There are many other ways in which we accept a lowering of expectations, a closure of categories, a donning of conceptual blinkers. The conditions of academic life, the need to finish theses, the need to get jobs, the pressure to get grants all push in the same direction. Everything tells us to focus on our own specialised fragment of knowledge, to forget the complexity of the world.

Complexity becomes the great alibi, both scientifically and morally. The world is so complex that we can think of it only in terms of fragmented narratives or, much more common in spite of the postmodernist fashion, in terms of positive and positivist case studies. The world is so complex that I cannot accept any moral responsibility for its development. Morality retracts: morality is about being good to the people around me; beyond that immediate circle the world is too complex, the relation between actions and consequences too complicated. When I stop my car at the traffic lights (for most academics in Mexico are of the car-driving class), I give (or do not give) a peso to the people begging there, but I do not ask what it is about the organisation of the world that creates more and more misery and how that organisation can be changed. That sort of question has become both morally and scientifically ridiculous. What is the point of asking it when we know that there is no answer?

The problem with this reduction of expectations, this closure of categories, this narrowing of the concept of scientific work, is not the quality of research. The research done may be very good; the results may even be "correct" in a certain sense. But the problem of the social sciences is not correctness. The problem of the social sciences is complicity. Our research may be very good, but if we accept the fragmentation that arises from disillusionment, if we abandon in our work the exploration of the possibility of radical change in a world in which exploitation and misery become daily more intense and the dynamic of exploitation goes far beyond any particular "identities," do we not then become accomplices in the exploitation of person by person, in the destruction of humanity, and ultimately in the deaths of our dead?

We are all accomplices of course. Just by living in this society, we play an active part in the destruction of humanity. There is no innocence. But there is a big question about how we relate to our guilt, about how we fight against our own complicity.

It is into this world of disillusionment that the Zapatistas stepped on January 1, 1994. They came like prehistoric people emerging out of their caves, talking of dignity and humanity. Did they not see how ridiculous they were? Had they not learned from the bitterness of history? Did they not know that the age of revolution was finished, that grand narratives were a thing of the past? Did they not know what had happened to all the Latin American revolutions? Had they not heard of the fall of the Soviet Union? Had they not heard of Pol Pot?

They had, of course, heard of all that. And even so, they decided to confront the fear of ridicule. They knew all about the bitterness of history, nobody better. Yet they reminded us that there are different ways of relating to that bitterness. Theodor Adorno, German, Jewish, communist, returned from exile at the end of the war saying, "After Auschwitz one has to ask if it is possible to go on living."[3] Ernst Bloch, German, Jewish, communist, returned from exile at the end of the war saying, "Now is the time to learn to hope."[4] As if echoing the words of Bloch, the Zapatistas rose up in the most ridiculous circumstances, when all good revolutionaries were either dead or resting in their beds, and said, "Now is the time to hope, now is the time to fight for humanity." History is bitter, but the bitterness of history does not necessarily lead to disillusionment. It can also lead to rage and to hope and to dignity:

> Then that suffering that united us made us speak, and we recognised that in our words there was truth, we knew that not only pain and suffering lived in our tongue, we recognised that there is hope still in our hearts. We spoke with ourselves, we looked inside ourselves and we looked at our history: we saw our most ancient fathers suffering and struggling, we saw our grandfathers struggling,' we saw our fathers with fury in their hands, we saw that not everything had been taken away from us, that we had the most valuable, that which made us live, that which made our step rise above plants and animals, that which made the stone be beneath our feet, and we saw, brothers, that all that we had was *dignity*, and we saw that great was the shame of having forgotten it, and we saw that *dignity* was good for men to be men again, and dignity returned to live in our hearts,

---

3   Theodor W. Adorno, *Negative Dialectics* (London: Routledge, 1973), 362–63.
4   Ernst Bloch, *Das Prinzip Hoffnung* (Frankfurt am Main: Suhrkamp, 1985), 1.

and we were new again, and the dead, our dead, saw that we were new again, and they called us again to dignity, to struggle.[5]

Dignity, a central category in the Zapatista uprising,[6] is the rejection of disillusionment: the rejection, therefore, of that which underlies the current development of the social sciences. It should be clear, then, that to speak of "Zapatismo and the social sciences" is not to constitute Zapatismo as an *object* of the social sciences but to see Zapatismo rather as the *subject* of an attack on the mainstream development of the social sciences. To treat Zapatismo as an *object* of social scientific inquiry would be to do violence to the Zapatistas, to refuse to listen to them, to force them into categories that they are challenging, to impose upon them the disillusionment that they are rebelling against.

In other words, the Zapatistas are not a "they" but a "we." "*Detrás del pasamontañas estamos ustedes*" ("Behind the balaclavas are the we that are you"), as Major Ana María said in her speech of welcome to the Intergalactic meeting of 1996. Or, to quote Antonio García de León, "As more and more rebel communiqués were issued, we realised that in reality the revolt came from the depths of ourselves."[7] Although the EZLN is almost entirely indigenous, they have insisted from the beginning that their struggle is not just an indigenous struggle but a struggle for humanity: "For Humanity and against Neoliberalism," as the slogan of the Intergalactic Meeting proclaims. From the beginning, and apparently at the insistence of those communities in which indigenous traditions are most strongly rooted, they have rejected the particular narrative of ethnic liberation and insisted (just as though they had never read Foucault or Lyotard or Derrida) on the grand narrative of human emancipation. "Behind us we are you ... behind, we are the same simple and ordinary men and women who repeat themselves in every race, who paint themselves in every colour, who speak in every language, and who live in every place."[8]

---

5   EZLN, *La Palabra de los Armados de Verdad y Fuego*, vol. 1 (México, DF: Editorial Fuenteovejuna, 1994), 122.

6   On the concept of dignity, see John Holloway, "Dignity's Revolt," in *Zapatista! Reinventing Revolution in Mexico*, eds. John Holloway and Eloína Peláez (London: Pluto, 1998).

7   Antonio García de León, in EZLN, *Documentos y Comunicados: 1° de enero / 8 de agosto de 1994* (México, DF: Ediciones Era, 1994), 14.

8   "Discurso inaugural de la mayor Ana María," *Chiapas* no. 3, 103.

When we feel excited by the words of the Zapatista communiqués, it is not they who excite us, it is ourselves. To be excited by the Zapatistas is to be excited by our own refusal of disillusionment.

To reject disillusionment is not, however, to ignore the bitterness of history. It is not to pretend that Auschwitz never happened. It is not to ignore all the tragedy precipitated in the name of the struggle for communism. Zapatismo is the attempt to rescue revolution from the rubble of history, but the concept of revolution that comes out of the rubble can have meaning only as something new. As Subcomandante Marcos put it in a comment on the first year of the uprising:

> Something broke in this year, not just the false image of modernity sold to us by neoliberalism, not just the falsity of government projects, of institutional alms, not just the unjust neglect by the country of its original inhabitants but also the rigid schemes of a Left living in and from the past. In the midst of this navigating from pain to hope, political struggle finds itself naked, bereft of the rusty garb inherited from pain: it is hope that obliges it to look for new forms of struggle, that is, new ways of being political, of doing politics: *a new politics, a new political morality, a new political ethic is not just a wish, it is the only way to go forward, to jump to the other side.*[9]

What is it that is new about Zapatismo? This is where we really have to confront the fear of ridicule not only by mainstream social scientists but also by orthodox Marxists. The core of the newness of Zapatismo is the project of changing the world without taking power. "We want to change the world but not by taking power, not to conquer the world but to make it anew." How absurd! Or rather, how absurd it would be if it were not for the fact that Zapatismo articulates something that has been in the air for thirty years or more, a rejection of state-centred politics that has been characteristic of much of feminism and of many explorations on the Left throughout the world, a rejection of power-focused politics that has received a new impulse in recent months, with the events of the UNAM, of Seattle, of Prague, of Quito.

Zapatismo moves us decisively beyond the state illusion. By the state illusion I mean the paradigm that has dominated left-wing thought for at least a century. The state illusion puts the state at the centre of radical

---

9   Subcomandante Marcos, quoted by Rosario Ibarra, *La Jornada*, May 2, 1995, 22.

change. The state illusion understands revolution as winning state power and transforming society through the state. The famous debate between Rosa Luxemburg and Eduard Bernstein a hundred years ago established the terms that were to dominate thinking about revolution for most of the twentieth century. On the one hand, *reform*, on the other, *revolution*. Reform was a gradual transition to socialism, to be achieved by winning elections and introducing change by parliamentary means; revolution was a much more rapid transition, to be achieved by taking state power and quickly introducing radical change. The intensity of the disagreements concealed a basic agreement: both approaches focussed on winning state power and saw the transition to socialism exclusively in those terms. Revolution and reformism are both state-centred approaches. Marxist debate was framed by a narrow dichotomy. Approaches that fell outside this dichotomy were stigmatised as being anarchist. Until recently, Marxist theoretical and political debate has been dominated by these three classifications: revolutionary, reformist, anarchist.

The state illusion dominated the revolutionary experience through-out most of the twentieth century: not only the experience of the Soviet Union and China but also the numerous national liberation and guer-rilla movements of the 1960s and the 1970s. The focus on the state shaped the way in which left-wing organising was conceived. The form of the party, whether vanguardist or parliamentary, presupposes an orientation toward the state and makes little sense without it. The party is in fact the form of disciplining class struggle, of subordinating the myriad forms of class struggle to the overriding aim of gaining control of the state. The state illusion penetrates deep into the experience of struggle, privileging those struggles that appear to contribute to the winning of state power and allocating a secondary role or worse to those forms of struggle that do not.

If the state illusion was the vehicle of hope for much of the century, it increasingly became the assassin of hope as the century progressed. The failure of revolution was in reality the historical failure of a particular concept of revolution, the concept that identified revolution with control of the state.

At the same time as the historical failure of the state-centred concept of revolution was becoming obvious, the development of capitalism itself was destroying the basis of the state illusion. The increasingly direct sub-ordination of the state to capital (even more obvious in the case of social democratic governments than in the case of openly neoliberal ones) has closed the door to the hopes of radical reformists. It has become increasingly clear that the relation between state and capital can be understood only as a relation between national state and global capital (and global society) and not as a relation between national state and national capital, and that therefore states are not the centres of power that the state-centred theory of both Luxemburg and Bernstein assumed them to be.

The great contribution of the Zapatistas has been to break the connection between revolution and control of the state. While so many people throughout the world have concluded that because revolution through the state is not possible, revolution is not possible (and so we must conform), the Zapatistas in effect have said: "If revolution through the state is not possible, then we must think of revolution in a different way. We must break the identification of revolution with the taking of state power, but we must not abandon the hope of revolution because that hope is life itself."[10]

The state illusion is, however, just part of a greater illusion, what one might call the power illusion. This is the idea that changing society is a matter of conquering positions of power, or at least of becoming powerful in some way. It seems to me that the sense of the Zapatista project is quite different, not to become powerful but to dissolve relations of power. This is surely the implication of their constant insistence on the principle of "commanding obeying"[11] and on dignity not just as the aim of the struggle but as the organisational principle of the struggle.

The Zapatistas take us beyond the state illusion and beyond the power illusion. But what does this mean? What does a revolution look like that is not focussed on the taking of state power or on becoming powerful in some sense? Are we not in danger of falling into complete absurdity? Are they not leading us into insanity?

Here it becomes clear that it is a grave mistake to speak of the Zapatistas as "armed reformists," as some have done. What the Zapatista uprising makes clear is that after the collapse of the Soviet Union, after the murder of Che and the tragedy of the Latin American revolutions, the notion of revolution can be maintained only if the stakes are raised. The revolutions of the twentieth century failed because they aimed too

---

10   This is not a quotation. I am putting words in their mouths.
11   "*Mandar obedeciendo.*"

low, not because they aimed too high. The conception of revolution was too limited. It is completely inadequate to think of revolution in terms of winning the state or conquering power. Something far more radical is needed, a much more profound rejection of capitalism. "We walk," they say, "we do not run, because we are going far." But the path that they invite us to walk on is vertiginous indeed. They invite us to go on a dangerous, dizzying walk to who knows where. And we accept, because there is no alternative. We do not have to look far to see that humanity is destroying itself. We cannot give up hope, yet the only hope that is now imaginable is a hope that goes beyond the state illusion, beyond the illusion of power.

What, then, does revolution mean if it does not mean taking state power or even becoming powerful? The answer is simple: we do not know, we have to learn. "Revolution," as Comandante Tacho puts it, "is like going to take lessons in a school that has not even been built."[12]

In a school that has not been built yet, learning cannot be a question of repeating the lessons that teacher taught us. If we wish to share the excitement of such a school, then we are forced to be subjects. We are forced to construct our own path, with only the utopian star to guide us. In this, of course, we share in the experience of others who have tried to follow the same star, but the bitter experience of history means that the star is no longer quite the same. What does revolution mean now? What can it mean to dissolve power relations? How can we take part in the struggle to dissolve power relations not just in our teaching practices or in our everyday lives but in the categories we use?

To think in the non-existing school of Zapatismo is exciting but frightening. Gone are the certainties of the old revolutionaries. After Auschwitz, after Hiroshima, there can no longer be a concept of historical certainty. When humanity possesses the capacity to annihilate itself tomorrow, there can be no guarantee of a happy ending. As Adorno correctly stressed, we must reject the notion of a dialectic that reconciles everything in the end; we must think rather of the dialectic as a negative dialectic, a movement through negation with no guarantees, a negative movement of possibility.

It seems clear too that the concept of revolution can no longer be instrumental. Our traditional concept of revolution is as a means to achieve an end, and we know that in practice this has meant using people as a means to an end. If dignity is taken as a central principle, then people

---

12   Yvon Le Bot, *El Sueño Zapatista* (México, DF, Plaza & Janés, 1997), 191.

cannot be treated as means: the creation of a society based on dignity can only take place through the development of social practices based on the mutual recognition of that dignity. We walk, not in order to arrive at a promised land, but because the walking itself is the revolution. And if instrumentalism falls as a way of thinking, so too does the lineal time that is implicit in the traditional concept of revolution, the clear distinction between before and after. There is no question of first revolution, then dignity: dignity itself is the revolution.

We are into a very shaky world where there seems to be nothing very firm to hold on to. We are walking a path on which we wish that we had at least the security of a tightrope under our feet. And gradually we realise that the firmness that we at first look for is the firmness of the power against which we are rebelling. Power is the establishment of laws, of definitions, of classifications. In one of the Zapatista communiqués, Marcos puts words into the mouth of Power: Power says to the rebels: "Be ye not awkward, refuse not to be classified. All that cannot be classified counts not, exists not, is not."[13] Define yourselves—that has been the devil's temptation to the Zapatistas since the very beginning, the temptation that, up to now at least, they have been able to resist.

This does not mean that the laws, definitions, and classifications do not exist. Of course they exist because power exists, but our struggle is against them. Our struggle is not so much undefined as anti-definitional, the struggle to liberate doing and thinking from the boxes in which capitalist Power holds them prisoner. Our struggle, in other words, is critical, is anti-fetishistic.

Hope is uncertain and therefore frightening. Hope means a present that is open, filled with the possibility of dignity but also full of Auschwitz, Hiroshima, and Acteal not only as past monstrosities but as screaming auguries of a possible future. Not just Bloch but also Adorno. Disillusion, with its blinkered categories, its fragmentation of the world into secure units with walls, into neat topics that can be encapsulated in research projects. Disillusion protects us against this insecurity. Disillusion shields us from the pain of the past and blots out the possibilities of the future. Disillusion locks us into the security of an absolute present, into the eternity of power. Disillusion sets our feet securely on the highway that leads toward the destruction of humanity.

---

13   Communiqué of May 1996, *La Jornada*, June 10, 1996.

To close your eyes to the bitterness of the past is to close your eyes to the possibility of the future. To close your eyes to the possibilities of the future is to dishonour the memory of the past, of our dead.

Fortunately for those of us who live in Puebla, we have an ever-present visual aid. We have in the volcano a constant reminder that a mountain is not a mountain, that the invisible has an explosive force, that the unthinkable is always thinkable and that there is nothing less secure than security.

This talk, like any talk, is a question. *Preguntando caminamos*.

ELEVEN

Zapatismo Urbano

I

I am not an indigenous peasant. Probably you, dear reader, are not an indigenous peasant either. Yet this issue revolves around an indigenous peasant uprising.

The Zapatistas of Chiapas are peasants. Our experiences are far removed from those of the Zapatistas of Chiapas. Our living conditions are very different from those of the Zapatistas of Chiapas, and our forms of struggle too. Yet the resonance of the Zapatista uprising in the cities has been enormous. Why? What does Zapatismo mean in the cities?

There have been two forms of reaction in the cities. The first is a reaction of solidarity: the struggle of the indigenous of Chiapas is a just struggle and we give it all the material and political support possible. Solidarity defines the struggle as being the struggle of a "them," and "they" are Indians who live in Chiapas. I do not dismiss this reaction, but it is not what interests me here.

The second reaction goes much further. Here it is not a question of solidarity with the struggle of others but of understanding that the Zapatistas and we are part of the same struggle. The Zapatistas of Chiapas do not give us a model that we can apply to our part of the struggle, but we see their forms of struggle as an inspiration for the development of our forms of struggle. In that sense we can speak of the spread of Zapatismo to the cities, the development of an urban Zapatismo, for which the EZLN is not a model but a constant point of reference.

There is no linear progression here. It is not the spread of an organisation that we are speaking of (though certainly the spread of the Frente

Zapatista within Mexico is part of the process). Neither is it really a question of the spread of influence from Chiapas. It is not that the decisions of the EZLN have an influence on struggles in Rome or Buenos Aires. It is rather a question of resonance and inspiration. The Zapatista uprising has had an enormous impact in the cities of the world because the themes that the EZLN raise and the orientations they suggest have resonated strongly with the preoccupations and directions of people in the cities. They have been a constant source of inspiration because they have formulated with particular clarity (not just in the communiqués but in their actions) directions and themes that were already present in the struggles of the cities.

The purpose of speaking of urban Zapatismo is twofold. On the one hand, it is a way of focussing more closely on this process. What is this resonance? Is it an imagined or real resonance? What are the differences between Zapatismo in the cities and Zapatismo in the countryside? What are the practical problems for the development of this sort of politics in the cities?

Second, to speak of urban Zapatismo is to speak of Zapatismo as a challenge. The Zapatistas do not ask for our sympathy or our solidarity. The commemoration of the tenth and twentieth anniversaries of the EZLN should not be a celebration of them but a challenge to us. They ask us to join in their struggle for a world of dignity.[1] How do we do it, we who live in the cities, we who write and read this essay?

II

The Zapatista uprising has been a fundamental point of reference for urban struggles over the last ten years. Yet there are obvious differences in the conditions and forms of struggle. We who live in the cities and look to the Zapatistas are not organised as an army. We do not live within the sort of communal support structures that exist in Chiapas. We do not have land on which to grow the basic foodstuffs necessary for survival, and we are not, on the whole, accustomed to the levels of complete poverty that is the daily experience of the Zapatistas of Chiapas.

There are aspects of the Zapatista uprising that have not found any echo in the cities. We urban Zapatistas generally do not want to be

---

1   On the question of dignity, see John Holloway, "Dignity's Revolt," in *Zapatista! Reinventing Revolution in Mexico*, eds. John Holloway and Eloína Peláez (London: Pluto, 1998).

organised as an army and often reject militarism as a form of organisation and concept of struggle. In the current debates in Italy, the Zapatistas
are even held up as a model in arguing for a complete rejection of all violence. The other aspect of the Zapatismo of Chiapas that has found little
resonance in the cities is their use of national symbols—the country's flag
and the national anthem. The urban Zapatista movement tends not to be
nationalist, and in many cases is profoundly antinationalist. It has been
not so much an international movement as a global movement, a movement of struggle for which global capitalism and not the nation state has
been the principal point of reference.

What, then, are the aspects of the Zapatista uprising that have found
echo in the cities of the world? The most obvious is the mere fact of rebellion—the fact that the Zapatistas rose up when the time for rebellion seemed
to have passed, their ¡Ya basta! to a world that is so obviously obscene.

But it is more than that. It is also that their ¡Ya basta! also turns against
a Left that had grown stale and stiff and alienating. It is the rejection both of
revolutionary vanguardism and of state-oriented reformism, the rejection
of the party as an organisational form and of the pursuit of power as an aim.

The rejection of the old forms of left-wing politics leaves us with an
enormous question mark. That itself is important. The Zapatista saying
"*caminamos preguntando*" (asking we walk) acquires a particular resonance because we are conscious that we do not know the way forward. The
world around us makes us scream, but where do we go with our scream,
what do we do with our scream?[2] The politics of rebellion is a politics of
searching—not for the correct line but for some sort of way forward, some
way of making our scream effective. There is no party to tell us which way
to go, so we must find it for ourselves.

The politics of asking leads on to certain forms of organisation. The
organisational forms of the Zapatistas of Chiapas are characterised by a
tension, as they themselves emphasise. This is the tension concentrated in
their principle of "*mandar obedeciendo*" (to lead by obeying). On the one
hand, they are organised as an army, with all that that means in terms of
vertical lines of command. On the other hand, the army is subject to the
control of the village councils, where discussion and consensus are the
guiding principles.

---

2   On the politics of the scream, see John Holloway, *Change the World without
    Taking Power* (London: Pluto, 2002).

The rejection of the party as an organisational form has meant (inevitably, perhaps) the revival of councilism, the revival of the council or assembly.[3] The council is the traditional form for expressing revolt that arises again and again in rebellions, from the Paris Commune to the neighbourhood councils of the recent revolt in Argentina. It is an expressive form of organisation, one that seeks to articulate the anger and worries of the participants. This can be contrasted with the party form, which is not expressive but instrumental, designed to attain the end of winning state power. As an expressive form, the council tends to be horizontal in structure, encouraging the free participation of all and aiming to reach consensus in its decisions. Seen in this way, the council is not so much a formal structure as an organisational orientation. This organisational orientation—the emphasis on horizontality, the encouragement of the expression of people's concerns, whether or not they are "revolutionary" or "political"—has been a characteristic feature of the current wave of urban struggle: not just of the neighbourhood councils of Argentina but equally of some of the *piquetero* groups, of the Madres de la Plaza de Mayo, of the Centri Sociali of Rome, Milan, or Turin, and of the altermundista movement in general.

Councilism is related to the question of community. In the Zapatista areas of Chiapas the community exists not as an idyll to be romanticised but simply because most of the people of a village have known one another all their lives, and because there are established practices of common work and decision-making. In the cities, there is often very little sense of community. People who work together do not necessarily live close together, and people who live close to one another often have no contact. The scream of protest that we feel is often experienced as an isolated and hopeless scream, a scream that we share at best with a handful of friends. The (re)construction of community bonds has, therefore, been a central concern of the movement in the cities. The construction of social centres or alternative cafés and the coming together of people in informal and changing movements create new patterns of community and mutual trust that are part and parcel of the development of councilist forms of organisation.

---

3   See, for example, Hernán Ouviña, "Las Asambleas barriales: apuntes a modo de hipótesis de trabajo," *Bajo el Volcán* (Puebla, 2002), 59–72; Raúl Zibechi, *La Genealogía de la Revuelta. Argentina: La sociedad en movimiento* (La Plata: Letra Libre, 2003).

Perhaps the central challenge of urban Zapatismo is the challenge of autonomy. Autonomy is simply the other side of saying that we want to change the world without taking power. Rejecting the pursuit of state power means rejection of the party as a form of organisation (understanding the party as a state-oriented form of organisation). But it means much more than that. It means also a change in the understanding of social conflict or class struggle.[4] The traditional concept sees class struggle as a struggle for power that inevitably determines the agenda, rhythms, and forms of struggle. Confrontation is then the pivot of social struggle. If, however, we say that we do not want to take power, then the whole conception of struggle shifts. What is central now is not the confrontation with the other side (capital) but the construction of our own world. We try to focus on our own doing, to push confrontation to one side. This is still class struggle, it is still confrontation with capital (inevitably, since capital is the imposition of an alien control of our activity). But insofar as possible, we seize the initiative, we seize the agenda. We make capital follow our agenda, so it becomes clear that the aggression comes from them not from us. We cannot be autonomous in a capitalist society, but we can push our autonomy as far as possible. Capital is the negation of autonomy, the ever-repeated negation of our self-determination. (As part of this, the state is the ever-repeated negation of the council.) If we see confrontation as the axis of struggle, then we are anticipating and therefore participating in this negation. By making the development of our own creativity (our own power-to-do) the centre of the movement, capital is revealed as a parasite, constantly forced to run after us. This is illustrated by the *Caracoles*, the establishment of their own Juntas de Buen Gobierno[5] by which the Zapatistas shrug off the state, turn their back on the state,

---

4   On this, see, for example, Holloway (2002); Zibechi, *La Genealogía*; Colectivo Situaciones / MTD Solano, *La Hipótesis 891: Más Allá de los Piquetes* (Buenos Aires: Ediciones de Mano en Mano, 2002); Florence Aubenas and Miguel Benasayag, *Résister, c'est créer* (Paris: La Découverte, 2002).

5   In August 2003, the Zapatistas established a number of Juntas de Buen Gobierno. This involved a reorganization of their own forms of government. One of the most important implications of this reorganisation is that, after years of unsuccessfully calling on the state to implement the Acuerdos de San Andrés on indigenous rights, the Zapatistas in effect declared that they would no longer make demands on the government but simply carry on with the implementation of the agreements themselves. In effect, they have turned their back on the state.

neither demanding anything of it nor openly confronting it, just doing their own thing.

But doing our own thing, developing our own creativity, is not the same in the cities as in the countryside. We do not possess land on which we can grow even the most basic food crops. It may be possible to occupy land for these purposes (as some of the piquetero groups in Argentina are beginning to do), but for most urban groups this is not an option. In order to develop our autonomy we are forced into contradictory situations, in which it is much better to recognise those contradictions rather than to gloss over them, just as the Zapatistas of Chiapas have had the great merit of recognising from the beginning the contradiction of their military organisation in a movement for human dignity. Urban autonomous groups survive either on the basis of state subsidies (sometimes forced by the groups themselves as in the case of the piqueteros who use the road-blocks to force the government to give money to the unemployed) or on the basis of some mixture of occasional or regular paid employment and state subsidies.[6] Thus, many urban groups are composed of a mixture of people in regular employment, people who are by choice or by necessity in irregular or occasional employment, and those who (again by choice or necessity) are unemployed and often dependent on state subsidies or some sort of market activity for their survival. These different forms of dependency on forces that we do not control (on capital) pose problems and limitations that should be recognised. At the same time, the significance of these limitations obviously depends on the collective strength of the groups: in the case of the piqueteros, for example, the payment of the state subsidies was imposed by road blocks and administered by the groups themselves.

All these different forms of dependency on capital are imposed by property, by the fact that all the wealth produced by human doing is congealed in the form of property that confronts and excludes us. The limiting of our autonomous self-determination appears in the form of property, behind which stand the forces of law and order that defend property. We seem to be forced back into a logic of confrontation in which we lose the initiative, or in which we are forced to focus on winning power so that

---

6 For a discussion of the practice of the piqueteros and especially of the MTD Solano, see Colectivo Situaciones/MTD Solano, *La Hipótesis 891*, one of the most enriching discussions of the possibilities and difficulties of urban Zapatismo.

we can control the police and change the laws on property. If we exclude this course (simply because control of the state tends to become control by the state), how can we go forward? Possibly by defetishising property, by seeing that property is not an established thing but a constant process of appropriating, a verb and not a noun. The problem then is not to conceptualise our own action in terms of the challenge to property but to focus on our own construction of an alternative world and to think about how to avoid the capitalist appropriation of the products of our own doing.

The problems indicated all point to the dangers of confusing an emphasis on autonomy with a concept of micropolitics. The notion of autonomy, as understood here, points to the centrality of our own doing and the development of our own power to do: if we see the world from this perspective, then it is clear that capital is a parasite and that the so-called rulers simply run after us all the time trying to appropriate the results of our creative doing. The problem of revolution is to shake off these parasites, to prevent them appropriating our creativity and its results, to make them irrelevant. This struggle does not require any central organisation (and certainly not any orientation toward the state), but its strength does depend on its massive character. What any particular group can achieve clearly depends on the strength of an entire movement pushing in the same or similar directions. The strength of the component groups depends on the strength of the movement, just as the strength of the movement depends on the strength of the component groups.

III

However we think of revolution, we are faced with the task of dissolving Reality. The transformation of the world means moving from a world ruled by objective reality to a world in which subjective creativity is the centre, in which humanity becomes its "own true sun."[7] The struggle for such a world means a constant process of criticism, a process of undermining the objectivity of reality and showing that it depends absolutely

---

7   See Karl Marx, "Introduction to the Contribution to the Critique of Hegel's Philosophy of Law," in Karl Marx and Frederick Engels, *Collected Works*, vol. 3 (London: Lawrence and Wishart, 1975), 176: "The criticism of religion disillusions man to make him think and act and shape his reality like a man who has been disillusioned and has come to reason, so that he will revolve around himself and therefore round his true sun. Religion is only the illusory sun which revolves round man as long as he does not revolve round himself."

for its existence on subjective creation. Our struggle is a struggle against the world-that-is, with its logic that tells us that "there is no alternative," with its language of prose that closes our horizons.

The poetry of the Zapatista uprising (of their communiqués and their actions) is not peripheral to their movement, is not the external decoration of a fundamentally serious movement, but is central to their whole struggle. The fact that the Zapatistas of Chiapas (and to some extent other Latin American indigenous movements) have made such an impact in the urban struggles of the world has much to do with the language they use. This is not just a question of pretty words or of Marcos's undoubted literary skills. It is above all that they offer a different way of seeing the world, a vision that breaks with the dominant logic of "there is no alternative."[8] Poetry and indeed other forms of artistic expression have come to play a central role in anti-capitalist struggle: poetry not as pretty words but as struggle against the prosaic logic of the world, poetry as the call of a world that does not yet exist.

Is this a dangerous romanticism? Are the Zapatistas unwittingly leading the rebellious youth of the world into forms of action that are dangerously unrealistic? Recently, as part of the 10/20 celebrations,[9] the Zapatistas have been emphasising the centrality of organisation in their struggle: Is this a way of countering the impression that their struggle is just poetry, just the power of the word?

Perhaps there is an element of romanticism in the resonance of the Zapatista struggle. There is sometimes undoubtedly a clash between expectations and reality for supporters who visit the Zapatista communities in Chiapas. In general, however, this is not the case. Those actively involved in struggle, whether in the cities or in the countryside, are aware of the difficulties they face and of the importance of organisation. The poetry of Zapatismo does not deflect people from the question of organisation. What it does is to open up perspectives in a world that seems so terribly closed. More than that, it suggests forms of action that break with

8   Former UK prime minister Margaret Thatcher's famous phrase to explain the necessity of subordinating politics to the market.
9   The "10/20 celebrations" commemorated the tenth anniversary of the Zapatista uprising (January 1, 1994) and the twentieth anniversary of the founding of the EZLN (November 17, 1983).

the logic of capital and are more difficult to integrate into the texture of domination.

The accusation of romanticism really has to do with the question of power. "Realism" is identified with a perspective that focuses on power and sees organisation and action as being *instruments* to achieve certain changes (whether minor changes or the radical change of society). What this realist perspective fails to see is that the very instrumentality of the approach leads to the adoption of forms of action and of organisation that defuse and demobilise the movement for change. It is precisely because instrumentalist realism has failed to achieve the objective of radical social change that people everywhere have turned away from this approach to forms of action that are *expressive* rather than instrumental. Part of this is the turn away from the goal of taking state power and from the party as an organisational form. The poetry of the movement is part of the same process.

Will this poetic romanticism prove more realistic than the previous socialist realism? We do not know. What we know is that the realism of power politics failed to achieve radical social change and that hope lies in breaking reality, in establishing our own reality, our own logic, our own language, our own colours, our own music, our own time, our own space. That is the core of the struggle not only against "them" but against ourselves, that is the core of the Zapatista resonance.

References

Aubenas, Florence, and Miguel Benasayag. *Résister, c'est créer*. Paris: La Découverte, 2002.

Colectivo Situaciones/MTD Solano. *La Hipótesis 891: Más Allá de los Piquetes*. Buenos Aires: Ediciones de Mano en Mano, 2002.

Holloway, John. *Change the World without Taking Power*. London: Pluto, 2002.

Holloway, John. "Dignity's Revolt." In *Zapatista! Reinventing Revolution in Mexico*, edited by John Holloway and Eloína Peláez, 159–98. London: Pluto, 1998.

Holloway, John, and Eloína Peláez, eds. *Zapatista! Reinventing Revolution in Mexico*. London: Pluto, 1998.

Marx, Karl "Introduction to the Contribution to the Critique of Hegel's Philosophy of Law." In Karl Marx and Frederick Engels, *Collected Works*, vol. 3. London: Lawrence and Wishart, 1975, 175–87.

Ouviña, Hernán. "Las Asambleas barriales: apuntes a modo de hipótesis de trabajo." *Bajo el Volcán*. Puebla, 2003, 59–72.

Zibechi, Raúl. *La Genealogía de la Revuelta. Argentina: La sociedad en movimiento*. La Plata: Letra Libre, 2003.

TWELVE

Stop Making Capitalism

I

In Mary Shelley's famous story, Dr. Frankenstein creates a creature, which then acquires an independent existence, a durable existence in which he no longer depends on the creative activity of Dr. Frankenstein. In another story, by Jorge Luis Borges, "Las Ruinas Circulares," a man creates another man not in a laboratory but by dreaming. The man created has all the appearance of being a normal man with an independent, durable existence, but in fact he is kept alive only by the constant creative activity, the dreaming, of the first man. His existence is not an illusion but his duration is: his existence depends, from one moment to another, on the creative activity of the dreamer.

The story of Frankenstein is often taken as a metaphor for capitalism. We have created a society that is beyond our control and that threatens to destroy us: the only way we can survive is by destroying that society. But perhaps we should think rather in terms of the Borges story: we have created a society that appears to be totally beyond our control, but that in reality depends upon our act of constant re-creation. The problem is not to destroy that society but to stop creating it. Capitalism exists today not because we created it two hundred years ago or a hundred years ago, but because we create it today. If we do not create it tomorrow, it will not exist.

Each day we create a world of horrors, of misery and violence and injustice. We take an active part in constructing the domination that oppresses us, the obscenity that horrifies us. We create surplus value, we respect money, we accept and impose unreasoned authority, we live by the clock, we close our eyes to the starving. We make capitalism. And now we must stop making it.

What does it mean to think of revolution not as destroying capitalism but as ceasing to create capitalism?

Changing the question does not solve the problem of revolution, it does not mean that now we know how to do it, but perhaps it can lead us to rethink the categories of revolutionary thought. Perhaps it opens a different grammar, a different logic of revolutionary thought, a different way of thinking about revolutionary politics. Perhaps it opens a new hope. That is what I want to explore.

II

The idea that revolution means destroying capitalism rests on a concept of duration, that is, on the idea that capitalism now is and will continue to be until we destroy it. The problem is that by assuming the duration of capitalism revolutionaries undermine the basis of their own call for revolution.

Any system of domination depends on duration, on the assumption that because something exists in one moment it will continue to exist in the next. The master assumes that because he ruled yesterday, he will continue to rule tomorrow. The slave dreams of a different tomorrow but often locates it beyond death, in heaven. She assumes in that case that there is nothing she can *do* to change the situation. The power of doing is subordinated to that which is.

This subordination of doing to being is a subordination of subject to object. Duration, then, is a characteristic of a society in which subject is subordinated to object, a society in which active subjectivity is assumed to be incapable of changing objective reality. Objective reality, or society-as-it-is, stands over against us: subject is separated from and subordinated to object. And verbs (the active form of speaking) are separated from and subordinated to nouns (which deny movement).

Under capitalism the separation of subject and object, and therefore duration, acquires a peculiar rigidity. This is rooted in the material separation of subject and object in the process of production. The commodity we produce stands over against us as something external, as an object that denies all relation with the work of the subject who produced it. It acquires an existence apparently completely separate from the work that constituted it. This separation between subject and object, doing and done, verb and noun is fundamental to the way that we subjects relate to each other under capitalism, so fundamental that it comes to permeate every aspect of social existence. In every aspect of our lives there is a separation of subject from object, doing from being, a subordination of subject to object, doing to being. Duration rules. This is expressed clearly in clock time, in which one minute is exactly the same as the next and the next and the next and the only revolution conceivable is the one that goes round and round.

To think of changing society, we must recover the centrality of human doing, we must rescue the buried subject. In other words, we must criticise—using genetic criticism, criticism ad hominem—the attempt to understand phenomena in terms of the doing that produces them. Marx's labour theory of value is such a criticism: at its core, it says, "The commodity denies our doing, but we made it." With that, the subject (our doing) is restored to the centre of the picture. The object claims to be independent of the subject, but in fact it depends on the subject. Being depends on doing. This is what opens up the possibility that we can change the world.

All criticism (understood in this sense) is an attack on duration. Once subjectivity is restored to the centre of society, duration is broken. It can no longer be assumed that one minute is the same as the next. It can no longer be assumed that tomorrow will be like today, because we may make it different. Criticism opens up a world of astonishment. When Marx says at the beginning of *Capital* that the commodity stands outside us, alien to us, but its secret is that we made it (labour theory of value), then our reaction is one both of horror and of hope. We are astonished that we should spend our lives making objects that deny our existence, that are alien to us and dominate us, but at the same time we see hope, because those objects depend totally upon us for their existence: our doing is at the centre of everything, our doing is the hidden sun around which everything revolves.

The object, which dominates the subject, depends on the subject that creates it. Capital, which dominates us, depends on our work, which creates it. The master who dominates the slave depends on the slave. There is a relation of domination and dependence in which the movement of domination is a constant flight from the dependence, a constant struggle by the master to escape from his dependence upon the slave—an impossible struggle, of course, because if he succeeded he would cease to be master. But in this relation of domination and dependence it is not so much the moment of domination (the traditional arena of left discourse) as the moment of dependence that interests us, because that is where hope is to be found.

All social phenomena, then, exist because they have been made by people: money or the state are just as much human products as the motor car. But more than that: all social phenomena exist only because they have been made and are constantly being remade. A car exists as a car only because we constantly recreate it by using it as a car; a state exists as a state only because we constantly recreate it by accepting its authority and its forms. Money exists only because we constantly reproduce it in our relations with others. If we stopped reproducing money in our social relations, the paper and the coins would continue to exist, but it would no longer be money. These phenomena are not like Frankenstein's Creature but like the creature produced by Borges's dreamer. They depend for their existence upon us, from one minute to the next.

The existence of capitalism is no illusion. What is an illusion is the separation of its existence from its constitution, in other words, its duration.

Duration, of course, is not just imaginary: it is generated in the real social separation of subject and object in the process of work, so that it is only through a complete transformation of the social organisation of work (doing) that duration can be destroyed. But the attack on duration is central to the attack on the capitalist organisation of work.

To attack duration is to demystify it, to show it to be an illusion. To demystify is to pierce the unreality of an enchanted world and to show that the world really revolves around human doing. However, it feels like just the opposite. We have always lived in the "enchanted, perverted, topsy-turvy world" of capitalism, the world of objects, of duration, of clock time. Consequently, the world into which criticism introduces us feels like a dreamworld, a Wonderland, a world of impossible intensity, a world in which everything is infinitely fragile because it depends on its constant re-creation.

In this Wonderland-world, in this communist-moving, nouns are dissolved into verbs, into doings. Nouns fetishise the product of doing, they tear the results away from that doing and enshrine them in a durable existence that denies that they are dependent on being constantly recreated. Marx criticised value to show that its core was human activity, work, but his critical method of recuperating the centrality of human doing can be extended to all nouns (but, in the duration-world in which we live, with its duration-talking, it is difficult to write without using nouns—so that critical thought really requires creating a new talking, what Vaneigem calls the poetry of revolution).

Communism, then, is not the culmination of history but the breaking of the continuum of history (Benjamin), the dissolution of the continuity of nouns into the absolute fragility of human doing. A self-determining society is a society in which it is explicit that only what is being done in the moment exists, a world of verbs. The notion of the culmination of history implies a positive movement, a movement of accumulation of struggle, a movement of extension. Breaking the continuum of history implies a negative movement, not an accumulation of struggles but the generation of new intensities incompatible with the dead identifications of capitalism. Perhaps we should think of totality, that concept that criticises the fragmented nature of bourgeois thought, not as a movement of extension but more as a movement toward the totalising of social existence into the intensity of each particular moment: the pursuit of an absolutely intense *Jetzt-Zeit*, or Nunc Stans in which time stops and capitalism explodes, or perhaps implodes. Communism would be a self-determining society, that is, a society without duration, without nouns: a terrifying, exhilarating thought.

III

What we want is a moment of terrible social intensity that shatters the continuum of history, a moment so intense that clock time is broken forever. Such moments occur: revolutions are like that. Everything stops, social relations are turned upside down as people go out on the streets and everything is concentrated in the act of saying NO.

But we cannot wait for the Great Revolutionary Moment. We cannot go on producing capitalism; we must break the continuum of history now. Individually and collectively, we must turn to capital and say, "Go on, now go, walk out the door, just turn around now, 'cause you're not welcome anymore. We will survive." "Go away, capital! ¡Que se vayan todos! All the politicians and all the capitalists. You're not welcome anymore. We will survive."

To say goodbye to capital is to break a relationship, to start afresh, to create a tabula rasa, to make the world anew. Breaking the continuum of history is like breaking the continuum of an oppressive relationship in daily life. While we are in the relationship, it seems impossible, inconceivable that we should ever break out of it, but it is not. Capital is beating us, killing thousands of us each day, but ¡Ya basta! Those who want to build a party and take state power would take us to marriage counsellors and the divorce courts before breaking the relationship. But no, we cannot wait. There is no intermediate step. Bye-bye, ciao, as simple as that.

Is it really so simple? No, of course not. But perhaps it is not as impossible as we usually think.

Capital exists because we make it. It depends absolutely on us. This is all-important: if there is no work, there is no capital. We create capital, and it is only by assuming our responsibility that we can understand our strength. Only if we understand that we make capital with all its horrors can we understand that we have the power to stop making it. State-oriented (and hegemony-centred and discourse-centred) approaches lose sight of this crucial axis of dependence: they turn our eyes away from the Achilles' heel of capitalism, its crucial point of vulnerability.

If capital depends upon us, then *refusal* is the key to our strength. If capital exists because we make it, then we must refuse to make it.

A sustained global mass strike would destroy capital completely, but the conditions for that do not exist at the moment. It is hard to see how everybody in the world could be persuaded to refuse to work for capital at the same time.

For the moment at least, the only way of thinking of revolution is in terms of a number of rents, tears, holes, fissures that spread through the social fabric. There are already millions of such holes, spaces in which people, individually or collectively, say, "NO, here capital does not rule, here we shall not structure our lives according to the dictates of capital." These holes are refusals, disobediences, insubordinations. In some cases (the EZLN in Chiapas, the MST in Brazil, the uprising in Bolivia, the piqueteros and *asambleas barriales* in Argentina, and so on), these insubordinations, these holes in the fabric of capital are already very big. The only way in which we can think of revolution is in terms of the extension and multiplication of these disobediences, of these fissures in capitalist command. Some argue that these disobediences, these fissures, acquire real significance only when they are institutionalised in the form of disobedient or revolutionary states, and that the whole movement of disobedience must be channelled toward that end. But there is no reason why disobediences should be institutionalised in state form and very many reasons why they should not.

These refusals are refusals of indignity, affirmations of dignity. Indignity is being commanded by others, being told what to do, as though one did not have the maturity to decide for oneself, in conjunction with others. Dignity then is the refusal of indignity, the refusal of alien command, the affirmation of oneself as part of the drive to social self-determination. There are two moments here: refusal and affirmation, No and Yes, a Yes present in the No. Stop making capitalism and do something else instead.

Refusal itself is not difficult. Most of us find it easy not to go to work under the command of others. Refusal is the crucial pivot in any attempt to change the world. But it is not enough for two reasons. First, refusal to work in present society confronts us immediately with the problem of starvation. If we do not sell our labour power, how do we obtain the means necessary to survive? In the richer countries, it is often possible to survive on state benefits, and this is what many of those in revolt against work do. But state benefits are very limited and in any case do not exist in most countries. Refusal to work under capitalist command is difficult to maintain unless it is accompanied by the development of some sort of alternative doing.

Second, and just as important as the need to avoid starvation, is dignity, the drive toward the social self-determination of our doing. This is the drive to do something that we judge to be necessary, desirable, or enjoyable. This is the struggle of doing against work, of the content against its capitalist form. Even in modern capitalism, where the subordination of doing to capital in the form of work is a very real subordination (or subsumption), there is always a residuum of dignity, of the insubordination of content to form. To be human is to struggle for the insubordination of doing to work, for the emancipation of doing from work. The worst architect always struggles against being converted into the best bee.[1] That is the meaning of dignity.

The struggle of doing against work, that is, the struggle for the emancipation of doing, is an everyday practice. It is common for people to work

---

1   Marx uses the comparison between architect and bee to distinguish between humans and animals: "A spider conducts operations which resemble those of the weaver, and a bee would put many a human architect to shame by the construction of its honeycomb cells. But what the distinguishes the worst architect from the best of bees is that the architect builds the cell in his mind before he constructs it in wax." Marx, *Capital*, vol. 1 (London: Penguin Books, 1990 [1867]), 284.

(or do) in-and-against capital, trying to do well what they do in spite of the capitalist form of organisation, fighting for use value against value. Obviously there are also many jobs in which it is very difficult to see any space for a revolt of doing against work. In such cases, perhaps the struggle of-and-for dignity can be understood only as a struggle of total negation (sabotage and other forms of refusal of work).

But there are clearly many examples that go beyond that of people occupying factories or schools or clinics and trying to organise them on a different basis, creating community bakeries or workshops or gardens, establishing radio stations of resistance, and so on. All these projects and revolts are limited, inadequate, and contradictory (as they must be in a capitalist context), but it is difficult to see how we can create an emancipated doing other than in this interstitial form, through a process of interweaving the different struggles of doing against work, knitting together the different doings in-and-against-and-beyond capital.

The emancipation of doing means the self-determination of doing. This implies some sort of council organisation, some form in which people come together to determine what to do and how to do it. The council (or soviet) tradition has a long history in the communist movement and recurs in different forms in all rebellions. Its central point is the insistence in the collective self-determination of doing. This means the rejection of leadership from outside, the acceptance that people here and now, with all their problems and weaknesses and neuroses, with all the habit inculcated by centuries of domination, should determine their own activity.

In these many experiments (whether or not they are imposed by the necessity to survive), the central theme is not survival but the emancipation of doing, the creation of a doing shaped not by profit but by what the doers consider desirable.

Any revolution that is not centred in the emancipation of doing is condemned to failure (because it is not a revolution). The emancipation of doing leads us into a different time, a different grammar, a different intensity of life. The emancipation of doing is the movement of anti-fetishisation, the recovery of creativity. Only in this way can the fissures become poles of attraction instead of ghettos, and only if they are poles of attraction can they expand and multiply. The revolutions in Russia and Cuba were initially poles of attraction for many who dreamed of another type of life: the fact that there was no real emancipation of doing in these societies meant that they gradually ceased to exert that attraction (although support and solidarity continue in the case of Cuba). And the same is true of many alternative projects today: if the only result of these projects is that the participants are poor, isolated, and bored, then the projects will not be poles of attraction. If rebellions are not attractive, they will not spread. In other words, ceasing to make capitalism has to be thought of as a realistic project, but if the realism is not a magic realism, it ceases to be realistic.

The struggle of doing against work is a struggle to create a different human richness: one shaped by social desires and not by capitalist appropriation, one that is not appropriated by capital. People produce an enormous richness each day, but nearly all of it is appropriated by capital, so that the only way in which we can have access to that richness is by bending low, bowing to the command of capital. It is easy to refuse to work for capital, but how can we survive without subordinating ourselves to capital?

Any attempt to gain access to the richness of human doing comes up against "property." Property is not a thing but a verb, a daily repeated process of appropriating the product of our doing. The process of appropriating (which is constantly being extended to new areas of doing) is supported by violence, but it depends greatly on the fetishisation of the process, on the transformation of the verb "to appropriate" into the noun "property." The resistance to the process of appropriation is part of constructing another doing, a doing that defetishises at the same time as it creates another sociality.

IV

Stop making capitalism: refuse. But this involves a second moment: do something else instead. This something else is a prefiguration, the embryo of a society yet to be born. To what extent can this embryo grow in the womb of existing society?

There are many unavoidable problems, and there is no model solution to apply. But one thing is clear: that we must stop making capitalism now, that we must stop creating the misery, oppression, and violence that surround us. ¡Ya basta! ¡Que se vayan todos! The slogans of recent years make it clear that very many people have had enough of capitalism.

After we say, "Go on, now go, walk out the door," there are still many forces that suck us back into the relationship. Yet the axis of our thought must be not continuity but discontinuity, break, rupture. We must stop making capitalism now. The problem of theorists is that perhaps we spend our time untying (or even tying) Gordian knots when what we need is to start from the energy of December 19–20, 2001, of Bolivia in October 2003, of January 1, 1994. Not domination but rupture is the centre of our thought.

Rupture does not mean that capitalism vanishes. The fissures do not mean that capitalism disappears. But rather than think of revolution as an event that will happen in the future (who knows when) and be relatively quick, it seems better to think of it as a process that is already under way and may take some time, precisely because revolution cannot be separated from the creating of an alternative world.

We see where we want to go. The new horizon shimmers in the morning mists like an island on the other side of the sea. But we cannot get there by putting stepping-stones and jumping from one step to another to another, building the party, winning control of the state, implementing social reform. That will not work, because the island we see shimmering in the mists is not in the sea but in the sky, and the only way to get there is to fly. It seems impossible until we realise that we are flying already.

THIRTEEN

1968 and the Crisis of Abstract Labour

The year 1968? Why talk about 1968? There are so many urgent things happening. Let's talk of Oaxaca and Chiapas and the danger of civil war in Mexico. Let's talk of the war in Iraq and the rapid destruction of the natural preconditions of human existence. Is this really a good moment for old men to sit back and reminisce?

But perhaps we need to talk of 1968 because, even in the face of all the real urgency, we are feeling lost and need some sense of direction: not to find the road (because the road does not exist) but to create many paths. Perhaps 1968 has something to do with our feeling lost, and perhaps it has something to do with making new paths. So let us talk of 1968.

It opened the door to a change in the world, a change in the rules of anti-capitalist conflict, a change in the meaning of anti-capitalist revolution, a change therefore in the meaning of hope. This is what we are still trying to understand. That is why I say that 1968 contributes to making us feel lost and is also a key to finding some orientation.

It was an explosion, and the sound of the explosion still echoes, difficult to distinguish from the sound of subsequent explosions that took up the themes of 1968—most important perhaps 1994 and the series of explosions that is the Zapatista movement. So when I speak of 1968, it is not necessarily with historical precision: what interests me is the explosion and how, in the wake of that explosion, we can think of overcoming the catastrophe that is capitalism.

The year 1968 was an explosion, the explosion of a certain constellation of social forces, a certain pattern of social conflict. Sometimes this constellation is referred to as Fordism. The term has the great merit of drawing our attention immediately to the core question of the way in which our daily activity is organised. It refers to a world in which mass production in the factories was integrated with the promotion of mass consumption through a combination of relatively high wages and the so-called welfare state. Central actors in this process were the trade unions, whose participation in the system of regular wage negotiations was a driving force, and the state, which appeared to have the capacity of regulating the economy and ensuring basic levels of social welfare. In such a society, it was not surprising that aspirations for social change concentrated on the state and on the goal of taking state power by electoral means or otherwise. Possibly it would be more accurate to speak of this pattern of class relations not just as Fordism but as Fordism-Keynesianism-Leninism.

I want to suggest that there was something even more profound at issue. The danger in restricting ourselves to the idea of the crisis of Fordism (or indeed Fordism-Keynesianism-Leninism) is that the term invites us to see this as one of a series of modes of regulation that would then be superseded by another (post-Fordism or Empire or whatever): capitalism is then seen as a series of restructurings or syntheses or closures, whereas our problem is not to write a history of capitalism, but rather to find a way out of this catastrophe. It is necessary to go beyond the concept of Fordism. Fordism was an extremely developed form of alienated or abstract labour, and what was challenged in these years was alienated labour, the very heart of capitalism.

Abstract labour (I use the term that Marx used in *Capital*, because it seems to me a richer concept) is the labour that produces value and surplus value, and therefore capital. Marx contrasts it with useful or concrete labour, the activity that is necessary for the reproduction of any society. Abstract labour is labour seen in abstraction from its particular characteristics, it is labour that is equivalent to any other labour and this equivalence is established through exchange. The abstraction is not just a mental abstraction; it is a real abstraction. The fact that the products are produced for exchange rebounds upon the production process itself and converts it into a process in which all that matters is the performance of socially necessary labour, the efficient production of commodities that will sell. Abstract labour is labour devoid of particularity, devoid of meaning. It produces the society of capital, in which the only meaning is the accumulation of abstract labour, the constant pursuit of profit.

Abstract labour weaves the society in which we live. It weaves the multiplicity of human activities together through the repeated process of exchange, through this process that tells us over and over again, "It does not matter what you enjoy doing, how much love and care you put into it, what matters is whether it will sell and how much money you can get for it." That is the way our different activities are woven together, that is the way capitalist society is constructed.

But the weaving goes much farther than that: relating to one another through the exchange of things creates a general thing-ification, a reification, a fetishisation of social relations. In the same way that the thing we create separates itself from us and stands against us, negating its origins, so all aspects of our relations with other people acquire the character of things. Money becomes a thing, rather than just a relation between different creators. The state becomes a thing rather than just a way in which we organise our common affairs. Sex becomes a thing rather than just the multiplicity of different ways in which people touch and relate physically. Nature becomes a thing to be used for our benefit, rather than the complex interrelation of the different forms of life that share this planet. Time becomes a thing, clock time, a time outside us that tells us that tomorrow will be the same as today, rather than just the rhythms of our living, the intensities and relaxations of our doing. And so on.

By performing abstract labour, we weave, we weave, we weave this world that is so rapidly destroying us. And each part of the weave gives strength and solidity to each other part of the weave. At the centre is our activity as abstract labour, but the empty meaningless abstraction of our labour is held in place by the whole structure of abstraction or alienation that we create: the state, the idea and practice of dimorphic sexuality, the objectification of nature, the living of time as clock time, the seeing of space as space contained within boundaries, and so on. All these different dimensions of abstract meaninglessness are created by and in turn reinforce the abstract meaningless of our daily activity, which is at its core. It is this complex weave that is blown in the air in 1968.

How? What is the force behind the explosion? It is not the working class, at least not in the traditional sense. Factory workers do play an important part, especially in France, but they do not play a central role in the explosion of 1968. Nor can it be understood in terms of any particular group. It is rather a social relation, the relation of abstract labour, that explodes. The force behind the explosion has to be understood not as a group but as the underside of abstract labour, the contradiction of abstract labour, that which abstract labour contains but does not contain, that which abstract labour represses but does not repress. This is what explodes.

What is the underside of abstract labour? There is a problem here with vocabulary, and not by chance, because that which is repressed tends to be invisible, without voice, without name. We can call it anti-alienation, or anti-abstraction. In the 1844 *Manuscripts* Marx refers to anti-alienation as "conscious life-activity" and in *Capital* the contrast is between abstract labour and "useful or concrete labour." This term is not entirely satisfactory, partly because the distinction between labour and other forms of activity is not common to all societies. For that reason, I shall refer to the underside of abstract labour as *doing*: doing rather than just anti-alienation, because what is at issue is first and foremost the way in which human activity is organised.

Capitalism is based on abstract labour, but there is always an underside, another aspect of activity that appears to be totally subordinated to abstract labour but is not and cannot be. Abstract labour is the activity that creates capital and weaves capitalist domination, but there is always another side, a doing that retains or seeks to retain its particularity, that pushes toward some sort of meaning, some sort of self-determination. Marx points right at the beginning of *Capital* to the relation between abstract and useful labour as the pivot upon which the understanding of political economy (and therefore capitalism) turns—a sentence almost totally ignored by the whole Marxist tradition.

Useful labour (doing) exists in the form of abstract labour, but the relation of form and content cannot be understood simply as containment: inevitably, doing exists in-against-and-beyond abstract labour. This is a matter of everyday experience, as we all try to find some way of directing our activity toward what we consider desirable or necessary. Even within our abstract labour we try to find some way of not submitting totally to the rule of money. As professors we try to do something more than producing the functionaries of capital, as assembly line workers we move our fingers along an imaginary guitar in the seconds we have free, as nurses we try to help our patients beyond the incentive of money, as students we dream of a life not determined totally by money. There is an antagonistic relation between our doing and the abstraction (or alienation) that capital imposes, a relation not only of subordination but also of resistance, revolt, and pushing beyond.

This is always present, but it explodes in 1968, as a generation no longer so tamed by the experience of fascism and war rises up and says, "No, we shall not dedicate our lives to the rule of money, we shall not dedicate all the days of our lives to abstract labour, we shall do something else instead." The revolt against capital expresses itself clearly as that which it always is and must be: a revolt against labour. It becomes clear that we cannot think of class struggle as labour against capital because labour is on the same side of capital, labour produces capital. The struggle is not that of labour against capital but of doing (or living) against labour and therefore against capital. This is what is expressed in the universities, in the factories, and on the streets in 1968. This is what makes it impossible for capital to increase the rate of exploitation sufficiently to maintain its rate of profit and hold Fordism in place.

It is the force of doing, that is, the force of saying, "No, we shall not live like that, we shall do otherwise," that blows apart that constellation of struggle based on the extreme abstraction of labour expressed in Fordism. It is a revolt that is directed against all aspects of the abstraction of labour: not just the alienation of labour in the narrow sense but also the fetishisation of sex, nature, time, and space and the state-oriented forms of organisation that are part of that fetishisation. There is a release, an emancipation: it becomes possible to think and do things that were not possible before. The force of the explosion, the force of the struggle, splits open the category of labour (opened by Marx but closed in practice by the Marxist tradition) and, with it all the other categories of thought.

The explosion throws us into a new world. It throws us onto a new battlefield that is distinctively open, characterised by a new constellation of struggles. This is crucial: if we leap to talk of a new mode of domination (Empire or post-Fordism), then we are closing dimensions that we are struggling to keep open. In other words, there is a real danger that by analysing the so-called new paradigm of domination, we give it a solidity that it does not merit and that we certainly do not want. The relatively coherent weave that existed before the explosion is torn apart. It is in the interests of capital to put it back together again, to establish a new pattern. Anti-capitalism moves in the opposite direction, tearing apart, pushing the cracks as far as it can.

The old constellation was based on the antagonism between labour and capital, with all that meant in terms of trade unions, corporatism, parties, the welfare state, and so on. If we are right in saying that the new constellation must be understood as having at its centre the antagonism between doing and abstract labour, then this means rethinking radically what anti-capitalism means, what revolution means. All the established practices and ideas bound up with abstract labour come into question: labour, sexuality, nature, state, time, and space all become battlegrounds of struggle.

The new constellation that showed its face clearly in 1968 and still struggles to be born is the constellation of doing against abstract labour. This means that it is fundamentally negative. Doing exists in and against abstract labour: insofar as it breaks through abstract labour and exists also beyond it (as cooperative, as social centre, as Junta de Buen Gobierno), it is always at risk, always both shaped and threatened by its antagonism with abstract labour. Once we positivise it, seeing it as an autonomous space, as socialism in one country or in one social centre, or as a cooperative that is not in movement against capitalism, it quickly converts itself into its opposite. The struggles against capital are fast-moving and unstable: they exist on the edge of evanescence and cannot be judged from the positivity of institutions.

The movement of doing against labour is anti-identitarian: the movement of nonidentity against identity. This is important for practical reasons, simply because capital's restructuring is the attempt to contain the new struggles within identities. The struggles of women, of blacks, of indigenous peoples, as long as they are contained within their respective identity, pose no problem at all for the reproduction of a system of abstract labour. On the contrary, the reconsolidation of abstract labour probably depends on the reshuffling of these identities as identities, the refocussing of struggles into limited, identitarian struggles. The Zapatista movement creates no challenge to capitalism as long as it remains a struggle for indigenous rights. When the struggle overflows identity, when the Zapatistas say, "We are indigenous but more than that." When they say that they are struggling to make the world anew, to create a world based on the mutual recognition of dignity, that is when they constitute a threat to capitalism. The struggle of doing is the struggle to overflow the fetishised categories of identity. We fight not so much for women's rights as for a world in which the division of people into two sexes (and the genitalisation of sexuality) is overcome, not so much for the protection of nature as for a radical rethinking of the relation between different forms of life, not so much for migrants' rights as for the abolition of frontiers.

In all transformation, time is crucial. Homogeneous time was perhaps the most important cement of the old constellation, the constellation of abstract labour, accepted by the Left as unquestioningly as by the Right. In this view, revolution, if it could be imagined at all, could only be in the future. That has gone. What was previously seen as an inseparable pair, "future revolution," is now seen to be pure nonsense. It is too late for future revolution. And anyway, every day in which we plan for a future revolution we recreate the capitalism that we hate, so that the very notion of future revolution is self-defeating. Revolution is here and now or not at all. That is implicit in 1968, with the movement's refusal to wait until the Party considered that it was the right moment. That is made explicit in the Zapatistas' ¡Ya basta! of January 1, 1994. Enough! Now! Not "We shall wait until the next Kondratieff cycle completes its circle."[1] And not "We shall wait until the Party conquers state power." But "Now: revolution here and now!"

What does this mean? It can only mean a multiplicity of struggles from the particular, the creation of spaces or moments in which we seek to live now the society we want to create. This means the creation of cracks in the system of capitalist command, moments or spaces in which we say, "No, we shall not do what capital requires of us; we shall do what we consider necessary or desirable."

Inevitably, this means an understanding of anti-capitalist struggle as a multiplicity of very different struggles. This is not a multiplication of identities but the rapid movement of anti-identitarian struggles that touch and diverge, infect and repel, a creative chaos of cracks that multiply and spread and at times are filled up and reappear and spread again. This is the polyphonic revolt of doing against abstract labour. It is necessarily polyphonic. To deny its polyphony would be to subordinate it to a new form of abstraction. The world we are trying to create, the world of useful doing or conscious life activity is necessarily a world of many worlds. And this means, of course, forms of organisation that seek to articulate and respect this polyphony: anti-state forms, in other words.

From the outside and sometimes from within, this polyphony seems to be just a chaotic, dissonant noise without direction or unity, without

---

1   Kondratieff proposed that capitalist development is characterised by long-term cycles or waves of growth and relative decline, often seen as lasting for about twenty-five years. The theory is often associated with a deterministic view of both economic and political development.

a metanarrative. That is a mistake. The metanarrative is not the same as before 1968, but there is a metanarrative, with two faces. The first face of this metanarrative is simply NO, ¡*Ya basta*! And the second face is Dignity: we live now the world we want to create, in other words, We Do.

Perhaps we can conclude by saying that 1968 was the crisis of the working class as prose, and its birth as poetry: the crisis of the working class as abstract labour, and its birth as useful-creative doing. The intervening years have shown us how difficult it is to write poetry, how difficult and how necessary.

FOURTEEN

Go on Now, Go

I'm so happy to be here, I feel I could sing a song.

The song grows out of a story, a simple but sad story of everyday life. Once upon a time there was a woman who lived with a man (their names don't matter), but it was not a happy relationship. He was rather brutal and insensitive. He would disappear for days and then return with no explanation, as if nothing had happened. The woman was very unhappy, but she was afraid to leave him. She was afraid to be alone, and each time he went away she just prayed for him to come back. But one day it got even worse and he was gone for two whole weeks and at last the woman thought, "That's it, I've had enough. ¡*Ya basta!*" So when she came home one evening and found him in the house, she said:

> Go on now, go
> Walk out the door
> Just turn around now
> 'Cause you're not welcome anymore
> Weren't you the one who tried to hurt me with goodbye
> You think I'd crumble
> You think I'd lay down and die
> Oh no, not I
> I will survive

And what happened then? We don't have all the details, but we do know that there was a dramatic shift in the whole dynamic of the relation and that at the centre of this shift was her proud declaration of dignity. "I will no longer serve you," she said, "I will no longer do what you tell me to do." And he was absolutely shocked, and he muttered and he stuttered and he said, "Please, please, please." And she said, "No, I am not negotiating, we are finished." And he said, "But just tell me what you want, and we can discuss it," and she said, "No, I am finished with a politics of demands. I demand nothing from you. I shall make my own life." And he said, "Well, at least wait until we can see a marriage counsellor or a lawyer." And she said, "No, I used to hope that you would be run over by a bus, but now I have understood that revolution is never in the future, it is us taking our lives into our hands here and now. Out." And he said, "You'll never survive. You're all on your own, an isolated individual." And she said, "No, you're wrong, I'm part of a movement that you don't even see. If I sing this song, it is the result of years of struggle by women all over the world. If I say I can survive, it is because the whole grammar of relations between women and men has been changed by these struggles." So he went away, but the next night he came back with his mates ready to beat sense into her. But of course she had already thought of that and mobilised hundreds of friends in her defence. It was difficult at first, but she did survive and lived happily ever after. Or at least that's what I think.

But there is a less optimistic version that says that she had great difficulty surviving, and after a few weeks she went back to him and said, "Please take me back, I'll do everything you want me to do," and the whole miserable relationship started up again and went on and on.

Let me tell you another story that is only slightly different, one that I call the "Solano flip." In the late 1990s, capital was abandoning a lot of workers in Argentina, and so you got the growth of an important unemployed workers' movement, the *piquetero* movement. The piqueteros started blocking roads in order to force the government to give them subsidies and to create jobs. "We want capital to come back," they said (or some of them), "We want jobs."

And then others, the more radical groups (most articulately the MTD Solano), began to say:

No, that's not true. We don't want capital back and we don't want jobs. We've done that, and we've had enough. ¡*Ya basta*! We want to do something meaningful with our lives. Capital is going away. Fine. Go on now, go, capital, walk out the door, just turn around now, 'cause you're not welcome anymore. We're going to force the government to give us resources (by blocking the roads), and we're going to decide collectively how to use those resources to develop activities that will improve the community: improving buildings, organising our own school, our own kitchens, our own bakeries, our own communal process of taking decisions.

And they were supported by the workers in hundreds of factories who, when capital said it was going away, said, "Fine, go on now, go, we shall take over the factory." And, in December 2001, when the government tried to introduce more repressive measures to get the situation under control, thousands and thousands of people took to the streets, calling "¡Que se vayan todos!" "Out with the lot of them!"

In these cases there is a radical change in the grammar of revolution that is not just peculiar to the particular struggle but part of a general shift over the last twenty (or perhaps forty) years. At the centre is the cry "¡Ya basta! We've had enough of that!" We've had enough of that, because we know that we are not only suffering capitalism, we are creating it. That is clear if we think of the woman in the song: as long as she stays with the man, she creates the relationship that she suffers. The same with capital: we create each day the capitalist social relations that we suffer. If capitalism exists today it is not because it was created in the eighteenth century, it is because we created it today. The question of revolution is not how we abolish capitalism in the future but how we stop creating it here and now.

To say "Go on now, go" is to say that we shall no longer go on creating a system that is catastrophic for humanity, that generates frustration, injustice, and violence, that now threatens to annihilate humanity. We refuse to create capitalism; we do something else. We break with the politics of demands and struggle for change by living now the society we want to create.

The anti-capitalist movement now faces a stark choice—in Ireland, in Greece, elsewhere. Faced with the flight of capital and rising unemployment and precariousness, we can either say, "Please come back, capital, we want jobs, we shall fight for the right to work." When we say that, we know it's not very likely to happen, and that to the extent that it does happen it will be under worse conditions than before. We know too that to demand more jobs is to close ourselves back into the system that is destroying the world. The alternative is to say, "Go on now, go, walk out the door, capital, just turn around now, 'cause you're not welcome anymore. You have failed, so fuck off. We do not want to devote our lives to the expansion of a catastrophic system. We want to create something else." It is clear that that is the only alternative that opens up the possibility of another world, the only revolutionary alternative. Somehow that is the perspective that we have to open.

In other words, we have to break open the unitary concept of labour. We need to say, as Marx did (but it gets lost in the Marxist tradition), that the category of labour conceals an antagonism between two different sorts of activity: on the one hand, what he called alienated labour or abstract labour or just plain "labour"; and on the other hand, an activity that we do not have a very clear name for: what Marx called "conscious life-activity" in 1844, or "concrete labour" in *Capital*. We have to say, as I think a host of struggles throughout the world, both within the factory and outside, are saying, "We are not labour. We do not like labour. Our struggle is against labour. We want to do something sensible with our lives. Labour is the subjection of our activity to the rule of money. That is not what we want."

It is not easy to see how we can just turn our back on labour, because then how do we survive? It is more difficult for us than it is for the woman in the song. If we think of it individually, it is very difficult. The more collective it is, the more feasible. (If you think of the millions of people who survive on less than one dollar a day, they do so on the basis of strong networks of social solidarity.) If we want to walk in the wrong direction, it is easier if we do it collectively, but the best way of doing it collectively may be to start off on our own and see who joins us. If we wait for everyone to be in agreement, we will never get anywhere. Revolution flows from the particular not from the totality.

The important thing is to connect in some way with an almost universal revolt against labour. Whether we are teachers or nurses or work in a factory or in an office, whether we are studying or unemployed, the tension between labour and doing something meaningful is something we feel intensely. Collectively or individually, we nearly all walk in the wrong direction in some sense. We try to create *no go* areas where we would say, "Here we shall not accept the rule of capital-and-labour. Here ... we reverse the flow of determination of our doing. Here we shall determine what we do, from below." There is a real rage in the world today against the rule of money. We must be careful not to deflect it into blaming banks, or finance capital, or the IMF: it is a rage against the rule of money, i.e., labour, i.e., capital.

This rage is expressed above all in cracks, in spaces or moments, large and small, in which people, by choice or necessity, and always in a contradictory manner, refuse to subordinate their activity to the rule of money and push toward self-determination of their own doing and living. The only way in which we can conceive of an anti-capitalist revolution today is as the creation, expansion, multiplication, and confluence of these cracks.

FIFTEEN

Crisis and Critique

I come home to *Capital and Class* with a mission, a challenge, an attack. I come to split the atom.

Critique is a splitting of the atom, the opening of categories that are closed, to reveal the antagonism within them. (In this sense the term "open Marxism," coined by Bonefeld, Gunn, and Psychopedis [1992], is a tautology, albeit a helpful one.)

Take a category, split it open. What do we see? Perhaps more categories. Take the commodity, for example, as Marx did. Split it open and we discover the antagonistic unity of value and use value. But that is not enough. We need to go to the core. We need to go ad hominem (as Marx insists). We need to reach an understanding of the category in terms of human action, going through layer after layer of conceptualisation if necessary. Why? Because it is only if we understand the social world in terms of human action that we can pose clearly the question of what human action is necessary to change it.

Take the antagonistic unity of value and use value and split it open, and then we come to the core, the pivot, a conceptualisation that refers directly to the antagonistic organisation of human activity, the dual character of labour as abstract labour and useful or concrete labour. "This point," says Marx in the opening pages of *Capital*, "is the pivot on which a clear comprehension of Political Economy turns" (1965 [1867], 41; 1990 [1867], 132). After the publication of the first volume, he wrote to Engels (Marx, 1987 [1867], 407): "The best points in my book are: 1) the twofold character of labour, according to whether it is expressed as use value or exchange value. *All* understanding of the facts depends upon *this*. It is emphasised immediately in the *first* chapter."[1]

We take the commodity for the sake of familiarity, but we could have started anywhere. Take the state if you like, split it open, and sooner or later you arrive at the same point, at the same critique ad hominem: it is the same self-antagonistic unity of abstract and concrete labour that explains the existence of the state. *Capital* is a critique of the categories of political economy, but the same principles apply to a critique of religion, politics, sociology, gender studies, or whatever: the question is always how do we understand the existence of the categories ad hominem, on the basis of the way in which human activity is organised.

We open the category and uncover the nature of the organisation of human activity. The categories of thought are expressions of the social relations that underlie them. "They are forms of thought expressing with social validity the conditions and relations of a definite, historically deter-mined mode of production." (Marx 1965 [1867], 76; 1990 [1867], 169). When we criticise the categories, we criticise the social relations that give rise to those categories. We open both. We see commodity and value as social relations and open them up to discover the dual character of labour that is at the root of both social relations and their conceptualisation.

What do we see then? We open the commodity and we see value and use value, but at first that is not really what we see. Our eyes focus on value. We open value and use value and see the dual character of labour as abstract and concrete labour, but the same thing happens. In reality our eyes focus on abstract labour. That is why there is so much discussion of value and so little of use value. That is why, in the recent turning of atten-tion to the dual character of labour, almost all attention focuses on one side of that dual character, abstract labour.

What we see first then is the dominant moment of the antagonistic unity. And something awful happens. Our critique degenerates into a theory of domination. Marxism becomes a theory of capitalist domination.

---

1   Marx continues: "2) the treatment of *surplus value independently of its par-ticular* forms as profit, interest, ground rent, etc.," but this does not concern us here. Note that Marx also saw this as his distinctive contribution: "I was the first to point out and to examine critically this twofold nature of the labour contained in commodities.": Karl Marx, *Capital,* vol. 1 (Moscow: Progress Publishers, 1965 [1867]), 42; Karl Marx, *Capital,* vol. 1 (London: Penguin Books, 1990 [1867]), 132.

Reactionary claptrap, in other words, a theory that traps us in the enclosure that it pretends to criticise. A theory of Cassandra, a theory that separates the analysis of capitalism from the movement of struggle, a theory that understands Marxism as the analysis of the *framework* within which class struggle develops. We do not want a theory of domination, we want a theory of struggle. We do not want to moan, we want to change the world.

Open the category and look again, look more carefully. Beneath and beyond the dominant moment of the antagonism we see the subordinate moment and it is moving, struggling. Beneath value we see use value, beneath the state we see anti-state forms of social organisation, beneath abstract labour we see concrete labour (or concrete doing). We do not see them very clearly, and we often do not have clear words to express what we see, because they all exist in the form of something else. Use value exists in the form of value, concrete labour exists in the form of abstract labour, social or communal organisation exists in the form of the state. They all exist, in other words, in the mode of being denied, as Richard Gunn puts it (1992, 14).

Denied but not annihilated. Contained but overflowing. Identified, defined, classified but breaking that identity, definition, class. Critique ad hominem, critique that takes us to the human roots of social phenomena, is inevitably anti-identitarian because it takes us to a restlessness that will not accept. Critique ad hominem takes us to ourselves, to the source of our own criticism, to our refusal, our rage, our dignity, our misfitting, our creativity, our inevitable schizophrenia. That which exists in the mode of being denied fights against its own denial, exists not only in but also against and beyond the mode of being denied. The force of our criticism lies inside that which we criticise, or, better, lies in-against-and-beyond that which we criticise. The force of our criticism of abstract labour lies in the fact that we the critics are part of the real movement of concrete labour in-against-and-beyond its own denial. The critical theorist is not the privileged intellectual but the subject, the doer, the concrete labourer who exists not only in the mode of being denied but also against and beyond it.

Take a category, split it open, and what we discover is not a philosophical contradiction but a living antagonism, a constant struggle, a clash between opposing movings. Abstract labour is a constant attack, a constant imposing on human activity of the ever-tightening constraints of socially necessary labour time. And concrete labour is a constant moving in the opposite direction, a moving toward the social self-determination of our own activity, the push of human creativity, the driving force of human production.

We uncover an antagonism, and our uncovering is part of the antagonism we uncover. Our opening is part of a social struggle to open. The conceptual splitting of labour is possible only because the struggles of 1968 split labour practically. And the other side, the moving of abstract labour, the abstracting of our doing into labour, is a closing. The abstracting of doing into labour is a closing of concepts and of social relations, the reaching out for other concepts in the process of closure, a social cohering of relations between people, a drive toward the formation of a system with its own laws of development, with its own identitarian logic, its own homogeneous time. The drive of formal rationality, the drive of the enlightenment. A cohering that gives them confidence and authority makes it all sound like the only possibility.

Genetic criticism, then, the derivation of the genesis of the different concepts (what Marx calls the return journey in the introduction to the *Grundrisse* [1973, 100]) is not the exposition of how capitalism *is*. Rather, it follows the movement of this closing, the moving toward a society subject to laws. We trace the movement not just of a past process but of present struggle.

But the closing is never complete, cannot be complete (because if it were complete we would not be here criticising). It is the closing of a ceiling over our heads, of walls around us, but we can still see beyond the ceiling, beyond the walls. The world of abstract labour is a closed world in which everything fits. But we do not fit. We are part of a world that does not fit. We mumble, we mutter, we are often incoherent, lacking in confidence, but we know that we do not fit. Concrete doing does not fit into abstract labour. Ours is the voice of misfitting, the voice of concrete doing.

We open a category and discover the misfitting that it conceals. We open the category and find that it conceals its own crisis. Critical theory is crisis theory, and crisis theory is critical theory. A plague on the preciousness of so much "critical theory" that thinks it can hold itself aloof from crisis and the social antagonism it indicates. A plague too on the boring emptiness of crisis theory, which sees itself as economics unburdened by the headaches of critical theory.

In the centre of critique is the opening of the most important atom of all, labour. Concrete labour (potentially conscious life activity) exists in the form of abstract labour, exists in-against-and-beyond abstract labour, exists as the crisis of abstract labour. Crisis is the moving of concrete doing in-against-and-beyond abstract labour, revolution is the breaking of concrete doing against-and-through abstract labour: of the creative force of human activity (force of production) against-and-through the dynamic social cohesion woven by abstract labour.

This is the pivot, the core of the newly emerging grammar of anti-capitalism. Why? Because if we split open labour, we can no longer conceptualise capitalism or class struggle as the antagonism between labour and capital. Labour (at least if we understand it as abstract labour) is the creator, day in, day out, of capital. Labour is on the same side as capital, and not just labour in the narrow sense but the whole world of theory and practice that springs from the dominance of abstract labour.

That is what the struggles are saying, inside and outside the factories: we are not labour; we do not like labour; we struggle against labour; we fight to emancipate our doing from labour. We want to dedicate our lives to what we want to do, what we consider important.

I said I came with a mission. That is my mission: to return to Marx in breaking open the atom of labour, not just in the sense of rediscovering the concept of abstract labour but seeing the revolt against abstract labour as the centre of class struggle, the hope for another world.

References

Bonefeld, Werner, Richard Gunn, and Kosmas Psychopedis. "Introduction," In *Open Marxism*, vol. 1, *Dialectics and History*, edited by Werner Bonefeld, Richard Gunn, and Kosmas Psychopedis, ix–xx. London: Pluto, 1992.

Gunn, Richard. "Against Historical Materialism: Marxism as a First-Order Discourse." In *Open Marxism*, vol. 2, *Theory and Practice*, edited by Werner Bonefeld, Richard Gunn, and Kosmas Psychopedis, 1–45. London: Pluto, 1992.

Marx, Karl. *Capital*, vol. 1. Moscow: Progress Publishers, 1965 [1867].

Marx, Karl. *Capital*, vol. 1. London: Penguin Books, 1990 [1867].

Marx, Karl. *Grundrisse*. London: Penguin Books, 1973.

Marx, Karl. "Letter of Marx to Engels, August 24, 1867." In Karl Marx and Frederick Engels, *Collected Works*, vol. 42. London: Lawrence and Wishart, 1897 [1867].

SIXTEEN

Rage Against the Rule of Money: The Leeds Lectures

I. Rage

Syntagma Square, Athens, June 15, 2011. Of the many images of the battle between police and protesters, one stands out. As the police attack time and time again and hurl canister after canister of tear gas, a group of musicians play their instruments in the centre of the square. Gas masks on their faces, they play on and on, a mocking repudiation of state violence, total asymmetry, turning rage into a thing of beauty: joyous rage, dignified rage.

We take up their tune, play variations, improvise, taking up themes as far as we can, and further. Surrounded by the noxious, evil-smelling gas of that's-the-way-things-are realism, we play on, making the music louder, spreading the melodies of revolt, the music of dignity.

We should all do this, in whatever way we can, singing songs, banging on a drum, whatever we know how to do. This is what I want to do in the only way that I know, writing these notes.

1. These Are Days of Rage

When the movements in North Africa and the Arab world started at the beginning of 2011 to proclaim Fridays as days of rage, days for the concentrated expression of accumulated anger, they set the tone for months to come. 2011, *a year in which rage ran through the world. Wonderful! And something to think about.*

Arab spring, European summer, American autumn, topped by a global day of rage on October 15. And now Occupy camps wherever I go. At their core is a No, we do not accept—a world that is unjust, a world that is corrupt,

238

that is attacking us, that ignores us, that tells us we are just the objects of history not its subjects. The rage is a rage-against, but it is more than that. It is also an amazingly creative rage, one that breaks with the existing institutions and opens up new ways of doing things. From being a critique of dictatorships, it quickly turned into a critique of democracies-as-we-know-them and a push toward new forms of social organisation and new ways of making decisions. We are seeing the development of a new grammar—or better a new anti-grammar of revolt. The assemblies, the people's microphones, the refusal to make demands, the repudiation of parties and of politicians left and right, the slogans: "Our dreams will not fit in your urns"; "This is not a question of Left against Right, it is those below against those above."

These are cracks in the domination of capital, spaces and moments of negation-and-creation, where we say No and create something different, exploring new paths, new logics, trying to open up different worlds. Not just autonomous spaces but cracks in the sense that they run with an amazing speed in unpredictable directions, cracks too in the sense that plasterers run around behind them, covering them up.

A war has been declared, one that may only be in its opening phases, perhaps still a phony war in some respects. Or perhaps the war was declared more than ten years ago, but we are only just beginning to respond to the viciousness with which we are being attacked. In this war I think of Greece as occupying a special place, because it is in Greece more than anywhere else that push has come to shove, that the master's roar of "Bow low! Submit!" coming from the Greek government, the European Union, and the money markets has confronted a massive No, a massive refusal from the Greek people. And Greece, perhaps more than anywhere else, forces us to think, and not just to celebrate, for despite the massive and repeated protests, despite the overwhelming repudiation of the government and of the political system by the Greek people (displayed for example in incidents all over the country on October 28), despite the forced resignation of Papandreou, there is no change in the austerity programmes, the government's repeated assaults against the living conditions and the way of life of the Greek people.[1] The massive protests of all shapes and sizes have not succeeded in stopping a dramatic fall in living standards. Lest we fall into an easy celebration of the great

---

1   Debtocracy, at http://www.debtocracy.gr/indexen.html.

struggles, we should remember the other side, as recounted in an article in the *Guardian*:

> Massive job losses, tax increases and galloping inflation have sapped the nation's energy. For pensioners forced to survive on less than 500 euros a month and families hit by unemployment that has reached a record 16%, there is no more room for manoeuvre. A new underclass has appeared: in the homeless and hungry who roam the streets; in the spiralling number of drug addicts; in the psychiatric patients ejected from institutions that can no longer offer them a place; in the thousands of shop owners forced to close and board up businesses; in those who forage through municipal rubbish bins at night; and in the pensioners who make do with rejects at fruit and vegetable markets. Suicides have also risen, with help lines reporting a deluge of calls—5,000 in the first eight months of 2011 compared with 2,500 for all of last year.

Dies irae indeed: day of wrath but with the crucial difference that, unlike the medieval hymn, the anger is not a judgement that comes down from a god on high but one that is exploding from below, exploding in the streets.

2. *This Rage Is Ours*

> Rintrah roars and shakes his fires in the burdened air;
> Hungry clouds swag on the deep.
>
> Once meek, and in a perilous path,
> The just man kept his course along
> The vale of death.
>
> But:
>
> Now the sneaking serpent walks
> In mild humility,
> And the just man rages in the wilds
> Where lions roam
> —William Blake, *The Marriage of Heaven and Hell*

We are the "just man" who rages in the wilds. The rage that runs through the world is our rage. We too are attacked, are indignant, are part of the 99%. In the war between rage and the power of the world-that-exists, there is no doubt, can be no doubt, on which side we stand. We stand on the side of rage: as experiential judgement and scientific responsibility.

It is not possible to stand outside rage. We live in a field of pain and anger. Anger is built in to the way in which the world is organised. Society is based on the rule of "faster! faster! faster!," sometimes referred to as the law of value. Usually the faster-faster-faster is imposed now not by the lash, as in slave societies, but by money, yet pain and anger is just as deeply encrusted into the social dynamic as if it were the lash that ruled, because the rule of money is the rule of stress, of unemployment, of feeling a failure, of gross inequality. It is a structural anger that is built in to the relation of oppression and that is present even when we feel happy. We have no difficulty in recognising that sort of structural anger when we see films of Robin Hood or Spartacus or slave plantations or the building of the pyramids: there is a righteous anger in the slaves or serfs even when they are having fun and laughing—even if they do not feel the anger in that particular moment, we recognise that it is inherent in the nature of serfdom or slavery. The anger is directed against those who benefit from the form of social organisation and take an active part in its imposition on the slaves and serfs. Now we live in a society in which the forms of imposition have changed, but the levels of alien determination of our daily activity are immeasurably greater and the differences between rich and poor far, far greater. Just as we now look back on the Russian serfs or the Egyptian slaves and wonder why they put up with it for so long, so it is be hoped that future generations will look back at us and wonder why we accepted for so long such pain, such obscenity.

In recent years capital has celebrated its orgies, the obscenity of the system has exploded beyond imagination. While millions and millions live on the edge of starvation or in the daily struggle for food, a tiny, tiny minority grow richer and richer and accumulate more and more power to impose themselves upon others.

This rage is ours, not just that of those who are camping in City Square or outside St Paul's or Wall Street or Puerta del Sol or Syntagma or Tahrir Square. Occupy everywhere! Or, more simply, occupy where we are! And where are we? In the university.

The rage is most definitely ours in the university. Around the world the universities have been at the forefront of the neoliberal attack. Everywhere there is a concerted assault to submit the universities to the logic of profit, the logic of the market. The decision by the government to triple fees in the

English public universities is probably the most grotesque example in the world, but everywhere there is a similar drive. These attacks limit access to higher education, make debt an even more central part of adult experience, and make market criteria the decisive factor determining the content and manner of education. The universities have become places of simmering rage, and in many cases of open eruption. Chile is the most outstanding example of such rage in the world at the moment.

But there is another sense in which rage is ours in the universities. Rage is the centre of scientific thought, anger is the core of rational thought. There is now surely only one scientific question left to us: How can we stop the headlong rush to human self-annihilation? If we think of scientific reflection or academic activity as related in some way to the future well-being of humanity, rather than as an impartial, disinterested record of our self-destruction, it is clear that it must be directed against the organisation of society that is pushing us in that direction. The sharpness of reason is the sharpness of the rage that runs through the world. As the beautiful letter of solidarity of October 26 to Occupy Wall Street from activists in Tahrir Square put it, "An entire generation across the globe has grown up realizing, rationally and emotionally, that we have no future in the current order of things."

Reason presents itself as the antithesis of rage. Reason, understood in this way, is the response from above that disarms, that says, "Let us be calm and think this thing out reasonably." "Be reasonable," says the spider to the fly, "Why do you get so excited?" But calm reason is reason within a framework of Reality, of that's the way things are. Let us be reasonable means: let us recognise Reality and reason from there to understand what is necessary. In response to the *indignados* of Spain and Greece: let us recognise the reality of money and understand what is necessary to maintain the integrity of the monetary system, and then we will see the irrationality of their protests. In recent months we have had an extraordinary flow of rational discourse from the newspapers, the politicians, and the academic commentators, in which the anger and pain of the people affected by and protesting against the current assault is simply blotted out. This has been particularly clear in discussions of the Greek financial crisis, where detailed discussions of the settlement between the European Union, the IMF, and the European Central Bank, of the size of the haircut that debtor banks will be required to accept and the scale of the necessary recapitalisation make little or no mention of the thousands and thousands of people protesting in the streets. Academic discourse is the discourse of the spider. This neutral, objective reason is the instrumental reason criticised by Adorno and Horkheimer, the positive rationality fustigated by Marcuse. It is rational irrationality, the rationality of an irrational world, the internal coherence of an obscene society.

Rage, then, rage against the false neutrality of academic and official discourse. Rage against the presentation of history as a process without a subject, without us.

3. Rage Faces Two Ways

Rage is a dangerous game, a two-edged sword.

On the one hand, it is the cutting edge of indignation, of offended dignity. The angers are there all the time, and not just the angers but the constant, often very patient, efforts to open cracks in the existing system of social relations, spaces or moments in which we do things in a different way and break the apparently irresistible logic of money. The great surges of social rage are a sudden flooding together of these angers, these cracks, these pushings in a different direction, a powerful flash of confluence. These are insurrectionary moments that transform people's lives and transform perceptions of reality. They are opportunities for accelerated and radical social change, probably even a necessary precondition for such change. The victim throws off her suffering and becomes an active subject, the many "I"s become a "We." This is dignified rage, righteous rage, the rage of hope.

But there is another side to rage. We only have to look back a few months to the English riots to see how ambiguous rage can be. Or look at the attacks on the Christian Copts in Egypt not very long after the Arab Spring. Or the way in which the demonstrations outside the Parliament in Athens turned into fighting between Communist Party supporters who wanted to defend the Parliament and the anarchists who wanted to attack it. Or look at the rage of the Tea Party in the United States or the rise of racism throughout Europe in recent years. Or look back at the form that social rage took during the last great crisis of capitalism. Rage can so easily become a rage of hatred and destruction.

One reason for starting with rage is that we live in a moment of intensifying rage. Crisis is the sharpening of social tensions, of frustrated expectations and the bitterness that grows from that frustration. More and more people cannot find employment. For those who do, the stress and the insecurity have become much greater than before. According to an article published in October 2011, unemployment among young people stood at 46 per cent in Spain, 43 per cent in Greece, 32 per cent in Ireland, 27 per cent in Italy, 22 per cent in the UK, and 24.6 per cent in the United States, with the expectation that it would continue to rise. Many, many young people cannot go to university because they do not have the money to pay for it. More and more people die simply because they lack access to healthcare. The number of people living in extreme poverty increases. There is more violence, both state and non-state. If there is a structural anger built in to the way that society is organised, then this is accentuated in periods of crisis. We are living in days of rage, and this social rage is likely to continue and intensify in the years that come. It makes no sense to say that it should not be so, that people should be reasonable. The rage is there and growing, and we are part of it. We cannot stand outside it. We are riding a tiger, and we cannot get off. What we can perhaps do is influence the direction in which it moves.

This is why I have chosen to focus on rage. It could be suggested that I should focus rather on joy or laughter or love as the driving force of the creation of a different world, and that this focus on rage is in fact dangerous because it can easily be seen as promoting a politics of violence, which is very far from being my intention. I understand the argument. Joy and laughter are at the centre of the struggle against the Grey Men of capitalist order: look at the music and the dancing in Syntagma Square with which we started. Yet, I choose to focus on rage for two reasons: because rage is the cutting edge of the push for social change, and because the rage is there, an exciting but also very dangerous force with which we have to come to grips.

Rage of hope, rage of destruction—they lead in very different directions yet there is a shared starting point: the frustrations and bitterness that arise from a system built on the exploitation and humiliation of the vast majority of people for the enrichment of a very few. How do we deal with this common basis? How do we distinguish between the rage of hope that pushes toward new worlds and the rage of destruction? Is it a question of ideology, of class consciousness, of social origin, of organisational form? How can we play a part in the flows of social rage? Where do we direct our rage?

The Zapatistas organised a big festival a few years ago that they called the Festival de la Digna Rabia, the festival of dignified or righteous rage. The title is important because it puts rage at the centre of the struggle, and characterising the rage as dignified or righteous clearly suggests that there is also an undignified rage or non-righteous rage, a rage to be rejected, a rage of destruction. But how can we distinguish between the two rages, or rather how (given that it is not a question of classifying rages), starting from the commonality of our rage, can we drive our rage in the direction of dignity? Perhaps there are two key issues. First, our rage is a rage-against but against whom or against what? Second, how do we express our rage?

This is what I want to explore in the rest of these notes.

II. The Rule of Money

4. *We Are Under Attack*

Our rage is a response to an attack. All over the world people are outraged not just because they are suffering the same problems as always, the same poverty, the same boredom at work, the same difficulties getting into universities, and so on. It is more than that. It is rather that people's expectations are being overturned or the basis of their way of living destroyed.

This attack is experienced in many different ways. The big indigenous march against Evo Morales's government in Bolivia in October was a reaction to a planned invasion of their territory by building a highway through the jungle. The big revolt by students in Britain, when it comes, will be in response to the repeated attacks on university life and what it means to study. The wave after wave of demonstrations in Greece are a response to the austerity measures that the government seeks to impose and that severely affect people's living standards and expectations.

Often the spark of rebellion is a defensive, even conservative, spark. They attack our jobs and we protest. They attack our schools, universities, and health services and we protest. They destroy our living as peasants and we protest. They attack us in the name of Progress, and we say that is not the Progress we want. Conservatism is a force to be respected, a force that has far more revolutionary than is often recognised.

This conservative defence against attack is an important part of the current wave of struggles around the world. Its core is a "No, we will not accept."

No, we will not accept you turning our lives upside down like this. We will not accept you destroying the schools and universities. We will not accept you destroying the countryside and eliminating the peasantry. No.

This is tremendously important and gives the struggles a solid strength.

The worm turns, and the worm that turns is a powerful beast to be feared. Defence bursts its own banks and overflows. If we say No to the attack on the universities, it leads us on to think about what exists. We do not accept the attacks of the government, but that does not mean that we think that the universities are great as they are. Increasingly, they have been subordinated to the logic of capital. All critical thought has been expelled from more and more institutions. Let us turn that around, let us turn every seminar and every lecture into a fight against the rule of the rich, the rule of capital. Defence, taken seriously, pushes us forward into an attack on that which exists. Their aggression has gone too far, and now we are on the offensive.

But against whom or what and how? How can we, the turning worm, the roaring, ranting, raging worm push against-and-beyond and beyond and beyond to reclaim our world and destroy the forces that are attacking us? What is it that is attacking us?

5. The Attack Is a Systemic One

In the protests in Budapest a few months ago, people marched under the banner of "I Don't Like the System." One of the slogans in Madrid makes a small but crucial correction: "We are not against the system, the system is against us."

But what does it mean? And what can we do about it?

6. The Attack Is Not a Personal One

Who is attacking us?

Perhaps the easiest way to react to our pains is to look for someone to blame. If we can find a person or a group of persons to blame, then it would seem to follow that we can change things by getting rid of those people and replacing them with others. And so we blame the politicians: we blame Papandreou and Zapatero and Cameron and Berlusconi and Mubarak and Gaddafi or, in other times, Stalin and Hitler. Or we blame the bankers, who pocket their million-dollar bonuses in return for destroying the planet. I was in Ireland just as the crisis was breaking, and there was a big move there to hold the bankers responsible and try to send them to prison.

At times, it seems as if the very act of raging drives us toward personalising that rage. There are, however, two great problems in personalising the blame, in directing our rage against certain groups of people. The first is that it falls into a way of thinking and talking that can lead to great destruction. The slogan "Kill the bankers! Kill the rich!" is enormously attractive but no different in structure from "Kill the Jews! Kill the immigrants!" In the same way, "Kill the fascists!" is a mirror image of "Kill the communists." Especially in the present period, we have to be careful not to reproduce the symmetries that have proved so disastrous.

The second problem is that personalisation of responsibility locks us into a cycle of hopelessness. Experience has shown repeatedly that changing people in positions of power makes very little difference. Papandreou and Zapatero and Cameron are to be blamed not because they have behaved badly as politicians, but simply because they have behaved as politicians, that is, as people who are part of a system that they do not control. As politicians, they dedicate their lives to implementing a system of aggression. It is the system of aggression that we have to dismantle: to change the agents of its implementation changes very little. The politicians are incapable of giving us what we want, simply because they are politicians, cogs in a wheel.

Yet it is hard to avoid completely the blaming of persons. For most people in the world, there was probably something deeply satisfying in seeing the Iraqi journalist hurl his shoe at Bush a few years ago, for example. And even if we understand that the actions of bankers obey a logic that is not the result of their volition, we are surely right in raging against the people who consciously reap the benefit of so much destruction. Certainly the bankers whose behaviour contributed to the crisis behaved simply as bankers do and must—as representatives of money in search of more money—yet anyone who chooses to be a banker at that level knows or should know that they are actively participating in a system that is causing death and destruction throughout the world. In that sense they are just as much to blame as the politicians like Bush, Blair, Cameron, Obama, and the many others who have acted as war criminals in recent years. Perhaps they should not be brought before the courts because that tends to absolve the system by individualising the blame, but some form of popular tribunal or public repudiation (as in the Argentinian *escraches*, for example) is surely appropriate. And it is magnificent that the politicians in Greece are afraid to show their faces on the streets.

The general point, however, is that to restrict our protests to the personal is not enough. We need to go beyond that.

7. *The Attack Is Not (Just) a Question of Policy*

A more sophisticated analysis presents the problem not in terms of individuals but of policy, of a line of action consciously adopted by politicians or imposed by the most powerful states. For the last thirty years or so, the policies of virtually all states, whatever the proclaimed complexion of their governments, can be seen as part of the neoliberal offensive: a political approach based on giving priority to the market, reducing the role of the state in providing education, healthcare, and other forms of social provision, promoting the privatisation of everything that can become a source of profit for the owners of capital.

There is no doubt that these policies have been promoted very consciously by specific political groups and theorists, yet the fact that similar policies have been adopted almost everywhere suggests that it is not simply a matter of political choice. The protagonists of these policies are simply swimming with the tide, with a great flow of social determination that they neither initiated nor control. If that is so, then it is not enough to direct our rage against neoliberal policies (the Washington Consensus) or to argue for a Keynesian welfare-state approach. All the experience of recent years indicates that politicians have very little capacity (or perhaps willingness) to change the direction of policies. Obama is perhaps the clearest current example of this: elected as a symbol of change, he has done very little to live up to that expectation.

It is precisely the fact that there is such little difference between the actions of governments of Left and Right that has led to such a massive repudiation of representative democracy in all the movements in this wave of indignation. "Where is the Left? Down there, on the right," as one of the slogans from Madrid put it. Perhaps more clearly than anything else, the current wave of rage has been directed against the bankruptcy of representative democracy, against its failure to represent the interests of the people. There is no more grotesque illustration of that than the vote in the Greek Parliament in the middle of June to accept the austerity measures imposed by the European Union and the IMF, while outside in the square hundreds of thousands of people hurled their defiance.

Representative democracy cannot represent the interests of the people if all governments and all representatives are being washed along by a tide that leaves them little room for action. We must take our rage a step further.

8. *Real Democracy Now! But the Issue Is Not Just Democracy*

Direct democracy has been the organisational form common to all the big uprisings in this year of rage: from Tahrir Square to Puerta del Sol to Syntagma Square to Occupy Wall Street and beyond. This is of enormous importance: we refuse to trust politicians or institutions; we reclaim the world as ours. We reclaim and assume our responsibility for the world. We want assemblies not just in the principal squares but, as the Occupy Wall Street website states: "We want to see a general assembly in every backyard, on every street corner because we don't need Wall Street and we don't need politicians to build a better society."

"*Democracia real*—real democracy" has been perhaps the central call of the movement, first raised by the indignados in the Puerta del Sol. Thousands and thousands of people have taken part in assemblies in over a thousand cities. A real movement from below that breaks institutional and party politics and links back to the long tradition of councils-assemblies-communes that has always been at the heart of the struggles for a different world.

Organisationally turning of the world upside-down is of fundamental importance. It brushes aside the state and the old institutionality of protest. It marks out a reclaiming of the world. Yet this reclaiming, to gather force, must be a process of breaking. To call for more direct democracy makes sense only if we understand democracy as breaking barriers and breaking reality. Decisions are always taken in a context, whether the decisions are individual or collective, authoritarian or anti-authoritarian. One can imagine that inside a prison it would be possible to organise a directly democratic process of deciding on meals and exercise times, but if the walls of the prison are not broken, the process could hardly be described as free. We have seen that politicians do not make decisions freely but are tightly constrained by a reality to which they constantly pay reverence. The simple act of creating an assembly to make decisions from below is a challenge to that reality. But it is only a first step.

We are in a prison surrounded by many walls. By occupying, we break one wall, the wall of political institutions. But the other walls are still there, and we must go on and on, breaking through one wall after another, if our push toward freedom is to be maintained. Just to take one example, a very interesting article by Mike Davis on the Wall Street occupation argues: "The great issue is not raising taxes on the rich or achieving a better regulation of banks. It's economic democracy: the right of ordinary people to make macro-decisions about social investment, interest rates, capital flows, job creation, and global warming. If the debate isn't about economic power, it's irrelevant." Interestingly, he breaks through two walls, those of taxation on the rich and regulation of the banks, and comes to the real issue of economic democracy, but then leaves the other walls intact. It is not that his (or indeed anyone else's) points are wrong, it's just that to give them real force we need to go on and on, breaking through wall after wall of apparent reality. What Davis omitted to say is that economic democracy means almost nothing as long as private property remains untouched and, above all, as long as the existence of money remains unquestioned.

That is what is so exciting about the present movements: the breaking of wall after wall and the unmasking (or partial unmasking) of the real enemy: Money. Money is the name of the assault on humanity. What an absurd thing to say!

9. Money Is the Attack

"We are not against the system, the system is against us." And the system that attacks bears a name: Money.

The system is not stable: it is an assault, an intensifying attack. The dynamic of the attack is the dynamic of money.

This is on the tip of the tongues of protesters all over the world. "Banksters-Gangsters, tremble in your suites! We're foreclosing on you in the streets!" (a slogan heard during the Oakland General Strike, Nov. 2) The attacks are on the banks and on the bankers but rarely directly on money. (Perhaps in general the challenge for theoretical reflection is to try and understand what is on the tip of movements' tongues, state it, and draw out the implications. Not just to celebrate the movements—though that is important—not to berate the movements and tell them they've got it wrong but to listen to them and try to push beyond.)

Perhaps people do not say that the enemy is money because it is too obvious, or perhaps too ridiculous, or perhaps both.

It is obvious enough. Look at the Greek referendum, for example. When Papandreou proposed a referendum to ask for the approval of the Greek people for the agreement he had already concluded with the European Union, the financial markets reacted sharply. It was not the bankers who were reacting, it was simply the movement of money, the functionaries of the movement of money placing it wherever they thought its prospects of securing a profit were best. Bankers are relevant only insofar as they behave as bankers, as servants of the movement and self-expansion of money. The real attack is not that of the bankers but of money.

Obvious, but if people do not say it, it is because it seems ridiculous. How can we blame money? Money is reality, isn't it? And anyway, aren't we fighting to have more money (more money for schools, hospitals, parks, ourselves), not to abolish it?

Certainly, we probably all want more money for ourselves, for our loved ones, or simply to achieve whatever we consider important. Money is the form that wealth takes in this society, and as the producers of that wealth, we all want to participate in it. In the present society, no matter how austerely we may (or may not) like to live, we need money to live and to realise our projects. So yes, we want more money for ourselves, for the universities, for schools and hospitals, for gardens and parks, for projects that point toward a different world, and so on. But that does not mean necessarily that we want a world that is ruled by money, that we want a world in which the richness that we produce takes the form of money. We can say, "Yes, in the present society we want money, because money is the key that gives us access to all sorts of things." But at the same time we know that this arrangement is terrible, that it is unjust, obscene, destructive. Probably most of us would be very happy if we had free access to social wealth without the medium of money.

But even if we leave aside the fact that we all want money, it still seems pointless to say that money is the enemy when it is hard to imagine a society without money: money seems identical to reality. What is the point of saying that reality is the enemy? It seems like saying, "Tough, it's a hard life, but we have to live with it."

Again, look at Greece: everything tells us that it is very simple: the Greeks just have to face up to Reality. They have been living beyond their means. They have had a binge and now have to accept the hangover that is the price for their excesses. Is this simple reality? Or is it an assault on humanity that bears the name of Money?

The notion that money is reality is absolutely central to the current attack on living conditions throughout the world. Discussing the impact of Berlusconi's resignation, a BBC commentator wondered whether the Italian people would have the "maturity" to accept the necessary measures of austerity.

We seem to be in a dilemma. It is easy to see that there is a force behind the banks and the corporations driving their insatiable greed, and that force is profit, the drive for more and more money. Yet money is so identified with reality that it seems nonsensical to call for its abolition. That is why the call remains on the tip of the tongue of the present movements, and indeed their enormous merit is to have brought the call to that point.

We seem to be trapped. Our rage seems to be based on a fundamental misunderstanding of the reality of society. Perhaps all those sober commentators, politicians, and bankster-gangsters who look down from suites at the occupiers of the world and shake their heads are right: perhaps we just need to mature and accept the logic of the world, the reality of a world ruled by money.

It is important to face this problem, to try and think it through, because if we do not, there is a danger that our brave cries of opposition will end in disillusionment. The wager of Occupy Wall Street and all the other occupies is that we subordinate the world to social control. But to do that, we have to think and act our way through the power of money.

The only way out of the trap is to break the reality of the existing world, to show that it is not reality.

10. Money Is Not Immutable, Eternal Reality—It Is a Historically Specific Form of Aggression

Money is a historically specific form of relating to other people, a historical form of social bond, social nexus, and social cohesion. It did not always exist, and there is no reason to think that it must always exist. What we do know is that the fact that it does exist has terrible, terrible consequences. It is a way of relating that has a built-in aggression that is also a dynamic of human destruction. I want to single out three aspects of this aggression (without claiming to present a general theory of money).

11. Money Is a Social Bond That Constantly Attacks Human Activity

Labour-labour-labour: faster-faster-faster. That is the centre of the money-aggression that is the attack at the core of money as a form of social cohesion.

Money is a social bond, a form of social cohesion, a form of relating our different productive and social activities. Money seems quite innocent, just a sensible way of relating your activity to mine. It seems to be just a simple medium of exchange. I am a carpenter and produce a table, and I want to sell that and buy a coat. Rather than spend my time looking for a tailor who happens to want a table, it is easier if I can just sell it to whoever for money and then go to a tailor and buy my coat.

It seems simple, but money is the original Frankenstein's Monster. It separates itself from the original process of exchange, and then turns against the original exchangers and attacks them. It does this by imposing its own laws on the process of exchange. What determines the rate at which the carpenter can exchange the table is the time taken to produce it, not the time she has taken but the time that is socially necessary to produce it. And since the time required to produce a table is constantly decreasing, this means that the carpenter must produce the table faster-faster-faster. If she does not, she will not be able to sell it at a price that reflects her work, or she may not be able to sell it at all. In other words, it is money that now tells her both how and how fast she must work. Money transforms the work process itself, converts a particular concrete activity into abstract or alienated labour, a mere means of making money. This does not mean that there is a total destruction of human creativity, but money hangs over every productive process, determining what will be produced and how.

This is raised to another dimension under capitalism when the carpenter begins to employ other people to produce the tables. The drive to produce everything faster-faster is now not just so that the carpenter can survive but becomes necessary to produce profit. The drive to make money is transformed into the drive to expand money, to make profits, and the faster-faster is turned against the workers. It is they who must produce faster-faster, and if they do not, they are simply excluded from the production process, they are made unemployed. Alienated or abstract labour, then, is not just labour that is alien and meaningless to us: it is a constant attack. Just as value production is constantly reformulated as the time socially necessary to produce a commodity falls, so abstract labour means a constant drive to produce things faster.

The rule of money is backed by punishment. Money, by virtue of being the universal medium of exchange, becomes the gateway that controls access to the products of human creation and the benefits of nature. If you do not obey the rules of money or cannot labour according to the money's requirements, then you will be excluded from human wealth. You will be poor, even to the point of starvation and death.

Money (or those who speak for money) is essentially saying, "Work harder, or you will suffer the consequences." Or rather, "Since you are too lazy, you must suffer. Now learn to work harder, or you will suffer more." This is the core of all the austerity plans and the financial crisis in Greece and the other countries. Jin Liqun, supervisory board chairman of China Investment Corporation, a sovereign wealth fund with $410 billion in assets under management, bluntly told Al Jazeera television: "If you look at the troubles which have happened in European societies, this is purely because of the accumulated troubles of the worn-out welfare society. The labour laws induce sloth and indolence rather than hard work." Or, as Alan Greenspan, the former head of the U.S. Federal Reserve, put it in the *Financial Times*, the real issue is a question of culture. And Kieran Kelly noted, "[I]f I lived in a country like this [Greece], I would find it hard to stir myself into a Germanic taxpaying life of capital accumulation and arduous labour. The surrounds just aren't conducive." For the euro to work, there must be some mechanism "to constrain aberrant behaviour."

The problem, of course, is that the type of labour imposed by money is destroying humans and destroying the world. It is causing more and more stress, excludes a very big proportion of the world's population, and is the basis of the process of destruction that is literally tearing the world apart.

12. *The Money-Attack Is the Movement of Monetisation of Social Relations, the Progressive Penetration of all Social Life*

Money has existed for a very long time, ever since the rise of commodity production (the production of things for exchange) from which it is inseparable, but for most of this time its impact has been relatively peripheral to people's lives. It is with the rise of capitalism that there is a progressive penetration of money into all of life. Once people are driven off the land and forced to sell their labour power in return for a wage in order to survive, their existence becomes dependent on having enough money to buy the commodities they need to live. It is with this that money becomes established as the dominant form of social cohesion.

The establishment of money as the dominant form of social cohesion and the ever-growing penetration of money into people's lives was achieved by bloody conquest and the violent destruction of previously established forms of social bonding. The struggle to impose, deepen, and maintain the monetising of social relations is continuing. This can be seen in the present barbarous destruction of the peasantry throughout the world, in the growing subordination of universities and education throughout the world to the logic of money, in the whole process of instructing young children that commodities have to be paid for with money, in looting, robbery, and the ever-growing number of those who police the rule of money. The existence of money as a form of social cohesion is constantly at issue. A huge apparatus of vigilance and oppression is required to impose and maintain the monetising of social relations and the unquestioned appearance of money as reality.

Money is not a thing but a social relation, and it is important to understand that it is an antagonistic one. Money is a process, a battle to impose discipline not only in the workplace but throughout society and in every aspect of life. Each banknote that we hold in our hands conceals a battlefield on which thousands and thousands of people die each day.

13. *Money Is an Attack Beyond All Social Control*
Money is an aggression that is not controlled by anyone.

The rich, the capitalists, benefit from the existence of money, they dedicate their lives to the expansion of money, but they do not control it. Governments may influence the movement of money, but they do not control it. Just look at the present moment, how the eyes of all governments are constantly on the money markets. See how the markets have just swept aside Papandreou in Greece and Berlusconi in Italy: certainly good riddance but also a display of the power of the money markets.

The autonomisation of the money form of social control is already present in the simplest form of money as a medium of exchange.

To return to my previous example of the carpenter and the tailor, the existence of money as a medium of exchange opens up the possibility that instead of buying the coat after selling my table, I may decide that I like the money and use it to buy something that I can sell at a higher price and so expand my money. The money and the commodities change places. At first the money was simply a means of exchanging commodities, now the commodities are simply a means of expanding money. Money has released itself from its humble origins. It was created as a social bond, a social nexus or form of social cohesion, but the social nexus acquires its own autonomy. It becomes an alien power over which nobody exercises control. It reacts upon the social processes that it was devised to bring together. I now produce chairs as commodities as quickly as possible, so that I can make more and more money. Money seeps into my whole way of working, transforms my daily activity into alien or abstract labour, under constant pressure to go faster-faster-faster. The only way to sell my chairs well is to produce them faster than my competitors, because it is the average speed of production that determines the price at which the chairs sell. Money begins to impose its own laws on everyone, and not just on humans but on other forms of life as well. If I find I cannot make enough money making chairs, I shall turn to something else more profitable, like drugs, arms, or indeed money itself. I shall forget about things and producing and lend my money to other people, making more money that way. Bliss, the pure self-expansion of money!

The self-expansion of money, the pursuit of profit, in other words, becomes the fundamental driving social force once capitalism develops. Labour power becomes a commodity, and money comes to penetrate all aspects of society. Accumulate! Accumulate! That is Moses and the Prophets! And accumulation is the accumulation of profit. This is the self-expansion of money, but money is only significant if it corresponds to something being produced. An expansion of money that does not correspond to an expansion of value means the present or threatened devaluation of the money. The self-expansion of money has as its base the expansion of value production, which in a capitalist context means the expansion of surplus value, of value that is surplus to the requirements of the reproduction of labour power and is appropriated by capital. But the basic point remains: there is a dynamic at work that no one controls—the dynamic of the self-expansion of money, the dynamic of capital accumulation. Capitalists seek to benefit from this dynamic, but they do not control it.

Why then focus on the power of money, rather than the power of capital? It is certainly not to suggest that money can be understood separately from capitalist exploitation: it is clear that the financial crisis must be understood as a crisis of the relations of production, a crisis of capital. First, because it is on the tip of the movement's tongue; second, because it is necessary to constantly refresh the language of revolt, to create fresh trails, rather than going down the well trodden paths of revolutionary discourse; third, because the focus on money confronts us with a more radical challenge that is at the same time more accessible, more within our grasp. It makes clear that the only way of abolishing class exploitation is through the abolition of money as a form of social cohesion: a challenge that clearly throws the ball into our court.

Money is the flow of capital, the flow of the faster-faster-faster that is at the centre of capitalist production into the further-further-further that is tearing up the earth. When capital meets obstacles in the process of production, it turns itself into money and flows further-further-further in pursuit of other ways of expanding itself, turning itself into mines that uproot peasants and destroy whole swathes of countryside, often turning its back on any form of production and seeking ways of making money from money, desperately pursuing the dream of the alchemists. What exists in the factory simply as capitalist command, the right to manage, to tell workers what to do and how to do it, becomes a flow of social determination throughout society shaping what is done and how, subordinating everything to its discipline. In the factory, the capitalist imperative of Accumulate! Accumulate! that is Moses and the Prophets translates directly into the imperative directed to the workers: bow low, bow low! Obey your lord and master! Money is the flow of this imperative throughout the world: bow low, bow low, obey your lord and master gives way to the Logic of Money! To which our rage, the rage of Tahrir Square, of Puerta del Sol, of Syntagma and Wall Street, says clearly, "Sorry, but no, we will not obey. We will not bow down!"

The aggression and the autonomisation of money from any form of social control goes a step further with the development of debt. Debt is the fragile separation of monetary expansion from value expansion. It is always a gamble on future value production. You do not have any money to do what you want, so you go to the bank and say, "Lend me some money. I assure you that I will have funds to pay you back in the near future." And the bank, keen to seize an opportunity to make profit, to make expand its money, says, "Yes." Both sides are gambling on an expectation, but the realisation of the expectation depends at the end of the day on the creation of the value that will substantiate it, on the creation of surplus value, in other words.

Of course the debt can multiply and become further and further removed from any production, but it is always based on a fragility, on the possibility that the necessary surplus value will not be produced, that the debtors will be unable to pay, and that their non-payment may lead to the collapse of the creditors who owe money to other creditors and to their collapse and so on in a cascade of non-payments and collapses that we know as financial crisis. Such a collapse destroys expectations and lives on a vast scale and, if all goes well for capital, restores a stable relationship between monetary expansion (the expansion of fictitious capital) and expansion of value production.

The expansion of debt is always a risk and is always dangerous, and this danger expresses itself as the threat of violence (because debt always involves a threat of violence, a "pay up or else") and also as increasing pressure on those who either produce surplus value directly (such as factory workers) or indirectly create the conditions for its production (like university workers). The money-attack becomes the debt-attack.

Crisis can express itself in many ways, but it is always an expression of a production of surplus value that is inadequate to meet the faster-faster-faster requirements of capital. Put simply, we are the crisis. We humans stand in the way of capital's drive to profit, money's drive to expand itself. Our humanity is what causes the problem: our attachment to silly little things that do not fit in with abstract labour, like doing what we like, spending time with friends, putting up resistance when too much is demanded, having a sense of justice and solidarity, not paying attention and walking off somewhere else. We are the crisis, our refusal to submit, our lack of adequate subordination.

Crisis is the clash between the drive of money (faster-faster, submit-submit), on the one hand, and our "Sorry, but we have other things to do," on the other. But it does not normally present itself in this way. There is a whole world of refracting images or fetishes that produce an appearance that is quite different. Money does not appear as the constant assault that it is, the organisation of the political in a multiplicity of states means that rivalries between states intervene, banks adopt new practices that attract popular blame, and so on. But the core of any crisis is always the same: there is not enough surplus value produced to provide the profit required to secure capital's reproduction, and there is not enough surplus value produced because capital's domination, however total it may appear, is not complete.

We must say loudly and with pride: we are the crisis of the system that is driving us toward our destruction. Of course capital tries in every way possible to overcome our resistance, telling us that money is simply a reality that we must be mature enough to accept, and by hitting us over the head when we are too immature to understand, by starving those who do not fit in because they were born in the wrong place or do not have the right skills or speak English, by bombing and killing those who do not fit in. The last great crisis of capital was resolved after the slaughter of about a hundred million people. That is why this time we are saying, "Enough! Enough of that stupid system! Game over!"

I want to conclude this section with a quote from the always irresistibly quotable Marcos, something that he said after the devaluation of the peso at the end of 1994 that should stand as a proud proclamation of the great movements of anger that we have seen in this year: "We have made the Power of Money tremble. It has realised there is something it cannot buy or sell, that dignity is starting to unite. The Power of Money is afraid, because the uniting of dignities signifies its downfall, its rapid transition to part of a nightmare that is coming to an end, the conclusion of a historical phase ruled by arrogance and stupidity."

III. Push Back the Rule of Money! Break the Rule of Money! Communise!

"The Beginning Is Near."
(a placard in the Oakland General Strike, November 2, 2011)

"We are not indignant, we are determined."
(Athens)

Break the power of money, because money is the key to the worldwide war against humanity. Break the power of money, because money is the social connection between us that has become more and more autonomous from us and more and more aggressive against us and now threatens to destroy us. Break the power of money, because otherwise whatever victories we achieve will be caught in the tentacles of the all-absorbing monster and turned against us.

Break the power of money: How can we even begin to pose this as an aim? An abstract call that is not grounded in the struggle makes little sense. It is only if it is already on the tip of the tongue of the struggle that it gains potential material force. But even if we say that it is already there, that it stands only thinly veiled just behind all the attacks on the banks and the bankster-gangsters, even then the question remains: How could we possibly abolish the power of money? Maybe we have to approach the point gradually, in small steps, each spilling over from the other.

14. *The Starting Point Is an Absolute No to the Assault of Money*
The first and perhaps the most important step is to say No. No, we do not accept. No. That is what protesters all over the world have been doing. It is what the students in England said on November 9 and what we are all saying today, what the students in Chile and now in Colombia have been

saying for months, what the Greeks have been saying over and over and over again to the government's austerity measures, what the occupiers from Puerta del Sol to Wall Street and beyond have been saying: No, we do not accept your logic, we do not accept your world, No.

The power of the absolute No should not be underestimated. In 1999, the university authorities at the National University in Mexico City wanted to raise student fees from a nominal £1 a year to about £50 a year — bad enough but nothing compared with tuition in England. Nonetheless Mexican students went on strike, completely shutting down the university (one of the largest in the world) for almost a year. The government sent in the police and arrested hundreds of students, but still the students won: the rise in fees was dropped and never mentioned since.

This is a repudiation of the rule of money. "No, here the writ of money does not run, keep your logic of death away from us."

15. *The Force of the No Turns the World Upside Down*

The simple No is more than a simple No. It is the reclaiming of our subjectivity, the rejection of a history that would roll on and over us, the repudiation of history as a process without a subject.

The No is a Here we are! We reclaim our space, our time, our history. We reclaim the world from those who are robbing it. We say to the politicians, "How dare you! You have it all wrong. You think you are our masters, but you are not. You are our servants, and you must obey us." This is the Zapatistas' *mandar obedeciendo*, rule by obeying. This is the Bolivian *pachakuti*, the affirmation of and insistence on a different perspective, a different pattern of social relations. You, politicians, must obey us, and if you do not we shall hold you responsible.

This turning of the world upside down is expressed beautifully in the letter of the comrades from Tahrir Square to the occupiers of Wall Street:

> We are not protesting. Who is there to protest to? What could we ask them for that they could grant? We are occupying. We are reclaiming those same spaces of public practice that have been commodified, privatized and locked into the hands of faceless bureaucracy, real estate portfolios, and police "protection." Hold on to these spaces, nurture them, and let the boundaries of your occupations grow. After all, who built these parks, these plazas, these buildings? Whose labour made them real and liveable? Why should it seem

so natural that they should be withheld from us, policed and disciplined? Reclaiming these spaces and managing them justly and collectively is proof enough of our legitimacy.

This reclaiming of the streets and parks and other places and times is already a movement against money. It is the refusal of a social bond that is alien to us; it is the transformation of space and time through the creation of different social connections. It is important to make this explicit, for money is always waiting in the wings, moving to reabsorb all protests.

16. Push Back the Rule of Money

Perhaps it seems too difficult, too extreme, to call for the breaking of the power of money. It is easier to think of pushing back the rule of money, of restricting its area of sovereignty.

The history of the twentieth century can be seen as the history of the struggle to push back the rule of money, or at least to keep it out of certain areas of human life. The century began with a huge wave of repudiation of the destructive effects of money, the high point of which was probably the Russian Revolution of 1917, which remained a major force until at least 1926. The fear that this revolutionary wave instilled in the servants of money combined with more limited struggles and in many countries led to the acceptance that some areas of human activity should not be immediately determined by money and the pursuit of profit. This huge drive, both revolutionary and reformist, to push back the rule of money, to exclude it from certain areas, had enormous consequences and, while we may be critical of the results in many ways, it would be wrong to fail to recognise the huge achievement of pushing money/capital out of the direct control of activity in large parts of the world and important areas of everyday life. The removal of education, healthcare, housing, pensions, and in some countries employment from direct determination by the criterion of profitability had a huge and generally very beneficial effect on people's lives. Being able to go to the doctor without worrying about whether you can pay for it transforms people's lives.

But the rule of money was not broken. Capital was forced to retreat and regroup, but it did not lose its dominance. There were three principal limitations to the success of the drive against the rule of money.

The first was the state. In both the welfare state and the would-be revolutionary variants of the drive against money, the state was understood as being a polar opposite to the rule of money, an alternative form of social cohesion. In fact the state as a form of social organisation complements the rule of money (that is, it is a particular form of the capital relation). In the welfare state countries, the state's primary role remained the attempt to promote optimal conditions for the accumulation of capital, and this always limited and shaped healthcare, education, and other systems apparently abstracted from the functioning of the market. In the regimes that were established on the basis of the Russian and Chinese Revolutions, the attempt to replace money with the state as the central principle of social cohesion failed: inevitably it was oppressive and inefficient not because it reduced the role of money but, on the contrary, because it excluded people from the control of the social. With this, the state effectively destroyed the only basis on which an alternative form of social cohesion could be woven. The result, in both cases, was a growing bureaucratisation of the areas apparently liberated from the rule of money.

Pushing back the rule of money does not have to involve the state. An example that comes to mind is that of the so-called War of Water in Cochabamba in Bolivia in 2000, where the people came together to reverse the privatisation of water and, after a confrontation with the army sent in to defend the interests of the French multinational that had been given the water concession, forced the company to withdraw, taking the water system into popular administration.

The second limitation was money itself. Although profitability was driven out as the main determinant of certain areas of activity, the prevalence of money as the dominant form of social cohesion was not questioned. In the case of the countries where the limited pushing back money was achieved under the banner of the welfare state, the overall dominance of money was never questioned. In the case of the Russian Revolution, after an initial period, the centrality of money was reestablished under the New Economic Policy (and defended theoretically in debates around the role of value in socialism—hence the importance of the work of theorists such as Rubin, who argued that value is a specifically capitalist form of social relations, and Pashukanis, who, in the same situation and with similar consequences for himself, argued that the state was a specifically capitalist form).

Linked with the state and money as forms of capitalist social relations is the most important limitation of all: labour. Money as a social bond shapes what it binds: it transforms human activity into labour, an alien, alienating activity determined not by us (individually or collectively) but by money's meaningless and unceasing drive to expand itself. It is this alien or abstract labour that is the substratum of money, and it is this shaping of human activity into labour that constantly produces and reproduces money as the dominant social connection. Breaking the power of money would have to be based on a different sort of human activity. Yet neither the welfare state nor the Russian and Chinese Revolutions questioned the nature of labour. On the contrary, labour (alienated, abstract labour) was understood as the basis both of the welfare state and of the socialist revolutions. Think of Lenin's espousal of Taylorism, and think of Stokhanov as the model for socialist workers. Labour, previously imposed immediately through the operation of money, was now imposed through the state, acting under the pressure of the international movement of money. The result was the same: the elimination of a self-determining social activity, which would be the only possibility of weaving alternatives to money as a social bond.

It is easy now to criticise both the socialist revolutions and the welfare state and to understand how their limitations weakened them and laid them open to the onslaught of money, yet it remains true that pushing back the rule of money was an aim widely shared and widely assumed to be obvious. For all our criticisms of social democracy and party communism, we need to pick up the fallen banners, make them ours, and declare that we too are fighting to push back the rule of money.

Push back the rule of money: that is probably something we can all agree on. Push it out of certain areas where its destructive effects are most obvious, like healthcare, education, housing, water, and electricity, and then keep on pushing. Money is far more noxious than tobacco, it causes far more deaths each day, far more pain and suffering. Perhaps we should declare the elimination of money as the aim and see how to eliminate it from one area after another. There is, however, an important difference from tobacco. The progressive elimination of tobacco smoking is promoted through the state: this is not problematic, because it is quite compatible with the state's role in promoting the accumulation of capital. In the case of money, however, it is different: to do it through the state would be to reproduce the limitations that characterised the welfare state and the socialist revolutions.

17. Break the Rule of Money! Communise!

Pushing back is not enough. This does not mean that there cannot be significant victories within the capitalist framework. There have been in the past, and there may well be in the future.

The most conceivable possibility in the present situation would be some sort of Keynesian solution, some sort of quantitative easing of money by which states would promote the continued expansion of debt and play a role as lender of last resort. (This would probably have to be the basis of any state-based pushing back solution.) It is being suggested by a number of commentators, for example, that this would be the only way of preserving the euro in the present crisis, but the problem is that the creation of the euro was specifically designed to exclude such flexible solutions, and there is at the moment no institution that could play the role of lender of last resort. In any case, any Keynesian solution of debt expansion is always a postponement of crisis, and while it may protect living standards to some extent, it does so at the cost of deepening the subjection of our lives to labour and money, of labour strengthening the position of money in the medium term and creating the likelihood of an even more enormous crash in the future.

We need desperately and urgently to break the destructive dynamic of money. Yet it is difficult to see how this could be done without the development of alternative forms of social cohesion, of different forms of coming together.

The socialists of the last century had a clear conception of the form of social cohesion that would take the place of money: the state and, crucially, state planning. This did not work because it was an attempt to replace one alien social bond with another. The result was oppressive, inefficient, and destructive.

The problem remains, then. If we want to get rid of the existing form of social cohesion, we need to develop an alternative form or, better, different alternative forms of social cohesion, because without some sort of social bonding we could not survive. This would probably be hopeless if we were not already doing it.

We can think of these processes of creating different social cohesions as the movement of communising. The money-attack is a constant process of destroying existing communities, existing structures of communal support and production, whether these are based on traditional communities or families or friendship. Money, as the process of monetising social relations, breaks existing bonds and replaces them with the money connection. Communising is the movement in the opposite direction: not backward but toward the creation of new relations of collaboration and support. This is more than pushing back the rule of money, it is the interstitial breaking of the power of money.

Three ways of thinking about this occur to me. First, there are movements that begin as movements of community defence. As I have mentioned elsewhere, the Zapatista uprising was in part a reaction to the threat to the their communities posed by the reform of the Mexican constitution and the undermining of collective forms of landholding. But the uprising has not just been a defence. It has been an affirmation and reorganisation of the communities, a development of new forms of self-government, and a complete repudiation of the state. A defence of the community that turned into a real reclaiming of communal power. And it is not just the Zapatistas. Indigenous movements throughout Latin America have played a very important role in recent years. Look at the big indigenous march in Bolivia last month (October 2011) that forced the government to reverse its plan to build a highway through the jungle. This too was in defence of a way of living in which money does not play an important role and forms of communal solidarity are very strong. Or if you do not want to go so far, you can think of the struggle in Rossport in the west of Ireland over Shell's Corrib gas pipeline as a struggle in defence of a communal way of life. These are all defences that overflow, defences where challenging the rule of money opens a push toward a different world.

Second, we can think of movements that consciously set out to do things in a different way, that deliberately seek to create quite different social relations as a way of living, to create a form of living based on cooperation and mutual solidarity. Think of the many Occupies of the world, the multitude of ecological communities throughout the world, the transition towns movement, with projects like Transition Heathrow, think of the Common Place here in Leeds and now The Space.[2] All can be seen as cracks, as quite conscious walkings in the wrong direction. There is no model, and

---

2   The transition towns movement is an international network of local community projects that aim to increase self-sufficiency, particularly in relation to energy consumption. Transition Heathrow is part of this network, operating in the particular context of Heathrow Airport in London. The Common Place was a social Centre in Leeds, as is The Space, where the last of these three lectures was delivered.

all are contradictory. Any attempt to break the rule of money and go the other way is going to involve compromises, a constant negotiating of the interface with the world we are trying to break from. It makes no sense to think in terms of purity—there are no pure solutions. I do not mean by that that we should not criticise different choices, but we cannot do it from the moral high ground of correctness.

Third, and especially important in the present situation, people are often pushed into communities of mutual support. If you think of the thousand million or so people who live on less than a dollar a day, it is not just that they live in great poverty, it is also that their lives are not monetised to the degree that ours are—they live on the basis of strong networks of mutual support. I remember hearing a Kenyan woman, Wangui M'bata, speak about that and how horrifying it was for her to see how old people are treated in Europe, simply because those networks of support have broken down to a large extent. This is important because what we are seeing now with the crisis of capitalism is the crisis of money as a social bond, as a form of social cohesion that allows people to survive. People are forced by necessity (and sometimes also by choice) to create alternative networks of support.

The cities of Argentina ten years ago provide a dramatic example of what that can produce; economic collapse was not just characterized by massive demonstrations that brought down one president after another but also by neighbourhood councils, recovered factories, barter networks involving millions of people, and unemployed workers' movements with their bakeries and kitchens and workshops and community gardens. Some of them declared that they were a movement of the unemployed, but they were not fighting to be employed, they had no desire to go back to being exploited but wanted to dedicate their lives to meaningful activities. To a lesser extent, similar processes took place in Greece: occupations of the public squares, neighbourhood assemblies, barter networks, creation of community gardens in the cities, people returning to cultivate the land there, organised non-payment of taxes on electricity bills and the reconnection of electricity for those who had been cut off, with the slogan: "No house without electricity!" The important thing is to see these not just as temporary expedients forced on people by necessity but as being attempts, in face of the failure of the money nexus, to create other forms of social connections that point toward a different sort of society and a different way of living.

The crisis is an attack on the way we live, but it is also a trap. Capital invites us, in effect, to tell it how much we miss it, how much we love it: "Come back capital, come back money, give us a job, let money flow into our lives!" That is the traditional politics of the Left: fight for the right to work! The challenge is to turn crisis around, break that eternal return to submission and say, "No, capital, we are your crisis. Our refusal to become robots is the rock on which your constant attack is broken. Now it is time for you to be gone because we have other things to do with our lives. We want to create a world that makes sense."

Can we do it? Perhaps we can.

SEVENTEEN

Communise

It has to be a verb, doesn't it? A noun cannot possibly express adequately the sort of society we want. Social organising that is self-determining cannot possibly be contained inside a noun. The notion of "communism" is grossly, nonsensically, dangerously self-contradictory. A noun suggests some form of fixity that would be incompatible with a collective self-creating. A noun excludes the active subject, whereas the whole point of the world we want is that the active social subject would be at the centre.

Ours is the revolt of verbs against nouns. It is the revolt of being-able-to against Power, of *poder* against *Poder*, *pouvoir* against *Pouvoir*, *potere* against *Potere*, *machen* (and *können*) against *Macht*. The moving of self-determining (of communising) against alien determination can hardly be otherwise. Alien determination entraps our lives within coagulations, within barriers, rules, frontiers, habits—within social forms, in other words. Social forms are the moulds or jellies into which human action rigidifies.

Marx devoted his work to the critique of these forms. The challenge is posed in the first sentence of *Capital*, which tells us that under capitalism the immense richness of human creation "appears as an 'immense accumulation of commodities'" (1990, 125). It *appears* as such because that is the social form in which it exists. Or, as Marx put it in the *Grundrisse* (1973, 488): "[W]hat is wealth other than the universality of human needs, capacities, pleasures, productive forces etc.... [t]he absolute working-out of his creative potentialities, with no presupposition other than the previous historic development, which makes this totality of development, i.e. the development of all human powers as such the end in itself." The potentially unlimited force of human creation is really entrapped within the limits of the commodity form. An absolute horror, a total nightmare, a present catastrophe that threatens to lead us to complete self-annihilation. How did it happen? What does it mean? How can we break these social forms?

What is at issue is not just the forms that Marx criticises in *Capital* (commodity, value, money, rent, law, state, and so on) but the very rigidification of human interaction that constitutes these forms. It is not just a question of criticising capitalist social forms but of understanding social forms as such as being capitalist—a vertiginous, exhilarating thought. Or, to return to our opening formulation, the problem is not particular nouns but nouns as such, the very enclosure of verbs within fixities.

The noun is closely tied to the closure of identity, whereas a verb suggests nonidentity, an overflowing of identity, a bursting-beyond, a moving of anti-identity, an anti-identifying that can only be understood as a constant moving against the identity within which it is (and we are) entrapped, a subverting. Let the noun, then, stand for identity and the verb for the moving of anti-identity. Identity is the real but mendacious separation of constitution and existence, whereas it is clear that communising can only mean the overcoming of this separation. Love as passion not as habit.

Communising is the moving against what stands in the way of our social determination of our own lives. The obstacles that confront us are not just our separation from the means of production but all those social forms that proclaim their own identity, that negate their own existence as forms and simply say, "We are." Money, for example, says, "I am who am," pure timeless identity. It does not say "I am a form of social relations, a rigidification of the way in which people relate to one another in a historically specific social context." It does not say to us "I am a human product and can therefore be abolished by humans." Just the contrary: the force of money depends on the denial of that which produced and produces it. The power of money is based on the separation of its existence from its constitution, from its genesis. And, as with money, so with wife, table, state, commodity, Australia, man, dinner. All of these present themselves in their pompous, mendacious, self-sufficiency as identities, as existences liberated from their constitution, as nouns that have swallowed up the verbs that created them. All must be dissolved. Communising is the movement of dissolving them, the unchaining of our doing, the reclaiming of the world. To free our culinary doing, we must understand dinner from the point of view of cooking. We must reunite the existence of the dinner with its constitution, emancipate the verb from the noun that it has created. And, as with dinner, so with man, Australia, commodity, state, table, wife, and money.

Critique, then, is genetic and directed at recovering the genesis of these forms that deny their own origins. It seeks behind that which exists the process that constituted it, that gave rise to its existence. Crucially, it also asks, "What is it about the constituting that gives rise to an existence that denies its own constitution? What is it about our verb that creates a noun that swallows up the verb? What is it about our doing that creates a done that denies the doing?" It is not enough to understand money, wife, table, state, commodity, Australia, man, and dinner as human products. We must go to the root, understand what is wrong with our doing that produces these monstrosities, these children that deny their own parents.

What is wrong with our doing? Marx's answer is clear. In capitalist society our doing is self-antagonistic. It has a dual character, which Marx refers to as useful or concrete labour, on the one hand, and abstract labour, on the other. "This point is crucial to an understanding of political economy" (1990, 132). If we wish to understand why our activity produces a society that denies our activity, then we must look to the twofold nature of that activity.

Concrete labour is simply labour that produces wealth in all its manifold varieties. It is making a car, writing an article, cooking a meal, cleaning the street. Here there is nothing that leads to a separation between constitution and existence. I make a table, and I use it or give it to someone else to enjoy: its existence as a table speaks directly of my act of making it. There is a making and a thing made but no separation between them.

Abstract labour is the same activity but seen now from the perspective of producing commodities. I make a table, but what matters is not the individual characteristics of the table or my relation to it but its value or the price that it will receive on the market. The table, as a commodity, is a "thing outside me," totally indifferent to me. As a commodity, it is a thing to be bought and sold, to be measured in the quantitative relation it establishes with other products—measured generally in money. In the world of commodities what matters is the amount of value produced not its composition in terms of cars, articles, meals, or clean streets. There is an abstraction from the particular qualities of the concrete labour: these count now only as a quantity of abstract labour. There is an abstraction from the very act of producing: all that matters is the quantity of value produced. Abstract labour creates a world of things, a world of existences that separate themselves from their constitution, a world of identities that proclaim, "We are," a world of nouns indifferent to the verbs that brought them into existence, a world of fetishes (as Marx calls it). Abstract labour is dynamic and driven (by the pursuit of value, of profit), but it posits its creations as things independent of the act of creation. In other words, it is the existence of our activity (doing, concrete labour) as abstract labour that leads to the rigidification or coagulation of social relations into social forms. We can speak of abstract labour as a social form, as the form in which concrete labour exists, but it is the central form that generates all other forms. It is abstract labour that holds entrapped the endless potential and creativity of concrete labour, that is, of human doing; and, therefore, it is the key to all the other forms of entrapment or domination.

Wealth exists in the form of an immense accumulation of commodities, concrete labour (or human doing) exists in the form of abstract labour. Human doing (concrete labour) produces wealth; abstract labour produces commodities. In both cases the activity (doing or abstract labour) is inevitably social. There is a coming together of different activities, a cohering of diverse active subjects, some form of sociality, communality, some communing of doers, some form of communising. Wealth exists in all societies, but in present-day society it takes the form of an accumulation of commodities; human doing exists in any society, but in this one it exists in the form of abstract labour. In the same way, we can say that communising, or social cohering, exists in any society, but in capitalism it is present in a peculiar form. There is a more intense and extensive integration of doings than ever before, but the intense social integration is not accompanied by social determination of what is done but is subjected in the first place to private determination by the owners of capital; the private determinations by the capitalists are subject in turn to a social determination by money (ultimately value), a determination that is subject to no conscious control. Communising, like wealth, like doing or concrete labour, exists as a hidden substratum of a social form that denies its existence. We have, then, an indissoluble trinity (in no way formulaic)—wealth, doing, communising—that exists in the form of a counter-trinity, equally indissoluble—commodities, abstract labour, capitalism.

All eyes now turn to this "exists in the form of," or "appears as," or "presents itself as." When we say (with Marx) that in present-day society wealth "appears as an 'immense accumulation of commodities,'" it is clear that this is not mere illusion, not a false appearance. If wealth appears in this way, it is because it really exists in this form. It is equally clear that the expression does not indicate a simple identity: we are not saying that in capitalist society wealth *is* an immense accumulation of commodities, concrete labour *is* abstract labour, communising *is* capitalism. We are clearly talking of two things that are non-identical but *appear* to be identical. There is at very least a tension here, but what is the nature of this tension?

It is a tension of domination. If something exists in the form of something else, then clearly it is subject to that form. If wealth exists in the form of commodities, it is the commodity that dominates, just as abstract labour dominates concrete labour, and capitalism dominates the communal.

This domination is a negation. If wealth exists in the form of an accumulation of commodities, then in effect the commodity is proclaiming, "I am the only wealth," a wealth usually measured in the money-form of the commodity. This we know from constant experience: wealth is measured in money. The lists of the five hundred richest people in the world, for example, assume that richness is identical to the accumulation of money: they do not try to measure richness in terms of people's wisdom or affective relations or enthusiasm for what they do. Wealth-richness disappears from view and money-wealth takes its place. That which exists in the form of something else exists in the "mode of being denied," to borrow Richard Gunn's classic phrase (1992, 14).

The fact that something exists in the mode of being denied does not mean that it ceases to exist. On the contrary, inevitably, it struggles against its own denial. Domination without resistance and revolt is inconceivable. The very fact that we think of revolt means that subordination is not total. The tension is an antagonism between content and form, between that which is denied and that which denies it.

This is an antagonism of verbs not of nouns: an active struggle. Domination, if it meets resistance (as it always does), is an active dominating. Dominating is always a struggle; it can never be taken for granted. Moreover, it is characteristic of domination under capitalism that it cannot stay still. The fact that value is determined by the socially necessary labour time required to produce a commodity means that the enriching of human capacity to produce is metamorphosed into an intensification of abstract labour, a faster-faster-faster. Domination cannot afford the luxury of the stillness of a noun: it can only be a dominating that constantly struggles to find ways of achieving an ever-deeper subordination of life to its aim of self-expansion. And if dominating is a verb, then clearly resisting and rebelling are too. The forms of social relations must be understood as form-processes, processes of forming, not as established fact. Money as monetising, state as statifying, commodity as commodifying, man as manning, Australia as Australing, and so on: all fierce struggles, daily and often bloody fightings.

This is the key issue in Marxist theory and practice. It can be seen in the debates around primitive accumulation. In the traditional mainstream interpretation, primitive accumulation refers to the violent period of struggle that led to the establishment of capitalist social relations, a historical phase followed by a routine capitalist normality. There is in this interpretation a clear separation between constitution and existence. Primitive accumulation is taken to refer to the constitution of forms of social relations (value, state, capital, and so on), followed by a period in which these forms acquire a relative stability. If that is so, then these forms can be seen as nouns: nouns with a limited historical life, but nevertheless as nouns that have a degree of fixity as long as capitalism survives. Marx expresses the traditional view graphically in the *Grundrisse*:

> Therefore, the conditions which preceded the creation of surplus capital or which express the becoming of capital, do not fall into the sphere of that mode of production for which capital serves as the presupposition; as the historic process of its becoming, they lie behind it, just as the processes by means of which the earth made the transition from a liquid sea of fire and vapour to its present form now lie behind its life as finished earth. (1973, 392)

Constitution is clearly separated from existence. However, those of us who live just beside smoking volcanoes (in my case Popocatépetl, just forty kilometres away) know that the geological transition from a liquid sea of fire to solid earth is not as clear-cut as Marx suggests, and we strongly suspect that this is even more so in the case of social relations. Like onion soup, beneath the apparent solidity of money, for example, is a seething, bubbling liquid. It certainly cannot be taken for granted that money is a universally respected form of social relations: How else can we explain the vast amount of energy devoted to its enforcement? Money, like state, man, woman, Australia, Mexico, rent, is constantly at issue, constantly contested: the existence of all these social relations depends on their constant reconstitution. Although there may well be significant differences according to time and place, Marx was wrong to suggest such a radical separation between constitution and existence.

The capitalist form of social relations, this rigidification of social interactions into established patterns, is a process, a verb, a rigidifying or forming of social doings that always meets with opposition. Genesis refers not just to the past but to a constant process of generating and regenerating the social forms; genetic criticism is not just the uncovering of the past but also of the present generating. If wealth exists in the form of an accumulation of commodities, this means that there is a constant commodifying of the richness of human creation, and that this commodifying meets a resistance, a constant pushing by human creativity against the commodifying and a constant overflowing from commodification. In other words, if wealth exists in the form of an accumulation of commodities, this inevitably means that it exists not just in but also against and beyond the accumulation of commodities. It does not exist outside the accumulation of commodities, untouched by it: this would lead us to an ahistorical essentialism that would not be helpful. It does not float in the air: it is living daily struggle. The richness of our activity is constrained within the commodity form but also pushes against it and, at least sporadically, it breaks eruptively through the commodity form, establishing other ways of interacting. Indeed, both sides are constituted through the antagonism: it is clear that the accumulation of commodities is constituted through the struggle to commodify wealth, but the contrary is also true: wealth is constituted through the struggle in-against-and-beyond the commodity form. And what is true of wealth is also true of concrete labour and communality: they are not only trapped within their capitalist forms but also push against and beyond them.

We can go a step further. That which exists in the form of something else, that which exists in the "mode of being denied," is the hidden substratum of that which denies it, and thereby its crisis. That which appears on the surface—commodities, abstract labour, capitalism—is nothing without that which it denies: wealth, concrete labour, communality. The master depends on his servant, always. It is a mutual dependence, but the relation is highly asymmetrical. The master without his servant is nothing, unable to cook his supper or make his bed, but the servant, through her concrete labour, is potentially everything, as Hegel, La Boétie, and others have pointed out. Power, the noun, is visible, but it depends on the invisible "being able to." The possibility of radical change comes from below, from what is hidden, from what is latent, from what Power depends on. It is this dependency that is the key to the crisis of domination. Marx's theory of the rate of profit is an attempt to understand how capital's dependence upon labour (and therefore on the transformation of human activity into labour) manifests itself in the tendency of the rate of profit to fall. The latent is the crisis of the apparent, the verb the crisis of the noun.

Enough, then, of the absurd, degrading idea that the crisis is the fault of the capitalists! We are the crisis of capital. We, who are not just invisible but latent, the latency of another world. We, who are the verbs that the nouns are incapable of containing. We, whose concrete doing will not fit in to abstract labour, whose wealth overflows from the immense accumulation of commodities, whose communality bursts through the false community of individuals and citizens. We who will not be contained, who have not yet accepted our role as robots. We who are the hidden volcanic substratum upon which the whole edifice of power is so fictively constructed. We who reclaim the earth because it is ours.

Communising is the moving of this crisis. Crisis is most visible in falling rates of profit, falling growth rates, rising unemployment, and so on, but beneath these manifestations lies the incapacity of capital to subordinate human doing sufficiently to the logic of its dynamic. Beneath the statistics lie the volcanic eruptions of insubordination, the ever-growing No, the overflowing of this No into "No, we will not accept that. We shall do things differently, in a way that we decide." Navarino Park in the centre of Athens, where the people tore down the walls of a car park to create a community garden, a place of children's games and cultivating vegetables and playing music, a place for talking and making revolution. A large part of the state of Chiapas, where the road signs proclaim, "Bad government stay out, here the people rule!" The recovered factories in Argentina, where the workers have shown that there can be a life without bosses. Abahlali baseMjondolo, the shack-dwellers in Durban, who are creating a living communism in their settlements. And so on and on and on. We can all think of examples, fill page after page with them. Communisings large and small, often so small as to be invisible, even to the participants—but nonetheless crucial, for crisis can probably not be explained in terms of overt resistance, but it certainly can be understood as resulting from the combined effect of open insubordination and the constant and ubiquitous non-subordination and refusal to subject our lives totally to the ever-intensifying exigencies of capitalist production. Communisings of many different types, all experimental, all filled with the active fragility of verbs, all contradictory, with one foot caught in the filthy mire of capitalism while they reach for something else, a different doing, a different richness, a different coming together.

Communising not just as verb but in the plural: communisings. The flowing of many babbling brooks and silent streams, coming together, parting again, flowing toward a potential sea. There is no room here for institutionalisation, however informal. Institutionalisation is always an attempt to block the flow, to separate existence from constitution (is that not the meaning of institutionalisation?), to subject the present to the past, to hold still the flow of doing, whereas communising is the opposite: the push to free ourselves from past determination, to give explicit articulation to the unity of constitution and existence.

Not communism-in-the-future but a multiplicity of communisings here and now. Does this mean that there can be no radical break with capitalism? Certainly not. We have to break the dynamic of capital, but the way to do it is not by projecting a communism into the future but by recognising, creating, expanding, and multiplying the communisings (or cracks in the texture of capitalist domination) and fomenting their confluence. It is hard for me to imagine the overcoming of capitalism other than through the confluence of communisings into a torrent that marginalises capital as a form of organisation and renders its violence ineffective. Then indeed we could think of the journey ending in a homecoming, but even that could not be a communism but only a constant communising in a more favourable climate (as indeed home is never the noun that the child imagines but a constant recreating by those involved).

Communising is simply the reclaiming of the world that is ours or, perhaps better, the creating of the world that is ours, in which we articulate practically the unity of doing and done, of constitution and existence, the communality of our doings.

Communise, wherever you are now.

References

Gunn, Richard. (1992) "Against Historical Materialism: Marxism as a First-order Discourse." In *Open Marxism*, vol. 2, edited by Werner Bonefeld, Richard Gunn, and Kosmas Psychopedis, 1–45. London: Pluto, 1992.

Marx, Karl. *Capital*, vol. 1. London: Penguin Books, 1990 [1867].

Marx, Karl. *Grundrisse*. London: Penguin Books, 1973.

EIGHTEEN

Opening Speech

1

My opening speech has a title: Opening Speech. When Daniel sent me the programme and I saw that I was due to give an opening speech, I thought, "Yes, yes, yes! Just what we need. A talk that opens. A dream, a wonderful dream!" Thank you, Daniel, for the suggestion. But is it possible? A talk that really opens, a talk that opens a world that is closing. Maybe even a talk that opens a festival that opens.

I want a talk that is not just the first talk in the festival. Of course that is already fantastic, a great honour, it is beautiful to be in Graz again, to be in the Dom again, to be on the stage after Kate Tempest. All that is wonderful. But I want more than that.

2

An opening talk (a talk that opens) walks in the wrong direction. It moves against the closing of the world. Just like the student protests of five years ago here in Austria. Those protests were directed against the closing of the world that the Bologna Process means: a closing of spaces within the universities, a closing of the possibilities of critical thought, a closing of the mind, a tighter subordination of the universities to the requirements of the system.

This closure is not restricted to the universities. A certain logic is being increasingly imposed on all aspects of life: the logic of money, the logic of profit, the logic of closure. In the universities, this logic tells us, "Don't think too much, just learn the correct answers." In the countryside it says, "Don't think that you can just live in the same way as your parents and grandparents, keeping some cattle and planting the crops you need to live. Now you must make way for agricultural mass production with all the chemicals and insecticides required." Or, ever more frequently, "Now you must make way for the mines, the dams, the motorways, the high-speed trains. In fact, why don't you just get out of the way altogether?" Millions upon millions of people are forced off the land into the world's slums every year. While in the cities the logic of money tells us, "Don't just think you can do what you want with your lives, you need to earn your living, and that means you need to do something that will increase profits, increase the power of the wealthy." That is what is happening: an obscene concentration of wealth all over the world, a huge increase in the power of the wealthy, in the power of money.

Money presents itself as a world of freedom, as an opening of possibilities for all. In fact it is just the opposite. The logic of money is the logic of closure. It is the weaving together of all human activity into a world totality, a system that nobody controls but that follows a simple law: more, more, more profit. And if you do not want to follow the rule of money, if you want to do something else with your lives, then you must be mad or criminal and should certainly be locked up. Money is a prison, supported by multiple lines of closure that are becoming more and more violent: borders, for example. The dynamic of money is the shattering of the hopes and dreams of youth, and we see it over and over again: dreams broken on the reality of unemployment or, often worse, the reality of employment.

3

It is not just that we live in a world of enclosure, but that the enclosure is becoming tighter all the time. Money has a dynamic. Money is capital and it cannot stand still. The rule of capital is "faster-faster-faster." And the rule of faster-faster-faster means "out of the way with the people who are holding things up, out of the way with the protesters and into the prisons with them, or into the mass graves that are multiplying throughout the world." The walls are closing in on us and threatening to crush us completely. The dynamic of money is the closure of life itself.

The dynamic of money is the dynamic of death. And the servants of money are the servants of death. Look closely at them, whether they be capitalists, like Gates or Slim or Buffett, or their political lackeys, like Obama or Cameron or Putin, and you will see that their faces are death masks. The apparent masters of the world are the servants of a system that is destroying us.

It is not just a question of future doom through climate change or shortage of water or nuclear war. The twilight is already upon us. The death of communities, the death of species, the death of many, many people. There is a real possibility that this is the closing of humanity's day on earth. Neoliberalism it is often called, but it is not a question of policy: it is capital that is celebrating its orgies—it is money as a form of social organisation that is reaching its limit.

A time of depression, perhaps, a time when most parents expect life to be more difficult for their children than it was for them, a time when the possibility of radically transforming the world seems to have faded.

4

That is why an opening speech is necessary, a speech that really opens. "Now is the time to learn hope," as Ernst Bloch wrote after the experience of the Nazis and the war. Not just a silly, empty hope that everything will turn out all right in the end, because it's not like that. It must be a grounded hope, a *docta spes*, as Bloch calls it.

In Bloch's day, hope was still tied to the Party and the idea of winning control of the state. But all that has gone, the party is over. We have to relearn hope, rethink hope, learn to open our eyes and open our minds and see beyond the closing walls of capitalism.

Hope lies not in building the party, not in winning control of the state, an institution absolutely integrated into capitalism that cannot be used to overcome it. Hope now lies in the millions and millions of us who say: No we will not accept your destruction and your mines and your dams and your guns and your wars. We will not accept the rule of money. We shall do things in different ways, connect to one another in different ways. We do not want your totality of death. We do not want any totality. We saw in the last century what happens when one totality is replaced by another, one closure replaced by another—the shameful tragedy of communism as it was. And now we say No. We break away from the totality of capital-death in a million different ways. We communise, fight to take control of the earth before they destroy it completely. We fight to open a gap between the future of capitalism, which can only be death, and the future of humanity, which can still be life.

Bloch pinned hope to the power of the Not Yet, the power of that world that does not yet exist, and therefore exists not-yet in our refusals, in our dreams, in our experimental creations, in our pushings against and beyond. It is a question of learning to listen and, hearing, to extend and strengthen. Arundhati Roy expresses this beautifully: "Another world is not only possible, she's on her way. . . . On a quiet day, if I listen very carefully I can hear her breathing."

Listen carefully, then. This Opening Speech, this Opening, this Festival, is part of the breathing of a world struggling to be born. There will be no closure.

Index

"Passim" (literally "scattered") indicates intermittent discussion of a topic over a cluster of pages.

About the Author

John Holloway is a professor of sociology at the Instituto de Ciencias Sociales y Humanidades in the Benemérita Universidad Autónoma de Puebla, Mexico. He has published widely on Marxist theory, on the Zapatista movement and on the new forms of anti-capitalist struggle. His book *Change the World without Taking Power* has been translated into eleven languages and has stirred an international debate. He is also the coeditor of *Beyond Crisis: After the Collapse of Institutional Hope in Greece, What?* (2019) and the author of *In, Against, and Beyond Capitalism: The San Francisco Lectures* (2016).

ABOUT PM PRESS

PM Press was founded at the end of 2007 by a small collection of folks with decades of publishing, media, and organizing experience. PM Press co-conspirators have published and distributed hundreds of books, pamphlets, CDs, and DVDs. Members of PM have founded enduring book fairs, spearheaded victorious tenant organizing campaigns, and worked closely with bookstores, academic conferences, and even rock bands to deliver political and challenging ideas to all walks of life. We're old enough to know what we're doing and young enough to know what's at stake.

We seek to create radical and stimulating fiction and nonfiction books, pamphlets, T-shirts, visual and audio materials to entertain, educate, and inspire you. We aim to distribute these through every available channel with every available technology—whether that means you are seeing anarchist classics at our bookfair stalls, reading our latest vegan cookbook at the café, downloading geeky fiction e-books, or digging new music and timely videos from our website.

PM Press is always on the lookout for talented and skilled volunteers, artists, activists, and writers to work with. If you have a great idea for a project or can contribute in some way, please get in touch.

PM Press
PO Box 23912
Oakland, CA 94623
www.pmpress.org

PM Press in Europe
europe@pmpress.org
www.pmpress.org.uk

FRIENDS OF PM PRESS

These are indisputably momentous times—the financial system is melting down globally and the Empire is stumbling. Now more than ever there is a vital need for radical ideas.

In the years since its founding—and on a mere shoestring— PM Press has risen to the formidable challenge of publishing and distributing knowledge and entertainment for the struggles ahead. With over 300 releases to date, we have published an impressive and stimulating array of literature, art, music, politics, and culture. Using every available medium, we've succeeded in connecting those hungry for ideas and information to those putting them into practice.

Friends of PM allows you to directly help impact, amplify, and revitalize the discourse and actions of radical writers, filmmakers, and artists. It provides us with a stable foundation from which we can build upon our early successes and provides a much-needed subsidy for the materials that can't necessarily pay their own way. You can help make that happen—and receive every new title automatically delivered to your door once a month—by joining as a Friend of PM Press. And, we'll throw in a free T-shirt when you sign up.

Here are your options:

- **$30 a month** Get all books and pamphlets plus 50% discount on all webstore purchases

- **$40 a month** Get all PM Press releases (including CDs and DVDs) plus 50% discount on all webstore purchases

- **$100 a month** Superstar—Everything plus PM merchandise, free downloads, and 50% discount on all webstore purchases

For those who can't afford $30 or more a month, we have **Sustainer Rates** at $15, $10 and $5. Sustainers get a free PM Press T-shirt and a 50% discount on all purchases from our website.

Your Visa or Mastercard will be billed once a month, until you tell us to stop. Or until our efforts succeed in bringing the revolution around. Or the financial meltdown of Capital makes plastic redundant. Whichever comes first.

DEPARTMENT OF ANTHROPOLOGY & SOCIAL CHANGE

Anthropology and Social Change, housed within
the California Institute of Integral Studies, is a small
innovative graduate department with a particular focus
on activist scholarship, militant research, and social change. We offer both masters
and doctoral degree programs.

Our unique approach to collaborative research methodology dissolves traditional
barriers between research and political activism, between insiders and outsiders,
and between researchers and protagonists. Activist research is a tool for "creating
the conditions we describe." We engage in the process of co-research to explore
existing alternatives and possibilities for social change.

Anthropology and Social Change
anth@ciis.edu
1453 Mission Street
94103
San Francisco, California
www.ciis.edu/academics/graduate-programs/anthropology-and-social-change

In, Against, and Beyond Capitalism: The San Francisco Lectures

John Holloway
with a Preface by Andrej Grubačić

ISBN: 978-1-62963-109-7
$14.95   112 pages

In, Against, and Beyond Capitalism is based on three
recent lectures delivered by John Holloway at the
California Institute of Integral Studies in San Francisco. The lectures focus on what
anticapitalist revolution can mean today—after the historic failure of the idea that
the conquest of state power was the key to radical change—and offer a brilliant
and engaging introduction to the central themes of Holloway's work.

The lectures take as their central challenge the idea that "We Are the Crisis of
Capital and Proud of It." This runs counter to many leftist assumptions that the
capitalists are to blame for the crisis, or that crisis is simply the expression of the
bankruptcy of the system. The only way to see crisis as the possible threshold to a
better world is to understand the failure of capitalism as the face of the push of our
creative force. This poses a theoretical challenge. The first lecture focuses on the
meaning of "We," the second on the understanding of capital as a system of social
cohesion that systematically frustrates our creative force, and the third on the
proposal that we are the crisis of this system of cohesion.

*"His Marxism is premised on another form of logic, one that affirms movement,
instability, and struggle. This is a movement of thought that affirms the richness of
life, particularity (non-identity) and 'walking in the opposite direction'; walking, that
is, away from exploitation, domination, and classification. Without contradictory
thinking in, against, and beyond the capitalist society, capital once again becomes a
reified object, a thing, and not a social relation that signifies transformation of a useful
and creative activity (doing) into (abstract) labor. Only open dialectics, a right kind of
thinking for the wrong kind of world, non-unitary thinking without guarantees, is able
to assist us in our contradictory struggle for a world free of contradiction."*
—Andrej Grubačić, from his Preface

"Holloway's work is infectiously optimistic."
—Steven Poole, the *Guardian* (UK)

"Holloway's thesis is indeed important and worthy of notice"
—Richard J.F. Day, *Canadian Journal of Cultural Studies*

Beyond Crisis: After the Collapse of Institutional Hope in Greece, What?

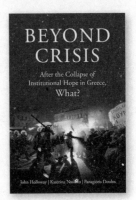

Edited by John Holloway, Katerina Nasioka, and Panagiotis Doulos

ISBN: 978-1-62963-515-6
$21.95   256 pages

The government led by Syriza in Greece, elected in January of 2015, seemed, at least in its initial months, to be the most radical European government in recent history. It proclaimed itself as the "government of hope" and became a symbol of hope throughout the world. It represented for many the proof that radical change could be achieved through institutional politics. Then came the referendum of July 2015, the vote to reject the austerity imposed by the banks and the European Union, followed by the complete reversal of the government's position and its acceptance of that austerity.

The dramatic collapse of the Syriza government's radical discourse showed the limits of institutional politics, a lesson that is apparently completely overlooked by the enthusiastic followers of Jeremy Corbyn and Bernie Sanders. But it also poses profound questions for those who reject state-centered politics. The anarchist or autonomist movement in Greece has been one of the strongest in the world yet it has failed to have a significant impact in opening up alternative perspectives in this situation.

Is there then no way out? Is there nothing beyond the world of capitalist destruction or can we still see some possibility for radical hope? The essays in this collection reflect on the experience of the crisis in Greece and its political implications for the whole world. They do not point a way forward but seek to open windows in the darkening sky of apparent impossibility.

"Beyond Crisis *does not look on the bright side. It looks straight into the eye of the storm and unfolds the hopelessness of conventional left politics in Greece and how it became part of the unfolding cycle of state violence and austerity. And it unfolds the community of hope, its courage of resistance and negativity, that has come to fore in Greece, and elsewhere too, as the direct democracy of a society of the free and equal."*
—Werner Bonefeld, professor of politics, University of York, England

"With Jeremy Corbyn calling for a 'new way of doing politics' and offering hope to millions, the publication of this book about Greece's erstwhile 'Government of Hope' is timely. The questions it asks are essential. How does rage, hope and optimism turn into to despair and depression? Why can't the institutional Left break through the 'Wall of Reality'? And, if not Syriza, Podemos or Corbyn's Labour, then what?"
—David Harvie, The Free Association

A Letter to My Children and the Children of the World to Come

Raoul Vaneigem
with an afterword by John Holloway

ISBN: 978-1-62963-512-5
$15.95   128 pages

Readers of Vaneigem's now-classic work *The Revolution of Everyday Life*, which as one of the main contributions of the Situationist International was a herald of the May 1968 uprisings in France, will find much to challenge them in these pages written in the highest idiom of subversive utopianism.

Some thirty-five years after the May "events," this short book poses the question of what kind of world we are going to leave to our children. "How could I address my daughters, my sons, my grandchildren and great-grandchildren," wonders Vaneigem, "without including all the others who, once precipitated into the sordid universe of money and power, are in danger, even tomorrow, of being deprived of the promise of a life that is undeniably offered at birth as a gift with nothing expected in return?"

A Letter to My Children provides a clear-eyed survey of the critical predicament into which the capitalist system has now plunged the world, but at the same time, in true dialectical fashion, and "far from the media whose job it is to ignore them," Vaneigem discerns all the signs of "a new burgeoning of life forces among the younger generations, a new drive to reinstate true human values, to proceed with the clandestine construction of a living society beneath the barbarity of the present and the ruins of the Old World."

"*In this fine book, the Situationist author, whose writings fueled the fires of May 1968, sets out to pass down the foundational ideals of his struggle against the seemingly all-powerful fetishism of the commodity and in favor of the force of human desire and the sovereignty of life.*"
—Jean Birnbaum, *Le Monde*

"*A startling and invigorating restatement for the present ghastly era of humanity's choice: socialism or barbarism.*"
—Dave Barbu, *Le Nouveau Père Duchesne*

Re-enchanting the World: Feminism and the Politics of the Commons

Silvia Federici
with a Foreword by Peter Linebaugh

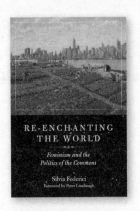

ISBN: 978-1-62963-569-9
$19.95   240 pages

Silvia Federici is one of the most important contemporary theorists of capitalism and feminist movements. In this collection of her work spanning over twenty years, she provides a detailed history and critique of the politics of the commons from a feminist perspective. In her clear and combative voice, Federici provides readers with an analysis of some of the key issues and debates in contemporary thinking on this subject.

Drawing on rich historical research, she maps the connections between the previous forms of enclosure that occurred with the birth of capitalism and the destruction of the commons and the "new enclosures" at the heart of the present phase of global capitalist accumulation. Considering the commons from a feminist perspective, this collection centers on women and reproductive work as crucial to both our economic survival and the construction of a world free from the hierarchies and divisions capital has planted in the body of the world proletariat. Federici is clear that the commons should not be understood as happy islands in a sea of exploitative relations but rather autonomous spaces from which to challenge the existing capitalist organization of life and labor.

"Silvia Federici's theoretical capacity to articulate the plurality that fuels the contemporary movement of women in struggle provides a true toolbox for building bridges between different features and different people."
—Massimo De Angelis, professor of political economy, University of East London

"Silvia Federici's work embodies an energy that urges us to rejuvenate struggles against all types of exploitation and, precisely for that reason, her work produces a common: a common sense of the dissidence that creates a community in struggle."
—Maria Mies, coauthor of *Ecofeminism*

Revolution at Point Zero: Housework, Reproduction, and Feminist Struggle

Silvia Federici

ISBN: 978-1-60486-333-8
$15.95   208 pages

Written between 1974 and 2012, *Revolution at Point Zero* collects forty years of research and theorizing on the nature of housework, social reproduction, and women's struggles on this terrain—to escape it, to better its conditions, to reconstruct it in ways that provide an alternative to capitalist relations.

Indeed, as Federici reveals, behind the capitalist organization of work and the contradictions inherent in "alienated labor" is an explosive ground zero for revolutionary practice upon which are decided the daily realities of our collective reproduction.

Beginning with Federici's organizational work in the Wages for Housework movement, the essays collected here unravel the power and politics of wide but related issues including the international restructuring of reproductive work and its effects on the sexual division of labor, the globalization of care work and sex work, the crisis of elder care, the development of affective labor, and the politics of the commons.

"Finally we have a volume that collects the many essays that over a period of four decades Silvia Federici has written on the question of social reproduction and women's struggles on this terrain. While providing a powerful history of the changes in the organization of reproductive labor, Revolution at Point Zero *documents the development of Federici's thought on some of the most important questions of our time: globalization, gender relations, the construction of new commons."*
—Mariarosa Dalla Costa, coauthor of *The Power of Women and the Subversion of the Community* and *Our Mother Ocean*

"As the academy colonizes and tames women's studies, Silvia Federici speaks the experience of a generation of women for whom politics was raw, passionately lived, often in the shadow of an uncritical Marxism. She spells out the subtle violence of housework and sexual servicing, the futility of equating waged work with emancipation, and the ongoing invisibility of women's reproductive labors. Under neoliberal globalization women's exploitation intensifies—in land enclosures, in forced migration, in the crisis of elder care. With ecofeminist thinkers and activists, Federici argues that protecting the means of subsistence now becomes the key terrain of struggle, and she calls on women North and South to join hands in building new commons."
—Ariel Salleh, author of *Ecofeminism as Politics: Nature, Marx, and the Postmodern*

Anthropocene or Capitalocene? Nature, History, and the Crisis of Capitalism

Edited by Jason W. Moore

ISBN: 978-1-62963-148-6

$21.95   304 pages

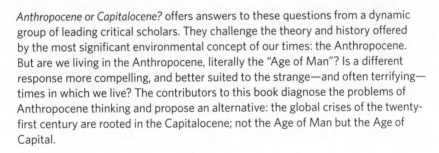

The Earth has reached a tipping point. Runaway climate change, the sixth great extinction of planetary life, the acidification of the oceans—all point toward an era of unprecedented turbulence in humanity's relationship within the web of life. But just what is that relationship, and how do we make sense of this extraordinary transition?

Anthropocene or Capitalocene? offers answers to these questions from a dynamic group of leading critical scholars. They challenge the theory and history offered by the most significant environmental concept of our times: the Anthropocene. But are we living in the Anthropocene, literally the "Age of Man"? Is a different response more compelling, and better suited to the strange—and often terrifying—times in which we live? The contributors to this book diagnose the problems of Anthropocene thinking and propose an alternative: the global crises of the twenty-first century are rooted in the Capitalocene; not the Age of Man but the Age of Capital.

Anthropocene or Capitalocene? offers a series of provocative essays on nature and power, humanity, and capitalism. Including both well-established voices and younger scholars, the book challenges the conventional practice of dividing historical change and contemporary reality into "Nature" and "Society," demonstrating the possibilities offered by a more nuanced and connective view of human environment-making, joined at every step with and within the biosphere. In distinct registers, the authors frame their discussions within a politics of hope that signal the possibilities for transcending capitalism, broadly understood as a "world-ecology" that joins nature, capital, and power as a historically evolving whole.

Contributors include Jason W. Moore, Eileen Crist, Donna J. Haraway, Justin McBrien, Elmar Altvater, Daniel Hartley, and Christian Parenti.

"We had best start thinking in revolutionary terms about the forces turning the world upside down if we are to put brakes on the madness. A good place to begin is this book, whose remarkable authors bring together history and theory, politics and ecology, economy and culture, to force a deep look at the origins of global transformation."
—Richard Walker, professor emeritus of geography, UC Berkeley, and author of *The Capitalist Imperative, The New Social Economy, The Conquest of Bread,* and *The Country in the City*

Practical Utopia: Strategies for a Desirable Society

Michael Albert
with a preface by Noam Chomsky

ISBN: 978-1-62963-381-7
$20.00   288 pages

Michael Albert's latest work, *Practical Utopia* is a
succinct and thoughtful discussion of ambitious
goals and practical principles for creating a desirable
society. It presents concepts and their connections to
current society; visions of what can be in a preferred, participatory future; and an
examination of the ends and means required for developing a just society. Neither
shying away from the complexity of human issues, nor reeking of dogmatism,
Practical Utopia presupposes only concern for humanity.

Part one offers conceptual tools for understanding society and history, for
discerning the nature of the oppressions people suffer and the potentials they
harbor. Part two promotes a vision for a better way of organizing economy, polity,
kinship, culture, ecology, and international relations. It is not a blueprint, of course,
but does address the key institutions needed if people are to be free to determine
their own circumstances. Part three investigates the means of seeking change
using a variety of tactics and programs.

"*Practical Utopia immediately struck me because it is written by a leftist who is
interested in the people winning and defeating oppression. The book is an excellent
jumping off point for debates on the framework to look at actually existing capitalism,
strategy for change, and what we need to do about moving forward. It speaks to many
of the questions faced by grassroots activists who want to get beyond demanding
change but who, instead, want to create a dynamic movement that can bring a just
world into existence. As someone who comes out of a different part of the Left than
does Michael Albert, I was nevertheless excited by the challenges he threw in front of
the readers of this book. Many a discussion will be sparked by the arguments of this
work.*"
—Bill Fletcher Jr., author of *"They're Bankrupting Us!" And 20 Other Myths about
Unions*

"*Albert mulls over the better society that we may create after capitalism, provoking
much thought and offering a generous, hopeful vision of the future. Albert's
prescriptions for action in the present are modest and wise, his suggestions for building
the future are ambitious and humane.*"
—Milan Rai

Archive That, Comrade! Left Legacies and the Counter Culture of Remembrance

Phil Cohen

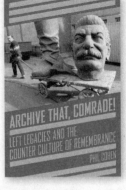

ISBN: 978-1-62963-506-4
$19.95   160 pages

Archive That, Comrade! explores issues of archival theory and practice that arise for any project aspiring to provide an open-access platform for political dialogue and democratic debate. It is informed by the author's experience of writing a memoir about his involvement in the London underground scene of the 1960s, the London street commune movement, and the occupation of 144 Piccadilly, an event that hit the world's headlines for ten days in July 1969.

After a brief introduction that sets the contemporary scene of 'archive fever,' the book considers what the political legacy of 1960s counter culture reveals about the process of commemoration. The argument then opens out to discuss the notion of historical legacy and its role in the 'dialectic of generations'. How far can the archive serve as a platform for dialogue and debate between different generations of activists in a culture that fetishises the evanescent present, practices a profound amnesia about its past, and forecloses the sociological imagination of an alternative future? The following section looks at the emergence of a complex apparatus of public fame and celebrity around the spectacle of dissidence and considers whether the Left has subverted or merely mirrored the dominant forms of reputation-making and public recognition. Can the Left establish its own autonomous model of commemoration?

The final section takes up the challenge of outlining a model for the democratic archive as a revisionary project, creating a resource for building collective capacity to sustain struggles of long duration. A postscript examines how archival strategies of the alt-right have intervened at this juncture to elaborate a politics of false memory.

"Has the Left got a past? And if so, is that past best forgotten? Who was it who said, 'Let the dead bury their dead'? Phil Cohen's book is a searing meditation on the politics of memory, written by someone for whom 'the '60s' are still alive—and therefore horrible, unfinished, unforgivable, tremendous, undead. His book brings back to life the William Faulkner cliché. The past for Cohen is neither dead nor alive. It's not even past, more's the pity."
—T.J. Clark, author of *The Sight of Death*

Autonomy Is in Our Hearts: Zapatista Autonomous Government through the Lens of the Tsotsil Language

Dylan Eldredge Fitzwater
with a Foreword by John P. Clark

ISBN: 978-1-62963-580-4
$19.95   224 pages

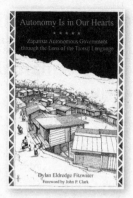

Following the Zapatista uprising on New Year's Day 1994, the EZLN communities of Chiapas began the slow process of creating a system of autonomous government that would bring their call for freedom, justice, and democracy from word to reality. *Autonomy Is in Our Hearts* analyzes this long and arduous process on its own terms, using the conceptual language of Tsotsil, a Mayan language indigenous to the highland Zapatista communities of Chiapas.

The words "Freedom," "Justice," and "Democracy" emblazoned on the Zapatista flags are only approximations of the aspirations articulated in the six indigenous languages spoken by the Zapatista communities. They are rough translations of concepts such as *ichbail ta muk'* or "mutual recognition and respect among equal persons or peoples," *a'mtel* or "collective work done for the good of a community" and *lekil kuxlejal* or "the life that is good for everyone." *Autonomy Is in Our Hearts* provides a fresh perspective on the Zapatistas and a deep engagement with the daily realities of Zapatista autonomous government. Simultaneously an exposition of Tsotsil philosophy and a detailed account of Zapatista governance structures, this book is an indispensable commentary on the Zapatista movement of today.

"This is a refreshing book. Written with the humility of the learner, or the absence of the arrogant knower, the Zapatista dictum to 'command obeying' becomes to 'know learning.'"
—Marisol de la Cadena, author of *Earth Beings: Ecologies of Practice across Andean Worlds*

"Autonomy Is in Our Hearts is perhaps the most important book you can read on the Zapatista movement in Chiapas today. It stands out from the rest of the Anglophone literature in that it demonstrates, with great sensitivity, how a dialectic between traditional culture and institutions and emerging revolutionary and regenerative forces can play a crucial role in liberatory social transformation. It shows us what we can learn from the indigenous people of Chiapas about a politics of community, care, and mutual aid, and—to use a word that they themselves use so much—about a politics of heart. A great strength of the work is that the author is a very good listener. He allows the people of Chiapas to tell their own story largely in their own words, and with their own distinctive voice."
—John P. Clark, from the Foreword

Occult Features of Anarchism: With Attention to the Conspiracy of Kings and the Conspiracy of the Peoples

Erica Lagalisse
with a Foreword by Barbara Ehrenreich

ISBN: 978-1-62963-579-8
$15.95   160 pages

In the nineteenth century anarchists were accused of conspiracy by governments afraid of revolution, but in the current century various "conspiracy theories" suggest that anarchists are controlled by government itself. The Illuminati were a network of intellectuals who argued for self-government and against private property, yet the public is now often told that they were (and are) the very group that controls governments and defends private property around the world. Intervening in such misinformation, Lagalisse works with primary and secondary sources in multiple languages to set straight the history of the Left and illustrate the actual relationship between revolutionism, pantheistic occult philosophy, and the clandestine fraternity.

Exploring hidden correspondences between anarchism, Renaissance magic, and New Age movements, Lagalisse also advances critical scholarship regarding leftist attachments to secular politics. Inspired by anthropological fieldwork within today's anarchist movements, her essay challenges anarchist atheism insofar as it poses practical challenges for coalition politics in today's world.

Studying anarchism as a historical object, *Occult Features of Anarchism* also shows how the development of leftist theory and practice within clandestine masculine public spheres continues to inform contemporary anarchist understandings of the "political," in which men's oppression by the state becomes the prototype for power in general. Readers behold how gender and religion become privatized in radical counterculture, a historical process intimately linked to the privatization of gender and religion by the modern nation-state.

"This is surely the most creative and exciting, and possibly the most important, work to come out on either anarchism or occultism in many a year. It should give rise to a whole new field of intellectual study."
—David Graeber, professor of anthropology at the London School of Economics and Political Science, author of *Debt: The First 5000 Years*

Stop, Thief!
The Commons, Enclosures, and Resistance

Peter Linebaugh

ISBN: 978-1-60486-747-3
$21.95   304 pages

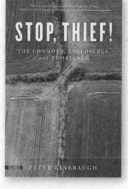

In this majestic tour de force, celebrated historian Peter Linebaugh takes aim at the thieves of land, the polluters of the seas, the ravagers of the forests, the despoilers of rivers, and the removers of mountaintops. Scarcely a society has existed on the face of the earth that has not had commoning at its heart. "Neither the state nor the market," say the planetary commoners. These essays kindle the embers of memory to ignite our future commons.

From Thomas Paine to the Luddites, from Karl Marx—who concluded his great study of capitalism with the enclosure of commons—to the practical dreamer William Morris—who made communism into a verb and advocated communizing industry and agriculture—to the 20th-century communist historian E.P. Thompson, Linebaugh brings to life the vital commonist tradition. He traces the red thread from the great revolt of commoners in 1381 to the enclosures of Ireland, and the American commons, where European immigrants who had been expelled from their commons met the immense commons of the native peoples and the underground African-American urban commons. Illuminating these struggles in this indispensable collection, Linebaugh reignites the ancient cry, "STOP, THIEF!"

"There is not a more important historian living today. Period."
—Robin D.G. Kelley, author of *Freedom Dreams: The Black Radical Imagination*

"E.P. Thompson, you may rest now. Linebaugh restores the dignity of the despised luddites with a poetic grace worthy of the master… [A] commonist manifesto for the 21st century."
—Mike Davis, author of *Planet of Slums*

"Peter Linebaugh's great act of historical imagination… takes the cliché of 'globalization' and makes it live. The local and the global are once again shown to be inseparable—as they are, at present, for the machine-breakers of the new world crisis."
—T.J. Clark, author of *Farewell to an Idea*

Capital and Its Discontents: Conversations with Radical Thinkers in a Time of Tumult

Sasha Lilley

ISBN: 978-1-60486-334-5
$20.00   320 pages

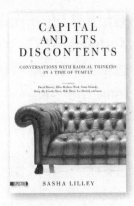

Capitalism is stumbling, empire is faltering, and the planet is thawing. Yet many people are still grasping to understand these multiple crises and to find a way forward to a just future. Into the breach come the essential insights of *Capital and Its Discontents*, which cut through the gristle to get to the heart of the matter about the nature of capitalism and imperialism, capitalism's vulnerabilities at this conjuncture—and what can we do to hasten its demise. Through a series of incisive conversations with some of the most eminent thinkers and political economists on the Left—including David Harvey, Ellen Meiksins Wood, Mike Davis, Leo Panitch, Tariq Ali, and Noam Chomsky—*Capital and Its Discontents* illuminates the dynamic contradictions undergirding capitalism and the potential for its dethroning. At a moment when capitalism as a system is more reviled than ever, here is an indispensable toolbox of ideas for action by some of the most brilliant thinkers of our times.

"These conversations illuminate the current world situation in ways that are very useful for those hoping to orient themselves and find a way forward to effective individual and collective action. Highly recommended."
—Kim Stanley Robinson, *New York Times* bestselling author of the *Mars Trilogy* and *The Years of Rice and Salt*

"In this fine set of interviews, an A-list of radical political economists demonstrate why their skills are indispensable to understanding today's multiple economic and ecological crises."
—Raj Patel, author of *Stuffed and Starved* and *The Value of Nothing*

"This is an extremely important book. It is the most detailed, comprehensive, and best study yet published on the most recent capitalist crisis and its discontents. Sasha Lilley sets each interview in its context, writing with style, scholarship, and wit about ideas and philosophies."
—Andrej Grubačić, radical sociologist and social critic, co-author of *Wobblies and Zapatistas*

Global Slump: The Economics and Politics of Crisis and Resistance

David McNally

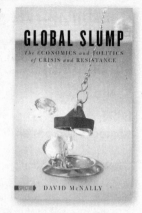

ISBN: 978-1-60486-332-1
$15.95   176 pages

Global Slump analyzes the world financial meltdown as the first systemic crisis of the neoliberal stage of capitalism. It argues that—far from having ended—the crisis has ushered in a whole period of worldwide economic and political turbulence. In developing an account of the crisis as rooted in fundamental features of capitalism, *Global Slump* challenges the view that its source lies in financial deregulation. It offers an original account of the "financialization" of the world economy and explores the connections between international financial markets and new forms of debt and dispossession, particularly in the Global South. The book shows that, while averting a complete meltdown, the massive intervention by central banks laid the basis for recurring crises for poor and working class people. It traces new patterns of social resistance for building an anti-capitalist opposition to the damage that neoliberal capitalism is inflicting on the lives of millions.

"In this book, McNally confirms—once again—his standing as one of the world's leading Marxist scholars of capitalism. For a scholarly, in depth analysis of our current crisis that never loses sight of its political implications (for them and for us), expressed in a language that leaves no reader behind, there is simply no better place to go."
—Bertell Ollman, professor, Department of Politics, NYU, and author of *Dance of the Dialectic: Steps in Marx's Method*

"David McNally's tremendously timely book is packed with significant theoretical and practical insights, and offers actually-existing examples of what is to be done. Global Slump *urgently details how changes in the capitalist space-economy over the past 25 years, especially in the forms that money takes, have expanded wide-scale vulnerabilities for all kinds of people, and how people fight back. In a word, the problem isn't neo-liberalism—it's capitalism."*
—Ruth Wilson Gilmore, University of Southern California and author, *Golden Gulag: Prisons, Surplus, Crisis, and Opposition in Globalizing California*